OPEN WEB LEARNING

Accompanying files online!

Visit our website *https://owl.institute* and download the accompanying material such as exercise files and solutions:

https://owl.institute/files
Download Code: 125fbb0cb322

Step-by-Step Guides

Marco Emrich and Christin Marit

Learning JavaScript: The non-boring beginner's guide to modern (ES6+) JavaScript programming Vol 1: The language core

Version 1.2.14 of August 19, 2018

— https://owl.institute —

About the Authors

Marco Emrich

Marco Emrich holds a university degree in computer science, is a passionate trainer and advocate of the software craftsmanship movement. He has wide experience as a software architect and developer in a variety of sectors. Marco heads the Web Engineering department of the Webmasters Akademie in Nuremberg, Germany. He also lectures regularly, holds workshops at leading software conferences and writes articles for technical journals. In his spare time, if he's not organizing meetings of the Softwerkskammer software craftsmanship community, you'll probably find Marco teaching his son how to program robot turtles.

https://github.com/marcoemrich
https://twitter.com/marcoemrich
https://www.linkedin.com/in/marco-emrich-47485388/

Christin Marit

Christin Marit is a qualified social pedagogue, certified web developer, photographer, blogger, world traveler and professional in the art of life. She works for the Webmasters Akademie in Nuremberg as a course developer, author and e-tutor. Christin feels that learning JavaScript should be as easy, wonderful and fascinating as life itself.

https://twitter.com/christinmarit
https://www.linkedin.com/in/christin-marit-7241a513b/

Do you know about our online training platform?

OPEN WEB LEARNING

Become a Certified Web Professional
Study Online at OWL Institute

Looking to boost your online knowledge? Discover our courses in web development, web design, and digital marketing at

https://owl.institute

Our classes encompass

- **Course material, developed by experts in the field**
- **Personal tutorial support**
- **Assignments, with personal feedback**
- **Quizzes**
- **Overview of your progress**
- **Professional certification**

Published by **The Open Web Learning Institute** at
Webmasters Akademie Nürnberg GmbH
Neumeyerstr. 22–26
90411 Nuremberg, Germany

© 2018 The Open Web Learning Institute at
Webmasters Akademie Nürnberg GmbH

Originially published in 2018 in Germany by Webmasters Press, Nürnberg, under the title
JavaScript: Aller Anfang ist leicht

Translated from German by Roland Galibert
Cover image: © iStock/binkski
Cover design: Frank Schad
Item number: 125fbb0cb322
Version 1.2.14 of August 19, 2018

Printed books made with Prince

For general information about our other products and services, please visit https://owl.institute.

Acknowledgements

We first want to thank all of our readers and reviewers for their invaluable feedback. We'd especially like to acknowledge Jan Teriete, David Seifert, Raimo Radczewski, Tom Scholz, Cord Mählmann and Thomas Metz. We also want to thank our editors Monika Beck †, Ulrike Walter and Thorsten Schneider.

Furthermore, we want to express our gratitude to the team at Think Geek Inc. for kindly allowing us to use their product images and texts for our fictional Nerd-World project.

And of course we also want to thank all the developers in the JavaScript community who tirelessly work on and work with improved technologies and who strive to maintain a constant exchange of ideas so that JavaScript will always be a language that makes programming really fun.

Table of Contents

Preface

JavaScript! JavaScript! JavaScript!

This language keeps popping up in more and more areas. Web developers agree: You just can't get around JavaScript! That opinion is backed up by a number of reliable sources, including the *RedMonk Programming Language Rankings*, a website which rates programming languages by their popularity. JavaScript currently holds the top spot there, followed by Java, PHP and Python.

The JavaScript language specification standard *ECMAScript 2015* is almost completely supported by modern browsers. Instead of starting with "old" JavaScript and then going on to show why things are better with the modern elements of the language, we'll teach you the "new" JavaScript right from the start. So let's throw away all the old baggage and get right to the "cool stuff".

Even though this is a beginner class and we try to break you into JavaScript as gently as possible, we also do place a high value on good code quality. *Even more important than code which runs is code which is well-written* — this means code which is easy to understand, easy to change and easy to extend. This is the belief already championed by the well-known *Software Craftsmanship Manifesto*, signed by thousands of software developers worldwide.

In short, our goal is to bring you, in the shortest possible time, up to the point where you're programming clean, up-to-date JavaScript code.

You already know JavaScript? Then let yourself in for a surprise and allow us to introduce you to a new programming style which takes advantage of the latest features of the language and leads to more concise, more succinct code.

As you work through this class, you might gradually come to suspect we had a lot of fun writing it. It's more than likely that was the case :) And we do hope you'll have at least as much fun reading it and programming.

With all that in mind: Let's get to the code!

Your authors, Christin & Marco

PS: Do not hesitate to contact me on *LinkedIn*[1] or follow me on *Twitter*[2]. It's always okay to ask me questions or give me feedback. I'd love to hear from you. — Marco

---

1. *https://www.linkedin.com/in/marco-emrich-47485388/*
2. *https://twitter.com/marcoemrich*

Everything You Always Wanted to Know About JavaScript

1

Even a journey of a thousand miles begins with a single step.

Japanese saying

1.1 JavaScript?

You've decided to learn JavaScript. You presumably already have some idea of what you can do with JavaScript. Nevertheless, it's possible we can still impress upon you how varied and universal the opportunities for using JavaScript really are.

JavaScript is everywhere!

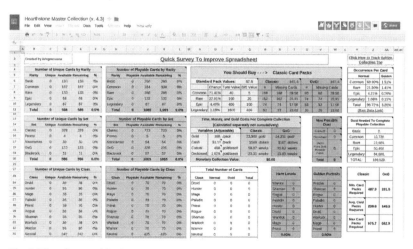

Fig. 1 *A Google spreadsheet*

JavaScript is present mainly in web browsers. You can use JavaScript to write programs which will run in your browser. The browser here plays the role of a platform — just like an operating system on which you can install programs. However, JavaScript applications don't need to be installed.

JavaScript provides a wide range of functionality. It starts with simple validation of form fields (e.g. checking whether an email address entered by a user is correctly formatted) and extends all the way up to complex applications like *Google Sheets*[3] (a browser-based spreadsheet application similar to Microsoft Excel fig. 1).

Modern e-shops (e.g. Amazon, eBay), video platforms (e.g. YouTube) and social sites (Facebook, Twitter) also use massive amounts of JavaScript. It would be impossible to imagine the modern Internet without JavaScript.

In addition to JavaScript, browsers can also run other languages, e.g. *Dart* (in Google Chrome) and *VBScript* (in Microsoft Internet Explorer). However, JavaScript is the only programming language reliably supported by all modern browsers. It also avoids, for the most part, the enormous loading times you may have experienced with Java applets or Flash.

Browsers aren't the only platform which can run JavaScript. For some time now, JavaScript has existed on other platforms such as PDFs, scripts for applications like Photoshop and control software in *robots*[4] (fig. 2).

As you see, you'll be able to use what you learn in this class practically anywhere. Still, we naturally want to concentrate first on JavaScript's most prominent purpose — its use in the Web.

Fig. 2 *Robot with Espruino board, photo: Pur3 Ltd*

JavaScript vs. Java

The term *Java* brings considerable danger of confusion. **Java** is also a programming language, but has as little in common with JavaScript as *car* does with *carpet* — in other words, practically nothing! Netscape licensed the name *JavaScript* from its contractual partner Sun Microsystems. This was presumably a marketing trick employed by Netscape to swim along in the popular waters occupied by the then highly successful Java language. Sun was then purchased by Oracle in 2009 for 7.4 billion dollars — meaning that Oracle is now owner of the *JavaScript* brand.

As a result, the name *JavaScript* is not especially favored by many developers. Experienced developers often refer to it simply as *JS*. This term is considered more

---

3. *https://www.google.com/sheets/about*
4. *http://www.espruino.com/distance_sensing_robot*

"hip" and avoids the reference to Java (*Java* is not exactly a synonym for "sleek and modern").

JS on the Server

JavaScript can also be executed on a server instead of in a browser — this allows web pages to be generated dynamically and provides an alternative to using a typical server language like PHP, Ruby or Java. Running JavaScript on a server is not a new concept. However, JS only became a practical language for server use by about 2010/2011, primarily because of the popularity of the *Node.js*[5] platform.

This opened up new possibilities for us as web developers. Previously, JS web developers were so-called **front enders** (front end developers) who were concerned mainly with the "look and feel" of a web application in the browser. These days, JS developers can also earn a living as **full stack** developers, implementing sophisticated server-side applications such as complex financial rules in addition to creating front end code intended strictly for browsers. Where previously web applications required two programming languages (JS on the client side and something like Java server-side), nowadays complete applications can be written entirely in JS.

JS in Embedded Systems

Finally, boards like *Espruino*[6] and *Tessel*[7] make it possible for you to run JavaScript directly on hardware. This will allow you to do things like automatically water your plants, *program musical instruments*[8], *control model helicopters using hand gestures*[9] or *keep an eye on your dog while you're asleep*[10]. The possibilities are endless.

We're not exaggerating when we say

> JS is everywhere these days!

---

5. *https://nodejs.org*
6. *http://www.espruino.com*
7. *https://tessel.io/*
8. *https://www.hackster.io/projects/e/841/841-making-sounds-and-music*
9. *http://tessel.hackster.io/rossetti211/tesselcopter*
10. *http://tessel.hackster.io/rickyrobinett/a-sleep-tracker-for-your-dog-using-tessel-and-twilio*

1.2   What This Class Is

This class concentrates on JavaScript in the browser. Since this is a class about basics, you'll also be able (with some exceptions) to implement what you've learned on a server — or in PDFs, to script Photoshop, to write mobile applications, to control robots, to make your coffee each morning or to save the universe (we admit we're not 100% certain about this last one).

If you're still not sure if learning JavaScript makes sense for you, perhaps the website *http://shouldILearnJavaScript.com*can help you decide.

> This class covers JavaScript language versions **ES6/EcmaScript 2015** up to **EcmaScript 2018**. You can find more information on JavaScript language versions in lesson 25.

1.3   What This Class Is NOT

If you use JS at some later point to develop software, you'll probably have to go back and look up some details. Unfortunately, this class has only limited value as a reference text. It's intended more as a guide which will give you a quick start to using JavaScript. We've organized the lessons in this class with the goal of optimizing your learning progress and not with the goal of helping you find a specific topic quickly. We also make no claims to completeness and in fact are consciously limiting ourselves to those topics which, for the moment, are most important to you as a beginner — in other words, the "big picture".

If in the future, as you're doing your day-to-day development work and find you need to reference JS in its entirety including all its gory details, we can recommend the following references:

➤ *www.mozdev.org*[11] — Mozilla Developer Network (MDN)
  The MDN much more than just a reference for the Firefox browser. You'll also find detailed information on the core JS language and on browser functionality. The MDN even includes tables describing what browser implements what feature as of what version, and often provides polyfills (code which allows earlier browser versions to support a feature they lack) for worst-case scenarios.

➤ *www.webplatform.org*[12]
  A joint documentation project from W3C, Microsoft, Adobe and other organi-

---

11. *http://www.mozdev.org*
12. *http://www.webplatform.org*

zations. Very good, highly detailed documentation of HTML5 and CSS. Documentation of JS is still in progress but already looks very promising.

➤ *www.nodejs.org*[13]
The official site of the Node.js server platform. Detailed documentation on the core JS language and all Node.js-specific extensions.

➤ *caniuse.com*[14]
Can I use a certain feature? This site will give you the answer! Detailed overviews of new features in HTML, CSS and JS, including information on browser versions as well as polyfills.

➤ **Speaking JavaScript** (Rauschmayer 2014, see References)
The book is considered *the* reference. It's up-to-date, detailed and precise.

➤ **JavaScript: The Definitive Guide** (Flanagen 2011, see References)
This is the standard JS work. Although it's no longer entirely up-to-date, it is very well structured and detailed.

➤ **Understanding ECMAScript 6** (Zakas, see References)
Zakas' work on all new features in ES6/ES2015 is available from Leanpub and also as *Open Source*[15].

If you need to Google for JS content, we recommend you add "mdn" to your search. This will land you directly on the right Mozilla Developer Network page — otherwise, you might get web pages in your hit list whose explanations are out-of-date or are simply wrong.

1.4   But What About Animations and the GUI?

If you've already flipped through the table of contents, you may have noticed that all the topics sound pretty technical and seem to have little to do with a graphical user interface (GUI). Not only that, our screenshots don't look like anything an artist would be too proud of. Are we serious?

---

13. *http://www.nodejs.org*

14. *http://caniuse.com*

15. *http://www.nczonline.net/blog/2014/03/26/announcing-understanding-ecmascript-6*

Absolutely! It's our experience that it's much easier to concentrate on the core of a language instead of struggling with highly polished animations. Concentrate on what's important — the language!

Once you understand the language, the rest is easy. As a result, you won't learn how to use JS to manipulate HTML and CSS until the second volume of this series. We hope this'll make your introduction to JS a little easier. But this doesn't mean the code and concepts you'll learn won't have any value in the real world. All our examples and exercises are based on problems and situations we've actually encountered in our day-to-day programming.

1.5   "NerdWorld" Project

Welcome to your first project! Naturally, your stated goal as a software developer is to earn enough money to settle down in the Caribbean as quickly as possible. But to do that, not only are you going to need clients — you're also going to have to satisfy them as best you can. This will bring you more clients, and in turn more money.

A Client Meeting

We'll say your first client is *Marty*. Marty owns a store and now wants to make his products available over the Internet as well. The name of his store is "*NerdWorld*" (this example is entirely fictitious — you can spare yourself the Google search :).

NerdWorld is an online shop where nerds, techies and other kindred spirits can buy their daily necessities: Nerf guns, UFOs with a USB connection, Klingon weapons for office use, caffeinated beverages, highly-caffeinated beverages, super-highly-caffeinated beverages, etc. In other words, everything a modern developer needs to survive in the office jungle.

Even though NerdWorld already has a static HTML site up, you can't buy any products through it yet. The new site is to consist primarily of the shop. In order to make the overall experience a little more interesting, existing features will be enhanced and additional features are also being planned. These include:

➤ a chat client through which customers can chat with salespeople/customer consultants

➤ an online newsletter through which the shop can keep customers informed about new products.

To make his dream reality, the shop's owner is now turning to an expert — you! You meet with him and he describes the situation:

 For years, we've been selling cool stuff geared to nerds and any other people who like that kind of thing. Our assortment of products ranges from items for Star Trek fans and paraphernalia for programmers, all the way up to smartphone-controlled mini-drones and joke items like an electroshock pen.

Throughout this course, we'll continue to refer back to the *NerdWorld Project*'s requirements to show you how JS can help you implement it. At the beginning, this will be only small set components which unfortunately you won't yet be able to use fully in an actual project. But at the least, the reference should show you that everything we cover is relevant to actual practice.

2 *Getting Started with Firefox Scratchpad*

2.1   So Where's My IDE?

Many developers write their JS code in a special development environment, a so-called **IDE** (integrated development environment). However, we'd like to spare you the trouble of installing and configuring one, as this can be quite time-consuming. Not only that, you won't need any special IDE features for your first steps into JS. All you'll need is to have the current version of **Mozilla Firefox** installed — Firefox alone will give you enough tools to develop small but complete JS applications. These include tools like **Scratchpad** and **Firefox Web Console**, which together alone already give you many features reserved to just IDEs.

You can download Firefox at *www.mozilla.org/en-US/firefox/new*[16] — be sure to select the version which corresponds to your operating system. You can also change the default language displayed on the Mozilla website (in this course, we'll be using the English version).

> **Walkthrough 1:**
>
> 1   Install and start Firefox on your operating system.
>
> 2   Start the Firefox **Web Console** from the Web Developer menu (fig. 3) or by using a keyboard shortcut: **Ctrl + Shift + K** or **Cmd + Alt + K**.

---

16.   *http://www.mozilla.org/en-US/firefox/new*

3

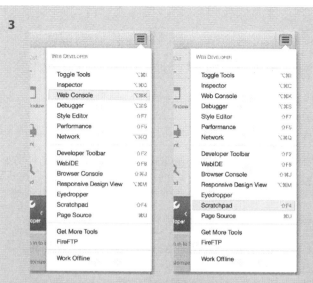

Fig. 3 *Firefox Menu: Web Console & Scratchpad*

Open **Scratchpad** from the Developer menu () or by using a keyboard shortcut: **Shift + F4** or **Fn + Shift + F4**

.

4   Arrange the two windows so that you have a complete view of both — either next to or under one another (fig. 4).

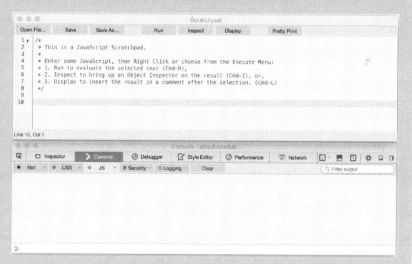

Fig. 4 *Firefox Scratchpad and Web Console*

And you're done! That's all you'll need in terms of setup. Now let's get started.

2.2   Helpful Shortcuts for Scratchpad and Console

The two tables below give you some helpful keyboard shortcuts for using Scratchpad and Web Console.

Windows / Linux	OS X	Function
Shift + F4	Fn + Shift + F4	Open Scratchpad
Ctrl + R	Cmd + R	Run your code in Scratchpad
Ctrl + Shift + R	Cmd + Shift + R	Reload & run — Reload page then run code
Ctrl + S	Cmd + S	Save file
Ctrl + O	Cmd + O	Open file
Ctrl + F	Cmd + F	Find
Ctrl + P	Cmd + P	Pretty print — Format code
Ctrl + J	Cmd + J	Jump to a specific line
Alt + up arrow	Alt + up arrow	Line up — Shift current line up one
Alt + down arrow	Alt + down arrow	Line down — Shift current line down one
Ctrl + /	—	Comment in/comment out a line

Table 2.1 Scratchpad keyboard shortcuts

Windows / Linux	OS X	Function
Ctrl + Shift + K	Cmd + Alt + K	Open Console
Ctrl + F	Cmd + F	Find
Ctrl + L	—	Clear — Delete all output

Table 2.2 Web Console keyboard shortcuts

2.3   "Hello World" with console.log

Learning a new programming language traditionally starts with printing out `Hello World`. To do this, all you need to do is to enter the following statement in Scratchpad.

```
1 console.log("Hello");
```

Listing 1 *accompanying_files/02/examples/hello.js*

As soon as you hit the **Run**button (or press the keyboard shortcut **Ctrl + R**), your output will appear in the console.

> ### Exercise 1: Logged into the Console
>
> Print out your name.

2.4   Sound the Alarm! My Console is on Fire!

Let's take a closer look at your JS code: `log` is what is known as a ***function***. Its job is to log messages to the `console` — just like in a log book.

As a result, `log` makes it possible for you to track the output and execution of your program, step by step — it's a feature intended more for programmers like us than for users.

Now replace `console.log` with `alert`:

```
1 alert("Welcome to NerdWorld");
```

Listing 2 *accompanying_files/02/examples/alert.js*

The `alert` function causes a so-called ***alert box*** to pop up in your browser window. `alert` is intended to make users aware of important warning messages.

The alert box is a **modal** window, meaning a user must first process it and close it before he/she may continue to use the corresponding web page. For reasons of general usability, we recommend you don't use `alert` unless you have a very good reason to do so. In addition, `alert` is a function only available in browser environments. For example, you can't use it if you're programming JS on a server using *Node.js*.

Both `alert` and `log` are functions. You can recognize a function call through the parentheses `()` which always follow the name of the function. These parentheses allow you to specify an **argument** for the function — such as `"Hello World"` in this example. What a function does with an argument depends upon the specific function. While `alert` outputs a warning message for users, `console.log` generates a log entry for developers like us.

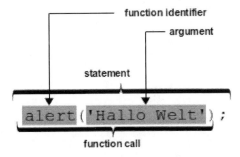

Fig. 5 *Illustration of terms used for function calls*

`alert` is a predefined function which comes with your browser. Your browser also provides `console`, a so-called *object*. You can then access the function `log` via `console`. For the time being, you'll only be using predefined functions like these which already come with your browser. When we get to the lesson 13 section, you'll learn how to define your own functions.

> ### Exercise 2: Sound the Alarm!
>
> Output the following text in an alert box: "*Alert! Your console is on fire! Hurry! Email your local fire department or tweet with the hashtag #helpMyComputerIsOnFire*"

For the sake of simplicity, we'll only be using `console.log` to output messages in this class. In real life, you also have a number of other options available to you in terms of output. However, since these aren't part of the core JS language, we won't be covering those options in this class.

2.5   Multiple Statements

Of course, you can also use multiple statements to log multiple messages one after the other:

```
1 console.log("a log message");
2 console.log("... and another one");
```

Listing 3 *accompanying_files/02/examples/logmessage.js*

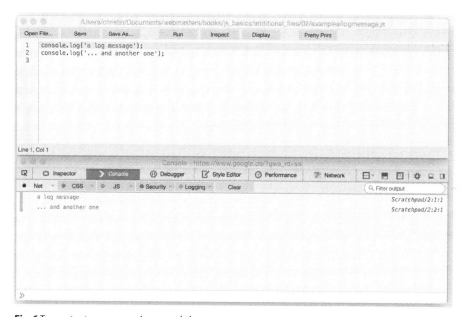

Fig. 6 *Two output messages using console.log*

Write each statement on a separate line. Here, we'll end each line with a semicolon (;). You can actually leave out the semicolon as well. In that case, JS will invoke a feature known as ***automatic semicolon insertion*** (***ASI***) and insert the semicolon for you automatically. Though this feature is quite practical, it also follows relatively complex rules which you should learn before using it.

In practice then, you have two options of entering statements:

1. semicolon-less style
2. semicolon style

Each style has its advantages and disadvantages (and of course its fanatical proponents). We opted for the second style in this class, but not because we feel it's definitely the better of the two — in the end, it's just a question of what you prefer. The main point in favor of the second style is that it's more widespread.

But why not go without?

You'll find arguments in favor of the semicolon-less school of style as well as related tips in

➤ *Marohnić 2010*[17]

➤ *Fuch 2013*[18]

➤ *Schlueter 2010*[19]

If you do want to work with fewer semicolons, you can try out your abilities on the *ASI Scanning Test Grounds*[20]. If you pass this test with flying colors, you may safely go ahead and (not) use semicolons as you see fit :-)

2.6   Coding Guidelines

As you can probably imagine, you're at liberty to make your own choices in terms of style in many areas of programming. This includes things like how you format your code, where you place semicolons, and so on. However, so that your code remains consistent and doesn't result in complete chaos, you should follow some specific rules for style. A collection of such rules is known as a set of ***coding guidelines***.

Software companies generally have their own coding guidelines, which may differ from company to company and even from project to project. It's essential here that the rules on each aspect of coding be consistent and that each team member follow these rules – only this will prevent unchecked growth and chaos. On the other hand, the precise wording of each rule is only of secondary importance.

A good example of a detailed coding guideline document is the *jQuery Style Guide*[21], which governs the code written by the developers of the jQuery library. Another fascinating source is *http://jscode.org* — this website allows you to click together your very own set of rules.

Coding guidelines are also important because you can never know where your code might wind up in the future and who's going to be making changes to your code. After a project is finished, the resulting software often remains in use for

---

17.   *http://mislav.uniqpath.com/2010/05/semicolons*

18.   *https://github.com/madrobby/zepto/blob/master/CONTRIBUTING.md*

19.   *http://blog.izs.me/post/2353458699/an-open-letter-to-javascript-leaders-regarding*

20.   *http://asi.qfox.nl*

21.   *http://contribute.jquery.org/style-guide/js*

years and years — development never stands still. Bugs will always need to be fixed, change requests will always need to be implemented, programs will always need to be adapted to changing conditions — all this comes under what is known as software **maintenance**. A programmer whose job is it to maintain, improve and adapt your code after you've finished developing it is your **maintenance programmer**. Be nice to your maintenance programmer! Help him or her to understand your code by sticking to common coding guidelines. (And if you're not nice enough, just think — your maintenance programmer might turn out to be a serial killer who knows exactly where you live…)

Maybe you'll even be the one who needs to make changes to your own code years later — so be nice to yourself!

> *Any fool can write code that a computer can understand. Good programmers write code that humans can understand.*
>   Fowler (1999)

From now on, we'll be developing our own coding guidelines. For each topic we cover, we'll establish appropriate rules to make our programming lives easier. Let's start right off with the following rules:

Coding Guidelines

➤ Always use exactly one line for exactly one statement.

➤ End each statement with a semicolon.

We'll be adding more coding guidelines very shortly.

2.7 Always Be "strict"!

In addition to coding guidelines, there's another thing you can do to make your life (and that of your maintenance programmer) a little easier:

Always be "strict"!

Don't worry — this doesn't mean you have to sit rigidly at attention all day as you're programming, or chew out your colleagues who write bad code.

What we mean here is moving JS into so-called **strict mode**. When it's in this mode, JS actually becomes stricter. More specifically:

> Certain guidelines which *standard mode* sees as just convention will actually lead to an error message in *strict mode*.

> Many obsolete language constructs (e.g. the `with` statement) are no longer accepted under this mode

> Code with minor errors or problems which JS will accept without a murmur in standard mode will now lead to a (usually) meaningful error message. This will allow you to detect problems early on and avoid an often time-consuming error search.

> Certain new language constructs (e.g. `let`) can only be used in strict mode in most environments.

Moving JS into strict mode is easy: Just add the statement

```
"use strict";
```

at the beginning of your JS file.

We'll do just that from now on, since this will create practically no disadvantages for us. After all, we don't have any legacy code (to be specific, code in old JS syntax) which needs to be supported. When we get to lesson 17, you'll learn even more about what using `"use strict";` will do for you. If you want even more information on strict mode, you'll find an *entry on strict mode*[22]in the MDN (Mozilla Development Network). This will explain to you all differences between the two modes.

2.8   Comments (or How to Put in Your Two Cents)

You can use *comments* to add useful explanations to your code or even to deactivate entire lines of code. Comments are invaluable in helping you quickly understand code which you or another programmer wrote previously.

> Well-placed comments will improve the readability of your code

The JavaScript interpreter ignores everything placed within comments. This even applies for complete JavaScript statements. There are two ways you can add comments to your JavaScript. You have a choice between

---

22. *https://developer.mozilla.org/en-US/docs/Web/JavaScript/Reference/Strict_mode/ Transitioning_to_strict_mode#Differences_from_non-strict_to_strict*

> ➤ *single-line* and

> ➤ *multi-line* comments.

You embed a single-line comment in your code using two slashes `//`.

```
1  // The following code contains a meaningful string.
2  console.log("I am a meaningful string");
```

In real life, you should only use comments to clarify more complex code and not for trivial code as in the example above. You haven't gained anything if you can't pick out your actual code because you've added too many comments.

Multi-line comments let you insert longer (multi-line) text comments into your code. These comments start with the characters `/*` and end with `*/`.

```
1  /*
2    TODO: Add a more spicy greeting here. Candidates are:
3      - Speak Friend and Enter
4      - Live long and prosper
5      - Welcome to the Future (in mystery Futurama Voice)
6  */
7  alert("Welcome to NerdWorld");
```

Listing 4 *accompanying_files/02/examples/comment.js*

3 Operators, Data Types and Other Priorities

3.1   JavaScript Calculations

All programming languages allow you to perform calculations. You can use JS, in a sense, as a replacement pocket calculator. For example, enter the following:

```
1 "use strict";
2
3 console.log(3 + 4);
```

Listing 5 accompanying_files/03/examples/calc.js

As expected, you get 7 as your result.

You can see a few key JS concepts just in this very small, simple example. 3 + 4 is an **expression**. Expressions are one of the most important concepts in JS. Expressions characteristically have a **return value** — in this case, the number 7 .

In turn, you can use return values in different places in your code, e.g. as an argument to a function call. Or to put this another way, JavaScript replaces expressions by their (return) values.

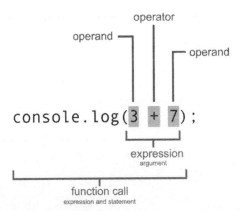

Fig. 7 Expressions

3.1.1   Expressions in Firefox Web Console

You can also enter expressions directly into Firefox Web Console. Try entering 3 + 4 in the input line (next to the double arrow ") (fig. 8).

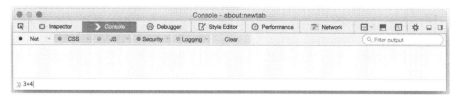

Fig. 8 *Entering expressions directly in console — input*

After you confirm your input with **Return**, the console will immediately display the return value (fig. 9).

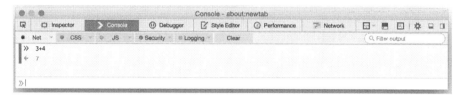

Fig. 9 *Entering expressions directly in console — output*

FYI, you can also use **Shift-Return** to input a multi-line statement, i.e. a single statement which runs over multiple lines. The entire statement is executed only after you hit **return**.

Alternatively, you can also select parts of expressions in Scratchpad and examine these using *Inspect* (**Ctrl-I / Cmd-I**). As you see in fig. 10, Scratchpad displays the result of `4 * 2` as `value: 8` in the side panel to the right.

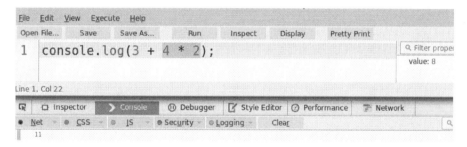

Fig. 10 *Inspect a selected (partial) expression in Scratchpad*

3.1.2   Notation

From now on, we'll often point out a value returned by some expression or which appears at the console. To do this, we'll insert a comment in the code and show the value in front of a `=>` — the so-called ***fat arrow***.

Example

```
1 3 + 4 // => 7
2 console.log(3 + 4 * 2); //=> 11
```

3.2   JavaScript as a Pocket Calculator: Arithmetic Operators

In addition to multiplication and addition operators, JS has corresponding operators for the arithmetic operations of *subtraction*, *division* and *modulus*. All of these operators fall under the group of so-called **arithmetic operators**:

Symbol	Operation
+	Addition
-	Subtraction
*	Multiplication
/	Division
%	Modulus — remainder of an integer division
**	Exponentiation (ECMAScript 2016+)

Table 3.1 Arithmetic operators

Example

➤   `5 + 4` returns `9`
➤   `5 - 4` returns `1`
➤   `5 * 4` returns `20`
➤   `5 / 4` returns `1.25`
➤   `10 % 3` returns `1` since 10 - 3 * 3 = 1.
➤   `5 ** 4` returns `625` since 5 * 5 * 5 * 5 = 625 .

> ### Exercise 3: 2000 Seconds
>
> How many minutes and remainder seconds are there in 2000 seconds? Use `console.log` to print out the answer.

Tips: The easiest way to solve this exercise is to use the modulus operator. Right now, we haven't taught you how to remove decimal places; we'll come back to that later.

3.3 Characters and Strings

Have you noticed anything about how numbers and text are coded differently? The `"Hello world"` at the beginning of the previous lesson was written out in quotation marks, while numbers were not. A text element is written out within quotation marks, and actually involves stringing or linking individual characters together — giving us the programming term ***string*** to indicate such text.

Two Types of Quotation Marks

You may use both single quotes or double quotes to delimit a string, but the marks at the beginning and at the end of the string must be the same.

Example
`"Some text string"` is allowed
`'Some text string'` is also allowed
`"Some text string'` is invalid

Most JS developers consistently use double quotes, and only use single quotes in exceptional cases, e.g. when they need to use double quotes within a string to indicate literal wording.

Coding Guidelines

You should normally use double quotes to delimit strings.

3.4 Determining Length

Sometimes you need to know how long a string is — i.e. how many characters are in it. As you do more and more development, you'll come across many situations where length is important.

For example, blogs, lists of products, and similar items sometimes provide a text preview which only shows part of the entire text. Before generating this preview, the length of the entire text item must first be measured to see whether the text actually needs to be shortened.

So at this point, we'd like to introduce you to the string property **length**. You can have a string return this property by typing *.length* after the string.

```
"length matters - sometimes".length // => 26
```

Then pack your statement into a `console.log` so you can see the response you need on the console:

```
1 "use strict";
2
3 console.log("length matters - sometimes".length);
```
Listing 6 *accompanying_files/03/examples/length.js*

Exercise 4: Lucky Numbers & Name Codes

Do you know about lucky numbers and code names? Here's an interesting way to come up with a name code:

Multiply the length of your first name (including your middle name(s) if you want) by the length of your last name and print out the result in the console. (Just to let you know, these are the numbers we got: 40 and 30.)

3.5   Literals: They Say What They Mean

Now that you've been introduced to strings and numbers, there's another important concept we need to tell you about: Basically, any value — whether a string or a number — which is specified literally in your code is known as a (you guessed it) **literal**. Literals always have a fixed value.

Examples

➤ 42
➤ "house"
➤ "green"
➤ 5.47
➤ 1998
➤ "Please enter your name"

3.6   Number & String Data Types

JavaScript literals have a so-called **data type**. As the term implies, a data type specifies what kind of data the literal represents, and in turn its possible values.

Up to this point, we've used the following data types:

Data Type	Permissible Values / Meaning	Example of Literal
String	Any text	"Hello"
Number	Any positive or negative number	246.5

Table 3.2 String & number data types

JavaScript encodes strings in so-called **UTF-16** character format [ECMA-262]. An encoding format is responsible for how characters are represented digitally. UTF-16 makes it possible for you to use a wide variety of special characters as well as specific letters from different languages (e. g. German umlauts, accented French characters, etc.).

The value range for numbers is also limited. However, as long as you don't carry out any astronomical calculations, you should be safe.

It's easy to find out the data type of a literal — just use the JavaScript operator `typeof`. `typeof` returns a string which tells you the literal's data type.

Examples

```
1 "use strict";
2
3 console.log(typeof 3764);         // => number
4 console.log(typeof "beautiful JS"); // => string
5 console.log(typeof 27.31);        // => number
```
Listing 7 accompanying_files/03/examples/type.js

Exercise 5: Hmmm...So What are You Really?

What is the data type of the following literal?
`"42"`

3.7   Precedences & Parentheses

3.7.1   Order of Operators

Take the expression `5 + 3 * 2` — what do you think is its result? The solution could conceivably be `16` or `11`.

The correct solution is `11`. When evaluating the expression above, JavaScript observes the arithmetic rule that multiplication takes priority over addition.

Since we have no specific rules established in this area (like the German "Punkt-vor-Strich" principle), JavaScript generalizes this principle even further, and specifies an order of evaluation for all operators. Since the addition operator (+) comes after the multiplication operator (*) in the order of evaluation, it's only evaluated after the multiplication operator. The following table shows the arithmetic operators we've covered so far in their order of evaluation (also known as *priority* or *precedence*):

Priority / Precedence	Name	Operator
1	Typeof operator	typeof
2	Multiplication, division, modulus	* / %
3	Addition, subtraction	+ -
4	Assignment operator	=

Table 3.3 Operators in their order of evaluation

Operators of the same rank are usually evaluated from left to right. *Usually* means that there are some exceptions to this rule. One example is the `=` assignment operator, which JS evaluates from right to left. From now on, you should follow the rules below when reading expressions:

1.   Evaluate the part of the expression whose operator has the highest priority.

2.   Replace this part of the expression with its result.

3.   Repeat steps 1 and 2 until the expression only contains operators of equal priority.

4.   Now you can evaluate what remains from left to right.

Example

3 * 4 + 7 / 2 - 3 results in **12 + 3.5 - 3** which results in**15.5 - 3** and finally results in **12.5**

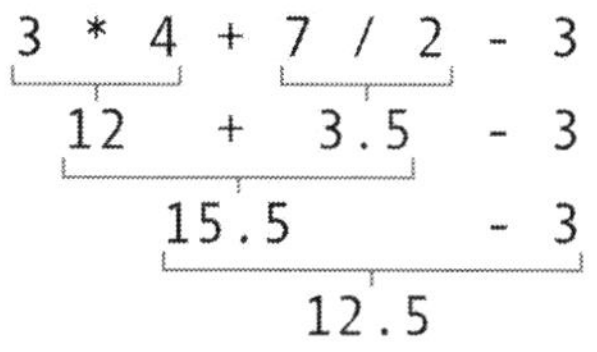

```
3  *  4  +  7 / 2  -  3
   12     +   3.5    -  3
      15.5            -  3
            12.5
```

Fig. 11 *Precedence*

3.7.2   Parentheses

Let's go back to the expression `5 + 3 * 2`. Let's say we did want `5 + 3` to be evaluated first, giving us a final result of `16`. You can use parentheses in cases like this to force JavaScript to observe a specific order of evaluation. The expression `(5 + 3) * 2` will now evaluate to `16`, just like we wanted.

Parentheses are themselves operators (the so-called ***grouping operator***) and have the highest precedence. If you use nested parentheses in an expression or part of an expression, JavaScript will evaluate it from inside out.

Example

(5 + 3) * 2 results in **8** * 2 which results in**16**

(12 / (2 +2) + 3) * 2 results in **(12 / 4 + 3)** * 2 which results in **(3 + 3)** * 2 which results in **6 * 2** and finally results in**12**

Let's add parentheses to our original precedence table (table 3.3):

Priority / Precedence	Name	Operator
1	**Grouping operator**	**Parentheses ()**
2	Typeof operator	typeof
3	Multiplication, division, modulus	* / %

Table 3.4 *Operators in their order of evaluation*

Priority / Precedence	Name	Operator
4	Addition, subtraction	+ -
5	Assignment operator	=

Table 3.4 Operators in their order of evaluation

Coding Guidelines

Don't try to be too sparing in your use of parentheses. If you're uncertain about operator precedence in an expression, it's better just to add a pair of parentheses. In cases where you have any doubt, extra parentheses are better than getting an unexpected result due to incorrect precedences. Extra parentheses, even when these are syntactically superfluous, also help to make an expression easier to read.

Example
(3 / a) + (7 + b) + (5 * c) is easier to read than **3 / a + 7 + b + 5 * c** or even **3/a+7+b+5*c**. We therefore recommend that you observe the following coding guideline:

➤ Use parentheses when you're unsure of the order of evaluation in an expression or if you think they'll make your code easier to read.

3.8   Exercise

Exercise 6: Just a Few More Calculations...

Expression	Return value
3 + 4	
3 * 12	
25 + 12	
(12 - 3) / 3	

Expression	Return value
12 % 3	
12 * (44 / 11) / 3 + 67	

4 *Variables (or, Keeping Reality in a Drawer)*

4.1   Really Quite Variable

Like many other programming languages, JS uses variables. Variables allow you to store values so you can retrieve and/or modify them at a later time.

4.2   Creating Variables

Think of variables as being the drawers in a chest of drawers. Each drawer contains a piece of information. A piece of information can be something like a user name, a background color for a website or the price of an item. But how can you find some piece of information when you need it? Or, going back to our analogy above, how would you find the right drawer in a chest of drawers without first opening each one?

Easy! Just label each drawer. You attach a label to each drawer which describes its contents, or the nature of its contents.

Fig. 12 *Concept of a variable*
`let price = 4;`

In JS and other programming languages, the counterpart to this label is called an ***identifier***. The term ***variable identifier*** is also used, especially when referring to variables.

When you want to create a variable, all you need to do is tell JS that the given element is a variable and what its identifier is. You let JS know something is a variable by using the specific keyword ***let***. By contrast, your identifier can be pretty much anything (though you do need to follow some rules — more on that later). For example, let's say you want to create a variable to store a user name. You write:

```
let username;
```

New in ECMAScript 2015

If you already have some experience in programming and are used to using *var* to specify variables, you may be a little surprised at *let*. ES5 and previous versions actually did use *var*. Even though *var* does still work, *let* definitely has an advantage — so-called ***local scoping***, which we'll touch on a little later.

The idea behind *let* may be best shown using an example.

Example

```
let username = "Oswine";
```
Let the username be Oswine.

Keywords

As you've just learned, **username** is a *variable identifier*, and the statement `let username;` is a *variable declaration*. On the other hand, the word *let* is a so-called ***keyword***. Keywords are a fixed component of a programming language. They have a specifically defined meaning and may not be used for any other purpose. FYI, keywords in JS must always be written in lowercase.

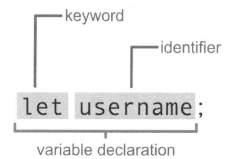

Fig. 13 *Declaration*

The identifier **username** is something we've freely selected. We could just as well have used ***userName*** or even just ***user***. This statement is called a ***variable declaration*** since it tells JS of the existence of a variable.

Good Identifiers

It's essential in programming to come up with good identifier names for your variables — doing so will make it much easier for you as well as others to understand your code. You shouldn't assume that you'll still remember what your variables mean in a few weeks, let alone a few months. Experience shows this just won't happen :)

In reality, programmers read code much more often than they write code. Don't shorten variable names just to make it easier for you to type out your code. Take steps to ensure that your variable names will remain understandable over the long run.

In the next lesson, we'll show you a few tips for coming up with good variable identifiers.

4.3   Assigning Values to Variables

Let's go back to our drawer analogy. You've taken one of your drawers and labeled it with the inscription *username*. But your drawer still doesn't contain anything.

To "pack" some contents into your variable, JavaScript uses the concept of assignment — i.e. you assign a variable its contents. Assignment in JS is expressed through the so-called **assignment operator**, represented by the equal sign `=`. It's essential in assignment that the variable identifier be on the left side of the assignment statement and the actual value be on the right side (e.g. the name *Ladislaus*):

```
username = "Ladislaus";
```

Direction is important — reversing the above statement

```
"Ladislaus" = username;
```

will result in an error. Think of it this way — you can pack some contents (e.g. a pen) into a chest drawer, but you can't pack the drawer into the contents themselves. (Try it for yourself if you don't believe us! ;)

A value can be stored in a variable, but a variable cannot be stored in a value.

The quotation marks here are also important. This allows JS to see the element is the value *Ladislaus* and not a variable called *Ladislaus*.

Now that you have a value stored in a variable, you can now use this value when-ever you need to, just by accessing it through the identifier **username**. The follow-ing line of code prints out the contents of the variable **username** to the console:

```
console.log(username);
```

This is the complete program:

```
1 "use strict";
2
3 let username;
4 username = "Ladislaus";
5
6 console.log(username);
```

Listing 8 *accompanying_files/04/examples/variable.js*

As expected, the console prints out the word *Ladislaus*. You may have already given some thought as to why we've been using quotation marks in all of our output statements up to this point. If you replace line 6 with `console.log("username");` your output will contain the text *username* instead of *Ladislaus*. Quotation marks make it possible for JS to differentiate between strings and variables.

If you already know what you want the value of a variable to be at the time you're creating it, you can make your code a little shorter — by using so-called *variable initialization*. To do this, you combine your variable declaration and value assign-ment into a single statement:

```
let username = "Ladislaus";
```

The complete program will then look like:

```
1 "use strict";
2
3 let username = "Ladislaus";
4 console.log(username);
```

4.4 Make Sure You're Prompt!

Of course, in real life you won't be using data you've specified yourself, but live data entered by a user. This is the only way your software (e.g. a website) can be interactive.

So let's add a live user name to our example — you won't be specifying this name yourself, instead, you'll let our fictitious user select it. To do this, let's make use of the function `prompt`:

```
prompt("Please let me know your name!");
```

Just like an alert box, a `prompt` will cause a window to pop up in the browser. However, unlike an alert box, the window for a prompt not only contains the text you specified (*Please let me know your name!*) but also an input field.

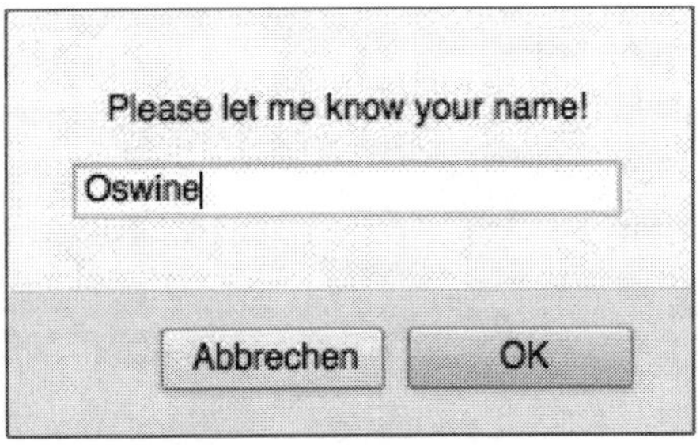

Fig. 14 *Window with input request (* `prompt` *function)*

Our user can now enter a name and confirm this with *OK*. However, given our code as it stands, that's all that happens. We can't make any use of the name our user entered because we haven't saved that input anywhere.

In the last section on assignment, we showed you how to store the name `"Ladislaus"` in the variable `username`:

```
let username = "Ladislaus";
```

So now let's replace the string `"Ladislaus"` by a call to the function `prompt`:

```
let username = prompt("Please let me know your name!");
```

After our user enters *Oswine*, our program will execute the following step:

```
let username = "Oswine";
```

(This code doesn't actually exist, we're just using it for illustration). The value replaced by the JS `prompt` (the string *Oswine* in the example above) is the value returned by `prompt`.

The string *Oswine* entered by our user is now stored in the variable `username`. This is the complete program:

```
1  let username;
2  username = prompt("Please let me know your name!");
3  console.log(username);
```

We can even make our code a little shorter:

```
1  "use strict";
2
3  let username = prompt("Please let me know your name!");
4
5  console.log(username);
```

Listing 9 accompanying_files/04/examples/prompt.js

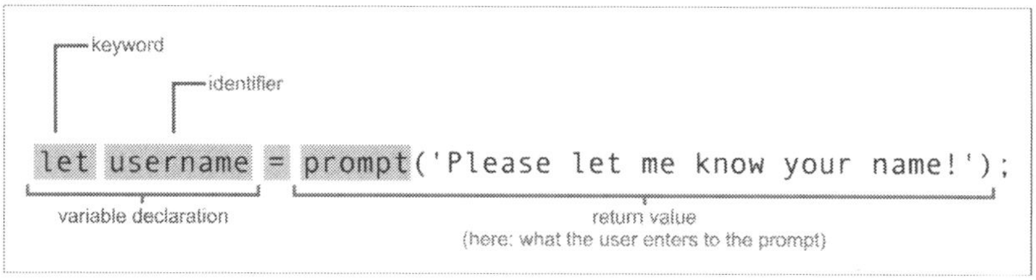

Fig. 15 Initialization

Exercise 7: But You Don't Ask Someone Something Like That!

Now use prompt to ask our user for his/her age, then store this in a variable and print it out to the console.
Also be sure to select a meaningful identifier for your variable.

4.5   Rock-Solid: Constants

How about trying out a program closer to the real world — say a small sales tax calculator? Our user will enter a net price for an item and get back its total price including sales tax. For the sake of simplicity, we'll assume a sales tax of 20%.

```
1  "use strict";
2
3  let netPrice = prompt("Net price for the shocking pen in $?");
4  let totalPrice = netPrice * 1.20;
5
6  console.log("Total price:");
7  console.log(totalPrice);
```

This works great! — the only problem is, our code isn't terribly elegant. When a number such as 1.20 appears in your code, it's often not immediately obvious what it means. In this simple example, it's probably easy enough to figure out what

1.20 means, but in practice things aren't always as simple. Experienced users call a value like this a **magic number** — just like it fell out of the blue.

Normally sales tax rates don't change while a program is running (and hopefully they won't change afterwards either...okay, maybe not). You should therefore make use of a so-called **constant** to hold numbers like sales tax and the like. A constant is very similar to a variable. The only difference is the value of a constant is not variable, but...er, constant.

```
1  "use strict";
2
3  const TAX_RATE = 1.20;
4
5  let netPrice = prompt("Net price for the shocking pen?");
6  let totalPrice = netPrice * TAX_RATE;
7
8  console.log("total price:");
9  console.log(totalPrice);
```

Listing 10 accompanying_files/04/examples/const.js

So we've now given the sales tax value in our code an actual name, and it's clear what line 6 is doing. Another advantage of constants is that they make it much easier for you to implement changes. Now, when the inevitable sales tax increase does come, you won't have to search for that value through the depths of your code, you can just change it directly (admittedly, with code of so few lines as in our example, the change is easy to find, but your programs won't always be this short).

In a sense, these constants serve to **configure your program**. If you follow these guidelines consistently, all your constants will appear at the beginning of your program, giving you a clear overview of all your "fine-tuning controls" at just a glance.

Note: Constants in Scratchpad

When declaring constants in Scratchpad, you need to be aware of a specific quirk in that tool. If you run your code twice by clicking **Run**, you'll get the following error (or one very similar):

```
Exception: TypeError: redeclaration of const
```

This occurs because Firefox has already created (declared) the constant the first time it runs your code, and now "remembers" it. The second time you run your code, the constant already exists under the same name and you get the infamous "redeclaration" error.

A reload will solve this problem — instead of reloading your browser manually, just use the menu item **Execute > Reload & Run**.

Finally, we'll define a few more coding guidelines to improve the readability of your code:

Coding Guidelines

➤ Avoid magic numbers.

➤ Write out constants which serve to configure your program all in uppercase, and use the underscore _ to separate words.

➤ Declare constants which serve to configure your program at the beginning of your code.

4.6   Battle of the Heavyweights: Variable vs. Constant

And in this corner…

Okay, seriously — how are constants different from variables? Apart from their different naming styles as dictated by coding guidelines and their different purposes, these two elements also have a strict technical difference.

While a variable can change its value at any time, constants cannot. As soon as you've tied a constant to a value, this value remains fixed until the end of your program. Let's look at a counterexample:

```
1  "use strict";
2
3  const TAX_RATE = 1.20;
4  TAX_RATE = 1.25;
```

The JS interpreter interrupts this code with an error message like "*TAX_RATE is read-only*" and terminates the program. This behavior is actually exactly what you want — this will ensure you can't accidentally overwrite your constant in another part of your program.

FYI, the exact error message you get will depend on the JS environment in which you're running your code (browser, Node.js, JS Bin, etc.).

Exercise 8: Imposing More Taxes

Prices would be so much nicer if it wasn't for that darned sales tax. But even though you have to pay the sales tax yourself, at least you can get someone

else to calculate the total price — JS! So write a program which will calculate and print out total price for you when net price is $150 (hint: it should be
$183).

The following definitions have already been provided for you:

```
1 "use strict";
2
3 const TAX_PERCENTAGE = 22;
4
5 let price = 150;
6
7 /* your code here */
8
9 console.log(totalPrice);
```

accompanying_files/04/exercises/tax.js

4.7   Compound Assignment Operators

You'll encounter the assignment operator `=` quite frequently in JS programs. Let's
go back to our NerdWorld project. Imagine that Marty now wants a button which
he can use to increase the price of an item by 10%. So you might find the following
snippet of code somewhere in the shop:

```
1 let price = 199; // in reality, this value is read from a
database somewhere
2 price = price * 1.10;
3 console.log(price); // => 218.9
```

In line 2, the program reads the old value for the price (here `199`), multiplies it by
`1.10`, then stores it back in the variable `price`.

The bad thing about this code is that the variable `price` appears twice in the
same line — each time, it refers to exactly the same variable. If you wanted to
come back later and change the name of this variable (e.g. to `productPrice`),
you'd have to change it in two places. If you forget to make the change in one
place, you'll get an error in your code. This is known as a **redundancy**. You'll often
encounter code like this throughout your programming career.

JavaScript provides a shorthand notation for cases like this. You can combine the
`*` and `=` into a new operator `*=`:

```
price *= 1.10; // same as: price = price * 1.10
```

The effect is exactly the same, but `price` now appears in the line just once — problem solved! In addition, any experienced programmer will be able to read and comprehend this line faster (it's even a couple characters shorter — though admittedly this isn't a significant advantage).

The `*=` operator is just one operator in the group of **compound assignment operators**. This trick of combination also works with all other arithmetic operators like `+`, `-`, `/` and `%` (modulus).

Just like assignment itself, these compound operators have a very low precedence and are therefore put at the very bottom of evaluation order.

Priority / Precedence	Name	Operator
1	Function call[a], Grouping operator	Function call, e.g. `prompt()` Parentheses ()
2	Typeof operator	typeof
3	Multiplication, division, modulus	* / %
4	Addition, subtraction	+ -
5	**Assignment operators**	= += -= *= /= %=

Table 4.1 Operators in their order of evaluation
[a]Although function calls are not operators, they can definitely be part of an expression.

You should be aware of a small detail when using compound operators: These operators expect to save a value back, and as a result they only work with variables.

```
199 *= 1.10; // wrong! doesn't work
```

The console will interrupt the above code with the error message "`ReferenceError: invalid assignment left-hand side`".

```
199 *= 1.10
ReferenceError: invalid assignment left-hand side
```

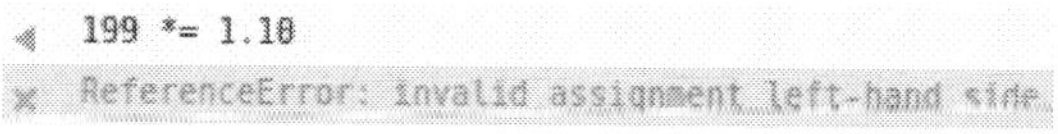

Fig. 16 Error message for `199 *= 1.10`

To be specific, the error occurs because the left side of the assignment statement isn't a variable — a number cannot be assigned a value (`199 = 218.9` just doesn't make any sense). The assignment is therefore invalid.

> The left side of an assignment (including a compound assignment) must always be a variable!

Coding Guidelines for Operators

As you saw in this lesson, it's a good idea to place a blank space before and after each operator (including an assignment operator). In principle, it actually doesn't make any difference whether you use one space, two spaces, five spaces or no spaces. JS ignores so-called white space (blank spaces, line breaks and tabs). Spaces are only significant when they're placed in quotation marks, since they must then be shown in the output. However, in general it's a good idea to use white space to make your code more readable. So we'll impose and observe the following coding guideline from now on:

> ➤ Put a blank space before and after each operator with two operands (e.g. addition operator, assignment operator, etc.).

Examples

> ➤ `3 + 4` is easier to read than `3+4`
> ➤ `let price = 3.88;` is easier to read than `let price=3.88;`

Identifying Good Identifiers

5

> *Much of the skill in writing unmaintainable code is the art of naming variables and methods. They don't matter at all to the compiler. That gives you huge latitude to use them to befuddle the maintenance programmer.*
>
> Roedy Green, How To Write Unmaintainable Code

We promised you we'd go into a little more detail about how you can (or should) name variables and other JavaScript language elements. The rules for identifiers in JS (see *Ecma International 2015*[23]) are pretty lax. Even though in principle you can use an identifier like `$27__Åööö`, in practice this makes little sense. As a result, we'll define much stricter coding guidelines than those imposed by Ecma International in order to help you select useful identifiers.

Not to worry, we didn't come up with these rules just off the top of our heads — they've been long-established within the JS community. You'll find that they're used outside of this course, in many real-world projects, books and websites (e.g. in Goodman (2004), Vermeulen (2000) and *Crockford*[24].

5.1   Meaningful Identifiers

You'll often find, in the source code of older applications, single letters used as variable identifiers. For example, you might see someone's age stored as the variable `x`, his last name stored as the variable `y` and his first name stored as `z`. Naturally, it's a little difficult to read through code which uses identifiers like these. As a result, it's necessary for us as programmers to select identifiers which are meaningful and self-explanatory (Goodman 2004, Münz 2003, Vermeulen 2000). You should be able to come back to your code in six months and know what exactly your identifiers mean. And ideally, other programmers should also intuitively understand the meaning of your variables just on the basis on their identifiers. It's very clear what `age` means. By contrast, you'll be able to figure out that `a` or `x` means age only through a time-consuming study of the code to determine the variable's context — assuming you can do this at all.

---

23. *http://www.ecma-international.org/ecma-262/6.0/*
24. *http://javascript.crockford.com/code.html*

Example

Use

➤ `age` instead of `x`

➤ `firstName` instead of `z`

➤ `price` instead of `p`

> **Use meaningful identifiers!**

And of course it goes without saying that you shouldn't chose an identifier which means something other than what its corresponding variable contains. This means `age` is a good identifier only if its related variable actually contains a value which describes age. For example, you shouldn't store the name of a person in your `age` variable.

Another indication of the meaningfulness of an identifier is its length. Variables which consist of just a single character are usually problematic (Kellerwessel 2002). Short variable names which don't fully describe the meaning of the variable are problematic as well. Beginner programmers often shy away from longer variable names because they want to save themselves some typing. However, based from experience, we can say that this normally isn't a problem in real world programing. In reality, programmers read code much more often than they write code.

> You should always concentrate more on making your code readable and understandable, and less on making it fast and easy to type.

On the other hand, an identifier should not be so long that it's difficult to read. For example, the identifier

`textForTheLinkInBoldAtTheTopRightOfTheMenu`

definitely needs to be shortened a little. However, it's difficult to come up with one definitive rule for the maximum length of an identifier — you need to strike a balance between what makes sense for your code's readability and what makes sense for its maintainability, and this can be different in each case.

5.2   No Special Characters

Another problem is the use of special characters. Although rules do allow the use of certain Unicode characters, it's better not to rely on this. Changes in encoding can always come up over the course of the (hopefully) long life of a file, all this would take is just an FTP upload to the server.

It's therefore a good idea to restrict identifier names to letters (A-Z, a-z), digits (0-9) and underscores (Kellerwessel 2002). Stefan Münz (2003) even considers this recommendation mandatory. --> In addition, identifiers should always begin with a letter (a-z).

5.3   No Made-Up Abbreviations

Abbreviating variable names can also bring problems. Naturally, most programmers feel the abbreviations they make up are completely obvious and self-explanatory. However, it's rather doubtful that in six month's time you'll still remember `itmp` stands for *itemPrice*. In particular, maintenance programmers — who without a doubt will at some point be holding your code in their hot little virtual fingers — will wonder in despair what could possibly be the difference between `itmp` and `itmpfrncrr` (*itmpfrncrr* actually stands for *item price in foreign currency* — believe it or not, this example comes from an actual project!) You're also better off refraining from AM (acronym mania).

Example

➤   `itemPrice` instead of `itp`
➤   `measurementValue` instead of `msval`

Excluded from this rule are commonly used abbreviations which would mean something to anyone, including maintenance programmers. You can always look these up in dictionaries of abbreviation and acronyms (e. g. *www.abkuerzungen.de/main.php*[25],*www.acronymfinder.com*[26]). You should also avoid little-known abbreviations, even when they are easy to look up.

Example

➤   `htmlCode` (for a code fragment in**H**yper**t**ext**M**arkup**L**anguage)
➤   `VAT` (for value-added tax)

---

25.   *http://www.abkuerzungen.de*
26.   *http://www.acronymfinder.com*

5.4   Variables in CamelCase

Another problem is separating words in identifiers which consist of multiple words. Blank spaces generally may not be used. Just stringing words together is also not a good solution. This impedes readability and can even lead to multiple meanings in some cases. For example, `endoffile` is not very clear.

Because of this, various standards on word separation have been established. One widely used standard in JS is **CamelCase** (more precisely **lowerCamelCase**). In CamelCase, every new word (or part of a word which can stand on its own) begins with an uppercase letter. The first word of the identifier is excluded from this rule and starts with a lowercase letter.

Example

`Use`

> `endOfFile` instead of `Endoffile`
> `numberOfLetters` (or `letterNumber`) instead of `Number of Letters` or `numberofletters`

5.5   Constants in SCREAMING_SNAKE_CASE

Constants which serve to configure your program are excluded from the Camel-Case rule. JS developers write out these constants all in uppercase and use under-scores (_) to separate words and word parts. This style of writing which uses underscores for separation is called **snake_case**, or **SCREAMING_SNAKE_CASE** when you write everything in uppercase.

Example

```
const TAX_RATE
```

5.6   JS Identifiers are Case-Sensitive

JS identifiers are **case-sensitive**. This means that JS differentiates between upper-case and lowercase — so JS actually sees `totalPrice` and `totalprice` as two completely different variables. If you accidentally write out the same variable in two different ways, JS won't be able to make a connection between the two and your program will result in some kind of error.

Using two different variables whose indicators only differ in terms of uppercase and lowercase lettering is also a dumb idea (hopefully we don't need to elaborate on that further :)

5.7   Nouns for Variable Identifiers

Express your variables using nouns (Vermeulen 2000).

Example

Use `color` instead of `coloring`.

5.8   Variable Identifiers in the Singular

The variables you've used up to this point can only take on one value. For example, at this point you can't save the names of several products in `productName`. As a result, you should always use the singular form when specifying identifiers for these variables (Vermeulen 2000).

Example

Use `productName` instead of `productNames`

5.9   Exercises

Exercise 9: Think Up Some Good Variable Identifiers!

Come up with some good identifiers for the variables in the following table:

Variable Description	Variable Identifier
Price of a book in an online shop	
Number of users currently logged in	
Title of a web page	
Cost of a house on a real estate site	
Model of a monitor on a manufacturer's website	
Vehicle identification number of a car being serviced on the website of a car repair shop	

Exercise 10: Improve on Some Bad Variable Identifiers!

What variable identifiers in the following list will create problems or should be avoided — and why? Describe the exact problem for those identifiers which don't make sense. When an identifier is problematic, give at least one suggestion for improvement.

Identifier	Variable Description	Problem / Recommendation(s)
imageNo	Number of an image on a website	-
imageid	ID of an image on a website	**Problem:** id is a permissible abbreviation, but image and id are separate word components **Recommandation:** `imageId`

Identifier	Variable Description	Problem / Recommendation(s)
imageCounter	Number of images uploaded	
counterForThe CurrentRowIn TheTableWhich ListsThe Users	Counter for current row in a table which lists users	
greatgrAndsonfirstnAme	First name of the son of a grandchild	
x	User's date of birth	
y	Number of current page	
f	File name	
faqHeading	Heading for a list of frequently asked questions	
menHeig	Height of a menu	
strName	Street name	
walc	Wall color	
ZiPcOdE	ZIP code	
ZIP	ZIP code	
zip	ZIP code	
2ndquestion	The second question	
number?	The quantity of a given product a user wishes to purchase, as an input field	
Important message!	This variable contains the text of an important system message	
pi	The number π (3.14…)	

6 *Give Your Program A Little Character — With Strings!*

6.1   A Fortunate Combination of Strings

You already know how to print out a name to the console. Next, we'll print out a complete greeting. First, think about how you print out a line of static text:

```
console.log("Hi Oswine. Welcome to NerdWorld!");
```

But in reality, you won't be able to print out the name of your user since you won't know it in advance. So instead of using *Oswine* or some other name, let's use a variable.

Right now our entire sentence is a string, so the console would print out the following for our user interaction.

```
Hi username. Welcome to NerdWorld!
```

Of course this isn't what we want. So change things so that the variable `username` doesn't appear within the string, and break your text up into static and variable fragments. To do this, you'll need the so-called **concatenation operator**, expressed in JavaScript by the plus sign (+). As its name implies, this operator allows you to chain strings together.

This means the character + in JS has two functions — when used with data of type `number`, it acts as an addition operator, and when used with strings, it acts as a concatenation operator.

```
1 console.log("Hi " + "Oswine" + ". Welcome to NerdWorld!");
2 // => Hi Oswine. Welcome to NerdWorld!
```

Right now we have three strings, and only the information in the middle string is variable and will change from user to user. So let's just replace this middle string with the variable *username*.

```
1 console.log("Hi " + username + ". Welcome to NerdWorld!")
2 // => Hi Oswine. Welcome to NerdWorld!
```

Here's the complete program:

```
1 "use strict";
2
3 let username = prompt("Please let me know your name!");
4
5 console.log("Hi " + username + ". Welcome to NerdWorld!");
```

Listing 12 *accompanying_files/06/examples/string_concat.js*

6.2   Template Strings — More than Just Placeholders

As an alternative to using the concatenation operator, you can also specify variables directly within a string. This so-called **template string substitution** spares you the trouble of having to juggle around quotation marks and + concatenation operators. Just like their name implies, **template strings** are special strings which function as a template, similar to a mail-merge document. Just like a mail-merge document contains placeholders for which you substitute actual addresses, salutations, etc., JS replaces the variables in template strings with their corresponding values.

You specify template string variables using the dollar sign $ and braces {}.

```
1 "use strict";
2
3 let username = prompt("Please let me know your name!");
4
5 console.log(`Hi ${username}. Welcome to NerdWorld!`);
```

Listing 13 *accompanying_files/06/examples/template_strings.js*

Note that the string in line 5 is not delimited using regular quotation marks but rather so-called *backticks* (see fig. 17). These backticks allow JS to recognize that the string is not a conventional string, but a template string.

Fig. 17 *Backticks on an US keyboard are normally just to the right of the shift key — you don't need to hold down any other key (e.g. Shift, Ctrl, etc.) in order to use it.*

Template strings will actually substitute for any expression, not just variables.

```
1 "use strict";
2
3 let currentAge = 28;
4 console.log(`In 10 years from now you will be ${currentAge + 10}
years old`);
```

Exercise 11: Mmmmmmmmm...

1   Ask your user for his/her favorite dish and favorite drink and save both of these in appropriately named variables.

2   Print out a sentence to the console which uses both variables, using the concatenation operator to combine the variables with the other parts of the sentence.

3   Repeat the last exercise, but this time use template string substitutions.

4   Finally, if you're feeling particularly industrious, try combining both versions (concatenation operator and template strings) to print out the same sentence.

6.3   Time For a Break

Up to this point, we've just been printing out one-line strings. This hasn't been a problem so far, since the examples we've been using have been relatively small. However, in real life programming, you'll quickly come to a point where you'll need to use line breaks.

We'll start out with an example that's (admittedly) a little meaningless. Just like before, we'll greet our user, but this time we'll also ask him/her a question.

```
Hey Oswine!
Great to see you again. How's everything going?
```

Your code might look something like this:

```
1 let username = "Oswine";
2 prompt(`Hey ${username}! Great to see you again. How's everything
going?`);
```

Let's try inserting a line break between the actual greeting and the question to make everything easier to read.

```
Hey Oswine!
Great to see you again. How's everything going?
```

One possibility would be to actually insert a line break at the appropriate place in the code. Unfortunately, this has some drawbacks:

➤ This only works with template strings (this would actually be okay in the example, since it is a template string)

➤ It often makes your code difficult to read

➤ If you try to indent the second line (so that your code is a little more readable), JS will treat the blank space at the beginning of the line as part of the string, and print this out as well.

So let's use a control character instead. Characters not only include visible characters such as letters, numbers, punctuation and special characters, but also so-called control characters. In the past, control characters were mainly used in text printers, to implement non-printing features such form feed, tab, bell, etc. These characters are represented in the **ASCII** standard. ASCII is a text encoding standard which was established by the American Standards Association (ASA), and is actually a subset of UTF-8.

By now, most of these control characters are only of historical interest, since only a few are still in use today. Right now, the only character you need to worry about is the **line break**.

A control character must be "escaped" so that it's not confused with a "normal" letter — this means you add a backslash (\ ) before the character. For example, a line break is written as \n . This will let you obtain the output you want in this statement:

```
1  "use strict";
2
3  let username = "Oswine";
4  prompt(`Hey ${username}\nGreat to see you again. How's everything
going?`);
```

Listing 14 accompanying_files/06/examples/linebreak.js

6.4   Further Backslash Escapades

This case comes up rarely, but it's certainly possible that you might actually need to print out a backslash followed by an n (instead of a line break) as part of your text.
One such example would be when you're specifying a Windows operating system directory:

```
1 prompt("Please enter the number of files for the following
directory:\nC:\important_folder\next_important_folder");
```

Please enter the number of files for the following directory:
C:important_folder
ext_important_folder

[   ]

                              Cancel   OK

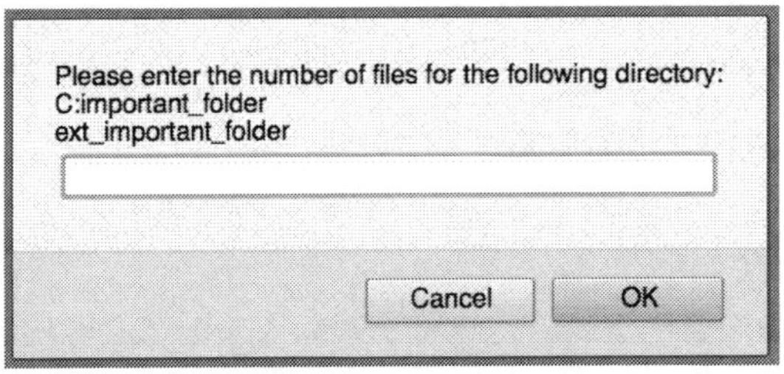

Fig. 18 *Multiple-line output using backslashes*

As you see in fig. 18, at the point where we placed the second `\n` in our code, the printout is missing the first n in `next_important_folder` and in its place we have an unintended line break. Not only that, none of the backslashes were printed out.

In cases where we need to use a backslash as part of the text, we need to escape the backslash itself. But don't worry, you don't need to learn anything else — you escape backslashes just by using another backslash.

```
1 prompt("Please enter the number of files for the following
directory:\nC:\\important_folder\\next_important_folder");
```

Please enter the number of files for the following directory:
C:\important_folder\next_important_folder

[42|]

                              Cancel   OK

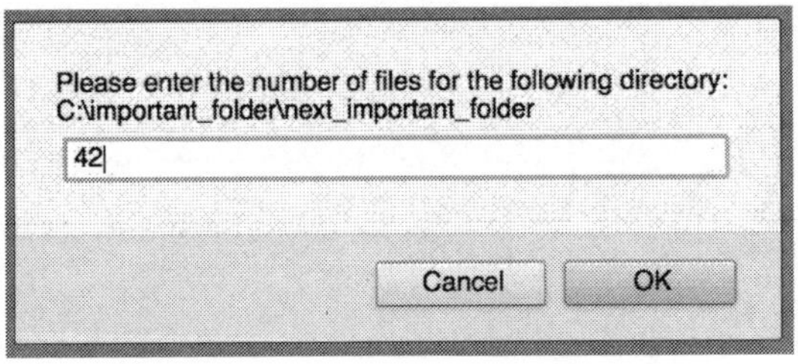

Fig. 19 *Multiple-line output using escaped backslashes*

Control Character	Description
\n	Line break
\\	Backslash (text required to print out an actual backslash)

Table 6.1 *Control character*

6.5 Exercises

Exercise 12: String "Calculations"

Expression	Return value
"Hello" + "world"	
"Hello" + " world"	
"1" + "1"	
1 + 1	
"1 + 1"	

Exercise 13: Errors in Detail

A few errors and irregularities managed to sneak their way into the following code.

```
1  "use strict";
2
3  let TALE = "Three hicks were working on a telephone tower –
   Steve, Bruce and Jed. Steve falls off and is killed instantly.
4
5  As the ambulance takes the body away, Bruce says, "Someone
   should go and tell his wife."
6
7  Jed says, "OK, I'm pretty good at that sensitive stuff,
   I'll do it."
8
9  Two hours later, he comes back carrying a case of beer.
10
11 Bruce says, "Where did you get that, Jed?"
12
13 "Steve's wife gave it to me," Jed replies.
14
15 "That's unbelievable, you told the lady her husband was
   dead and she gave you beer?"
16
17 Well, not exactly", Jed says. "When she answered the door,
   I said to her, 'You must be Steve's widow'."
18
```

```
19 She said, "No, I'm not a widow!"
20
21 And I said, "I'll bet you a case of Budweiser you are."
22
23 Console.log(tale)
```

accompanying_files/06/exercises/bugs_everywhere.js

Fix the code so that it prints out the following:

```
Three hicks were working on a telephone tower - Steve, Bruce and Jed. Steve falls off and is killed instantly.
As the ambulance takes the body away, Bruce says, 'Someone should go and tell his wife.'
Jed says, 'OK, I'm pretty good at that sensitive stuff, I'll do it.'
Two hours later, he comes back carrying a case of beer.
Bruce says, 'Where did you get that, Jed?'
'Steve's wife gave it to me,' Jed replies.
'That's unbelievable, you told the lady her husband was dead and she gave you beer?'
'Well, not exactly', Jed says. 'when she answered the door, I said to her, "You must be Steve's widow".'
She said, 'No, I'm not a widow!'
And I said, 'I'll bet you a case of Budweiser you are.'
```

Fig. 20 *Popular joke, source: http://jokes.cc.com/funny-dark-humor/nrihw9/sensitive-beer*

Type Conversion and Numbers Which Aren't Numbers

7

7.1   Implicit Type Conversion

It would seem obvious that, just like in a pocket calculator, the arithmetic operators used in programming expect numbers as operands, i.e. values of type `number`. But what happens if you use arithmetic operators to combine strings together instead of numbers? We can illustrate this question using the operators `*`, `/` and `-` (the `+` sign deserves special attention, so we'll come back to it in a moment). What values do the following expressions return? Try it out for yourself!

Examples
"5" * "4" returns?
"5" * 4 returns?
5 * "4" returns?

The result in all cases is `20`, with a data type of `number`. The explanation of this lies in the fact that the multiplication operator expects two numbers as operands. If one or even both operands are of type `string`, JS carries out a so-called **implicit type conversion**. Regardless of the data types of the two operands, the JS interpreter tries to convert their data types to `number` types. This form of type conversion is known as **implicit** since it happens automatically, i.e. without any involvement on the part of the programmer. The technical term for implicit type conversion is **coercion**.

The operators `/` and `-` use coercion as well.

Examples

"5" - "4" returns **1** (type: **number**)
"5" - 4 returns **1** (type: **number**)
5 - "4" returns **1** (type: **number**)
"5" / "4" returns **1.25** (type:**number**)
"5" / 4 returns **1.25** (type:**number**)
5 / "4" returns**1.25** (type: **number**)

7.2   Explicit Type Conversion

Unfortunately, JS can't always know what data type an application actually needs, and sometimes returns the wrong one. In such cases, it's up to you as the programmer to implement the type conversion yourself. The following example illustrates this problem.

Let's take the code for a simple cash register. A cashier enters the prices for three items, and the application is to calculate and display the total price for all three.

```
1 let price1 = prompt("Price of item 1?");
2 let price2 = prompt("Price of item 2?");
3 let price3 = prompt("Price of item 3?");
4
5 console.log("total: " + (price1 + price2 + price3));
```

Run the cash register program and enter a price of 1 for all three items. The application should now display

```
total: 3
```

Instead, you get:

```
total: 111
```

If this happened to you in the supermarket and you suddenly had to shell out $111 instead of $3, you probably wouldn't be too happy. So what went wrong here? To understand that, we need to look a little closer at types. Let's trying adding the following statement between line 1 and line 2:

```
console.log(typeof price1)
```

Run the application again — the console displays `string`.
The problem lies in the fact that the function `prompt` always returns a string regardless of the input you give it. This means that the value of `price1` is actually the string `"1"` and not the number `1`. Since the operands here are strings, `+` concatenates them. As a result, `"1" + "1" + "1"` returns the string `"111"`. Explicit type conversion will solve this problem. Explicit means that the interpreter doesn't automatically take care of the conversion — instead, it's now up to you as the programmer to handle this. If you change your code so that each variable is of type `number`, the cash register program will perform the calculation correctly. JS provides a function called (surprise!) `Number` for just this purpose. It expects a string as an argument and converts the type of this argument to a `number`.

Example

`Number("1")` returns `1` (type: `number`)

The return value of **prompt** is a string. However, since we need a number, you need to apply the function **Number** to the value returned by **prompt**. You can do this as follows:

```
Number(prompt("Price of article 1?"))
```

If a user enters the number 1 for the price of the first item, the `prompt` function will return the string `"1"`. `Number` then converts this to a number.

Here's the complete program:

```
1  "use strict";
2
3  let price1 = Number(prompt("Price of article 1?"));
4  let price2 = Number(prompt("Price of article 2?"));
5  let price3 = Number(prompt("Price of article 3?"));
6
7  console.log("total: " + (price1 + price2 + price3));
```

Listing 16 accompanying_files/07/examples/number.js

Run the program again with the same input as above (a 1 three times). This time we get the right output:

```
total: 3
```

Exactly how does `Number` work? The function analyzes the string you pass it to see if it's a number — after all, a string doesn't necessarily have to contain a numeric value. For example, `"Hello"` doesn't contain any numbers.

Number("25") returns **25** (type:**number**)
Number("Hello") returns **NaN** (type:**number**)

7.3   **The NaN Paradox**

You've probably been asking yourself just what is **NaN** (the value returned by `Number` in the preceding example). `Number` always returns `NaN` when you ask that function to convert a string like "Hello".

`NaN` stands for *not a number*. This value represents a numeric operation which has resulted in an error. This can occur both during explicit as well as implicit type conversion.

Examples

Number("NerdWorld") returns**NaN**
Number("NerdWorld 2") returns**NaN**
"Three" * 3 returns**NaN**

Just like *1, 2, 3* etc., *NaN* is also a value of type `number`. `NaN` can also be used as a literal — just try

```
typeof NaN
```

At first, it seems a little paradoxical to say: "Not a number is a number" — but this actually makes sense. Any place in your program where you can use a value of data type **number**, you can also use **NaN**. This allows your program to keep running even when an error occurs. Although the error does show up in the result, this is usually better than having your program terminate completely. A **NaN** which acts as an operand in a numeric calculation will again result in a return value of **NaN**.

Number("NerdWorld") * 3 returns **NaN**
NaN * 3 returns **NaN**
12 / "3products" returns **NaN**, but
12 / "3" returns **4** and
12 / Number("3products") returns **NaN**

7.4   Exercises

Exercise 14: Just Exactly What Kinds of Expressions are These?

What's the return value and data type of the following expressions?

Expression	Return Value	Data Type
"1.5" * 2		
"1,5" * 2		
"1.5" + 2		
Number("1.5") * 2		
Number("1,5") * 2		
Number("3 days") * 7		

Expression	Return Value	Data Type
Number("Page 20") + 5		
"9,2" + Number("11.7");		
(NaN - 2) * (4 / 2)		
alert(Number(17 / 2 + 1.3))		
typeof 12.25		
typeof typeof 12.25		

Exercise 15: Maximum Distance & Consumption

1 Write a program to calculate a car's fuel consumption. The user will enter the number of miles he/she has driven (distance) as well as the amount of gas consumed during the trip. The program then calculates fuel consumption per 100 kilometers and prints this out.
   Hint: Use the following formula:
   consumption [liters/100 km] = total gas consumed [liters] / distance [km] × 100

2 Add code to your program so that it also asks the user for the capacity of his/her tank and calculates the maximum distance the user can travel, in kilometers.
   Hint: Use the following formula:
   maximum distance [km] = tank capacity [liters] / consumption [liters/100 km]

8 *Math, Because the Whole is Greater than the Sum of its Parts*

8.1   Math Object

JS provides programmers like us with a wide variety of mathematical functions. These include functions which do things like round off values, return random numbers, perform angle calculations, etc. Instead of scattering around these functions all over the place, JS makes these functions accessible through a single `Math` object. For now, you don't need to be aware of any of the gory details surrounding objects. The sole purpose of the `Math` object is to group together all mathematically-related functions and constants so that they're easier to find. As a result, such an object is often also known as a ***utility object***. table 8.1 describes a small selection of the functions available to you via `Math`:

Function or constant	Purpose	Example
sqrt	Square root	`Math.sqrt(9)` returns 3
pow	Exponentiation	`Math.pow(2, 5)` returns 32
cos	Cosine	`Math.cos(0)` returns 1
PI	π	`Math.PI` returns 3.141592653589793

Table 8.1 *Math object functions and constants*

JS developers will often also refer to this object as the Math API. You can think of an ***API (application programming interface)*** as a human-machine interface which allows a programmer to access the functionality essential for developing software. Depending on the given situation, this functionality can involve definitions, protocols, etc. In JS, an API generally refers to a set of functions which all relate to a specific topic. For example, the Math API allows you to access all the mathematical functionality available in JS.

8.2 Some Well-Rounded Functions: floor, round & ceil

The Math object also provides commonly used rounding functions. Three such functions exist in JS: `round`, `ceil` and `floor`. The function `round` is a conventional function found in many programming languages. It behaves just like in the commercial work world: Any value after the decimal point which is 0.5 or greater is rounded up to the next highest integer, while values less than this are rounded down. By contrast, the function `floor` always rounds down, while `ceil` always rounds up.

Example

➤ `Math.round(3.1)` returns 3

➤ `Math.round(3.5)` returns 4

➤ `Math.floor(3.7)` returns 3

➤ `Math.ceil(3.1)` returns 4

8.3 Fixed Like New with toFixed

Sometimes you need to round a number to a specific number of decimal places. For example, we normally round off monetary amounts to two places, so we have a whole amount of cents in addition to the dollar amount.

However, contrary to what you might expect, you won't find this functionality in `Math`. Instead, you call the function `toFixed` directly from a number value.

Examples

```
1  3.4567.toFixed(3); // => 3.457
2
3  let price = 10;
4  price.toFixed(2) // => 10.00
```

The argument passed to `toFixed` specifies how many decimal places should be printed out.

8.4 Just As Luck Would Have It, A Random Function

Random numbers are used in many programs, e.g. in online games. The Math object again is responsible for generating random numbers.

As an example, let's program a die — in other words, random numbers between `1` and `6`.

To do this, we'll need the function `Math.random()`. It returns numbers from `0` up to but not including `1`.

For example, calling `Math.random()` will return values like `0.7881953510278985` or `0.399900033690243175`.

By multiplying this return value by `6`, we can obtain the number range we need for our example.

`Math.random() * 6` will return values like `4.6533273673689099115` or `2.364744869982669`.

Then use `Math.floor` to remove the unnecessary decimal places (a `round` would distort the probability and favor some numbers over others).

`Math.floor(Math.random() * 6)` will now return values like `3` or `5` or `0`.

However, we still have a problem — our expression is returning numbers from `0` through `5`, but never `6`. So just add 1 — and now we have a "real" die:

`Math.floor(Math.random() * 6) + 1` returns values like `3` or `1` or `6`.

8.5   Reference

Function or Constant	Purpose	Example
sqrt	Square root	`Math.sqrt(9)` returns 3
pow	Exponentiation	`Math.pow(2, 5)` returns 32
cos	Cosine	`Math.cos(0)` returns 1
PI	π	`Math.PI` returns 3.141592653589793
round	Rounding per normal business practice	`Math.round(3,678)` returns 4
floor	Round down	`Math.floor(3,678)` returns 3
ceil	Round up	`Math.ceil(3,678)` returns 4

Table 8.2 Math object functions/constants and toFixed

Function or Constant	Purpose	Example
max	Maximum value among (any number of) arguments	`Math.max(3, 7, 2)` returns 7
min	Minimum value among (any number of) arguments	`Math.min(3, 7, 2)` returns 2
abs	Absolute value of a number (magnitude without plus/minus sign)	`Math.abs(-3.678)` returns 3.678
random	A random number	`Math.random()` returns a random number from 0 up to but not including 1
toFixed	Round to specified number of decimal places	`3.0.toFixed(2)` returns 3.00

Table 8.2 *Math object functions/constants and toFixed*

8.6   Exercises

Exercise 16: 2000 Seconds, Part 2

Print out the results of your time calculation (exercise 3) so they're rounded off (no decimal places), in the following form:
mm:ss

Exercise 17: Lotto (or the "49-Sided Die")

A die is definitely useful and is a good option for generating random numbers from one to six. In all other cases, however, a random number generator is definitely an essential tool for generating random numbers in other ranges. For example, you might need some help for picking numbers the next time you play lotto.

So write a program which prints out exactly one random number between 1 and 49. Include the boundary values 1 and 49 as possible values, and do not print out decimal places.

Exercise 18: Maximum Distance & Consumption, Part 2

1   Round the output of exercise 15 (question 1 only) per normal business practice (i.e. round up all numbers greater than or equal to 0.5).

To Tell The Truth — Relational Operators & the boolean Data Type

9

The Truth is Out There

The X-Files

Our client Marty, the owner of NerdWorld, just had a long talk over lunch with Tanya, the head of his marketing department. The two came up with a new requirement for the website:

> Our marketing department had a great idea for a discount. From now on, we want customers who're buying three or more of an item to get a volume discount of 5% on the item. We think this will get customers who're ordering two of an item to think about maybe buying a third item as well. If a customer likes an item, perhaps he/she would also give it to someone else as a present — so this would be good chance to just dump another item from stock into the order.

9.1   Decisions, Decisions...

You find countless cases like this in the real world, in which a program needs to react to yes/no decisions, e.g.

➤ *"Should a discount be applied?"*
➤ *"Did the user enter the correct password?"*

To make these decisions, the program needs to know what's true and what's false and react accordingly. In the case of an incorrect password, this reaction would be an error message. And in the case of a discount, this reaction would be deducting the discount from the total price of the order.

An expression within the program must therefore:

➤ decide whether something is *true* or *false*.
➤ return the result of this decision.

To make a decision, an expression must compare two values with each other. So that you can check, say, whether the *quantity ordered for a certain product is greater than 2*, or whether *a string input by a user corresponds to his/her password*, you'll need so-called *comparison operators* (also called **relational operators**). Let's look at these in a little more detail.

9.2   Relational Operators and the Meaning of Truth

Relational operators make it possible for you to compare two values. You can interpret these comparisons as a question:

```
325 > 12
```

Is 325 greater than 12?

```
23.5 <= 23.9
```

Is 23.5 less than or equal to 23.9?

```
365 === 365
```

Is 365 equal to 365?

```
2 !== 5?
```

Is 2 not equal to 5?

The following table gives you an overview of these relational operators:

Operator	Operation
<	less than
>	greater than
<=	less than or equal to
>=	greater than or equal to
===	equal to
!==	not equal to

Table 9.1 *Relational Operators*

So now let's go back to our webshop and check whether a customer ordered at least three of the same item. You can do this as follows:

```
quantityOfCartItem >= 3
```

Here `quantityOfCartItem` is a variable which contains the quantity of a given item in a customer's cart.

9.3   The boolean Data Type

We expect answers to our questions — in other words, an appropriate return value. This return value is another common feature shared by relational operators, and is always **true** or **false**.

For example, the expression `quantityOfCartItem >= 3` would have a return value of `true` if the value of our `quantityOfCartItem` variable were 10, and a return value of `false` if its value were 1. In real life, the cart implementation would determine this value. To try this out, let's create a simple cart simulation using a `prompt`:

```
1 "use strict";
2
3 let quantityOfCartItem = prompt("Quantity of the item?");
4
5 console.log("Discount given: " + (quantityOfCartItem >= 3));
```
Listing 17 accompanying_files/09/examples/boolean.js

A `true` in the console means that the discount will be applied. You would then need to deduct the discount from the price (but we'll look at that later).

These `true` and `false` values are actually not strings, but rather values which stand on their own and represent a condition of *true* or *false*. As a result, JS provides a separate data type for these values — **boolean**. You can also use the console to see how this data type works:

```
typeof (3 < 7)
```

or

```
typeof true
```

An expression which returns such a boolean value is called a **boolean expression** or **condition**.

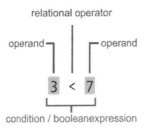

relational operator

operand ─┐ │ ┌─ operand

3 < 7

condition / booleanexpression

Fig. 21 *Boolean Expression*

A Short History Lesson

The **boolean** data type is named after mathematician *George Boole* (1815 - 1864), whose concepts form the basis of the calculations carried out by modern computers. He's therefore considered one of the founders of computer science, despite the fact that computers didn't even exist in his time.

Examples

Condition	Return Value
3 > 5	false
4567 === 4567	true
4567 !== 4567	false
"Ladislaus" === "Ladislaus"	true
"Oswine" === "Ladislaus"	false
321 <= 253	false
321 >= 253	true
12 >= 15	false
12 <= 15	true
7 <= 7	true
5 === 9	false
5 !== 9	true
"5" === 5	false

Why a Basic Equals Sign isn't Enough

The basic equals sign = is already being used as the assignment operator and therefore can't be used as a comparison operator. Comparison operators in JS include both double and triple equals signs. However, the two have a subtle difference which can result in some nasty bugs. Douglas Crockford (2008) even calls == the "evil twin".

The difference lies in the fact of how the two operators handle different data types. === is fairly easy to understand — if two values have different data types, they just aren't equal!

Examples

```
5 === "5"   // => false
0 === false // => false
```

== behaves differently. When two values are of different data types, it tries to convert their types so that it can carry out a comparison.

Examples

```
5 == "5"       // => true
0 == false     // => true
"0" == false   // => true
0 == ""        // => true
"0" == ""      // => false
```

While expressions like 5 == "5" are relatively straightforward, situations like "0" == false often result in bugs which are tough to find. The *rules for comparison in the ECMA standard*[27] are quite complicated, and it's tough to keep all of them in the back of your mind.

Fortunately, the operator is only used in very rare, very specific situations.

My recommendation: Just always use the triple equals sign ===, then you'll always be safe (Crockford 2008).

Finally, let's assign these new relational operators to our precedence table specifying the order of evaluation of all JS operators:

---

27. http://www.ecma-international.org/ecma-262/5.1/#sec-11.9.3

Priority / Precedence	Operator
1	Function call, e.g. `prompt()` Parentheses ()
2	typeof
3	* / %
4	+ -
5	< > <= >=
6	=== !==
7	= += -= *= /= %=

Table 9.3 Operators in their order of evaluation

9.4   Number or not Number...That is the Question

In addition to operators, many functions also return boolean values.

The function **isNaN** tests the argument you pass it to see if it's NOT a number (isNaN stands for *is Not a Number*). However, what we really want to look at is the value the function returns. The argument is either a number or it isn't. As a result, the function just returns `true` or `false` (meaning its return value is of type `boolean`).

Examples

`isNaN(3)` returns `false`
`isNaN("Hello")` returns `true`

Let's take a closer look at the function. What do you think the expression `isNaN("34")` will return?

Interestingly enough, the answer is `false`. Although the literal `"34"` is a string, isNaN sees it as a number. Why is this?

The function `isNaN` expects a value of type `number`. So it only returns true if the argument is the special value `NaN`. Let's try to make this a little clearer:

➤ `isNaN(NaN)` returns `true` because *NaN* means *not a number*

➤ `isNaN(-42)`, `isNaN(27)`, `isNaN(25.342)` all return `false` because their arguments are numbers.

If the function `isNaN` is passed an argument which is not of type `number` JS must then convert its data type. This conversion is an implicit type conversion as described in section 7.1. As a result, JS turns `"34"` (a string) into `34` (a number) and turns `"Hello"` into `NaN`.

The function is doing exactly what is expected of it. If the argument passed to `isNaN` winds up being turned into a number, the function returns `false`. This means that the answer to the question "*Is the argument not a number?*" is *no* — it is indeed a number! If instead you pass `isNaN` an argument which cannot be used numerically in a calculation, it'll return a value of *true*.

Examples

```
isNaN("17.7") returns false
isNaN("twenty-three") returns true
isNaN("3cars") returns true
```

9.5   String Greater Than String? Strings, Numbers and How They're Compared

Just like numbers, you can also test strings for more than just equality, so relational operators such as *less than* or *greater than* can be used with strings. What do you think `"Ladislaus" > "Oswine"` will return?

The return value for this expression is `false`. This doesn't mean that the JS interpreter actually knows these two guys and how much they weigh or anything else about them (though that definitely would be interesting). Instead, JS performs a simple **lexicographical** comparison. This means that JS first sorts the words according to their first letters, then by their second letters, etc. — just like the terms in an encyclopedia. Since L comes before O in the alphabet and is therefore considered smaller, the expression `"Ladislaus" > "Oswine"` returns a value of `false`. The expression `"Anton" > "Alan"` returns `true` — the first characters of the two strings are equal, but then `n` comes after `l` in the alphabet.

Just in case you can't get enough of comparisons...

If the strings you're comparing are numbers (or more precisely, digits), JS will also sort these in lexicographical order. Relational operators generally sort so that digits come before letters.

Example

➤ `"5" < "a"` returns `true`

➤ `"3" < "4"` returns `true`

JS also compares number strings character by character, without taking into consideration the actual value (of data type `number`) represented by the numerical sequence.

Example

➤ `300 < 4` returns `false` but

➤ `"300" < "4"` returns `true`

JS first compares the first characters of each string. `"3"` is less than `"4"`, so the result is already `true`, and `"00"` doesn't need to be checked further.

The interpreter performs a lexicographical comparison if both operands are of type `string`. If at least one operand is a number, the interpreter first converts both data types to `number` (see section 7.1). If this results in at least one operand being converted to `NaN`, the result is `false`.

Examples

➤ `"23" < 37` returns `true`

➤ `"300" < 4` returns `false`

➤ `"4" < 300` returns `true`

➤ `2 < "3cars"` returns `false`, since `"3cars"` is converted to `NaN`.

9.6 Exercises

Exercise 19: Just Exactly What Kinds of Expressions are These? — Part 2

What's the return value and data type of the following expressions? First try to figure out the results on your own and enter your answers in the table. Then use the console to see if your answers were correct.

Expression	Return Value	Data Type
"computer" === "problems"		
19 >= 19		
19 >= 19.2		
5 * 7 === 36 - 1		
3 + 3 !== 2 * 3		
"42" === 42		
"42" + 1 === 43		
"2" * "4" === Number(17 / 2)		
"42" === "forty-two"		
isNaN("3" + "4")		
"two" < "three"		
"seven" < "nine"		
"nine" < "seven"		

10 *Just in Case…if & else*

10.1   if…then

In the last lesson, you learned how to use relational operators to formulate expressions which return `true` or `false`. Instead of just printing out these boolean values, we'll now use them as conditions. Your program will then be able to make decisions based on these conditions.

Examples

> **Condition:** A player has answered a riddle correctly.
> **Decision:** The program congratulates the player on giving the right answer.

> **Condition:** A user has entered an invalid number in a form.
> **Decision:** The application points out the error to the user.

> **Condition:** The X-coordinate of a figure has reached the right side of the screen.
> **Decision:** The figure immediately stops moving to the right and starts to move downward.

And let's not forgot the new feature our client wants:

> **Condition:** A user's cart contains at least 3 of the same item.
> **Decision:** The discount is subtracted from the price.

Programming languages make decisions based on the *if-then* principle.**If** a certain condition is `true`,**then** execute one or more statements. This task in JS is handled by the ***if statement***. This statement consists of:

> the keyword `if`
> a condition (boolean expression) in parentheses
> a body, which contains statements surrounded by braces

Use the following syntax:

```
if (condition) {
   statement1;
   statement2;
   ...
}
```

Example

```
1  "use strict";
2
3  const SOLUTION = 42;
4
5  let answer = Number(prompt("What's the result of 6 * 7"));
6
7  if (answer === SOLUTION) {
8    console.log("42 is correct.");
9    console.log("Congratulations, You are a genius!");
10 }
```

Listing 18 *accompanying_files/10/examples/if.js*

This code first stores the correct answer to the riddle in the constant `SOLUTION` in line 3. Line 5 then asks the user the riddle and stores the answer in the variable `answer`.

In line 7, the `if` statement uses the equality operator to see if the user's input matches the specified solution. If so, the interpreter makes the decision to execute the statements in the body of the statement (i.e. those within the braces `{...}`). As a result, the user gets a response when he/she solves the question. If the answer input by the user is incorrect, the body is not executed and the script terminates without generating any output.

We can use a so-called activity diagram (see fig. 22) to illustrate branching in an `if` statement. Activity diagrams depict the different process flows (activities) within a program, allowing its branches and other possible program paths to be clearly illustrated.

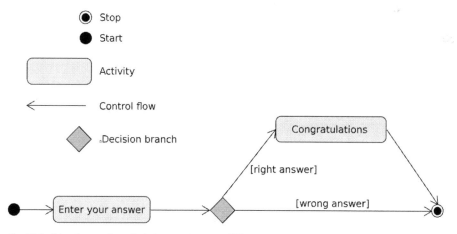

Fig. 22 *Activity diagram for calculation exercise using* `if`

The flow of a program branches when the program encounters an `if`. In other words, the program now has two possible paths. An `if` statement is therefore also referred to as **branching** and is part of the group of so-called **control structures**.

So now, how can we actually implement our newest client requirement?

```
 1  "use strict";
 2
 3  const DISCOUNT = 0.05;
 4
 5  let quantityOfCartItem = prompt("Quantity of the item?");
 6  let pricePerItem = 20; // just to simulate the real price here
 7  let totalPrice = quantityOfCartItem * pricePerItem;
 8
 9  if (quantityOfCartItem >= 3) {
10      totalPrice = totalPrice * (1 - DISCOUNT);
11  }
12
13  console.log("total Price: " + totalPrice);
```

Listing 19 *accompanying_files/10/examples/discount.js*

The `if` uses the condition from lesson 9. If you input a value of *3* or greater in the `prompt`, the condition returns `true` and the `if` executes the statement in line 10. This then reduces `totalPrice` by the discount (`DISCOUNT` constant). The `DISCOUNT` of `0.05` corresponds to the 5% in our requirement.

Awesome! We've successfully implemented the feature and our client is thrilled (whether NerdWorld actually sells more products now is another story...)

Exercise 20: The Dark Side of JavaScript

Now we'll program, little by little, a small quiz in which players will have to answer questions on JS and will therefore come up against errors and bad code — the dark side of JS. May the Source be with you!

1   Our first step is to ask the player for his/her name, store this in a variable then send him/her a greeting via an alert box. Start your program with the following code:

```
 1  "use strict";
 2
 3  let username = ...
 4  alert(...);
```

2   Let's ask our player whether he/she is actually fit enough to compete against the dark JavaScript. It might also be a good idea here to specify

the possible options for answering the question. Save the player's response in a new variable, then code an `if` branch. The body of the `if` statement should only be executed if our player confirms that he/she does indeed feel strong enough to start the game. We'll code an `alert` in the body to get confirmation that our player wants to start the game and also to spur our player on.

```
1  "use strict";
2
3  let username = ...
4  alert(...);
5
6  let playerFitness = ...
7
8  if (...) {
9    alert(...);
10 }
```

We also need to take into account the case in which our player is just too wimpy and the fitness level he/she enters is too low. Add another `if` branch to handle this case and send our player off in disgrace (while still being nice of course...however you want to do it :)

```
1  "use strict";
2
3  let username = ...
4
5  alert(...);
6
7  let playerFitness = ...
8
9  if (...) {
10   alert(...);
11 }
12
13 if (...) {
14   alert(...);
15 }
```

accompanying_files/10/exercises/dark_side_of_js.js

Tip: You should always test your program while you're actually developing it. Run your program again after every change you implement!

3   Now we're ready to start the game. Present the player with his/her first task. After the `alert`, declare a new variable to store the player's answer

to the following question:
*"Which operator has the higher priority: * or + ?"*

So that your program will be able to react to the player's answer, code
another `if` branch whose body is executed only if he/she gives the right
answer.

```
1  "use strict";
2
3  let username = ...
4  alert(...);
5
6  let playerFitness = ...
7
8  if (...) {
9    let fightOne = prompt(...
10   if (...) {
11     alert(...);
12   }
13 }
14
15 if (...) {
16   alert(...);
17 }
```

The `alert` here congratulates the player on a correct answer. If you like,
you can also include other branches with additional questions.

4   Add another `if` for the case in which the player gives an incorrect
     answer.

10.2   And If Not, Then What?

In our small calculation game (listing 18), the user got feedback when he/she per-
formed the calculation correctly. On the other hand, if our user hasn't yet mastered
the high art of multiplication, he/she will never know it.

You could add another `if` to check if `answer !== solution`, but the following
method is much more elegant:

```
1  "use strict";
2
3  const SOLUTION = 42;
4
5  let answer = Number(prompt("What's the result of 6 * 7"));
6
```

```
 7 if (answer === SOLUTION) {
 8   console.log("42 is correct.");
 9   console.log("Congratulations, You are a genius!");
10 } else {
11   console.log("Wrong. Math isn't exactly your strong point, is
it?");
12 }
```

Listing 21 *accompanying_files/10/examples/if_else.js*

Instead of using a second `if` branch, just add an **else** statement to the first. The body of the `else` statement is only executed if the body of the `if` statement is not executed. Expressed in words, our script might read something like the following description:

```
If the input is equal to the solution, then print out the
congratulatory message, otherwise display the "incorrect" message.
```

An `else` statement consists of:

➤ the keyword `else` and
➤ a body with statements.

`else` can never stand alone, since it's only an extension of an `if`. As a result, programmers normally call this construct an **if/else** statement. Its syntax is as follows:

```
if (condition) {
   statement1a;
   statement2a;
   ...
} else {
   statement1b;
   statement2b;
   ...
}
```

And here's an activity diagram of our code updated to include an else:

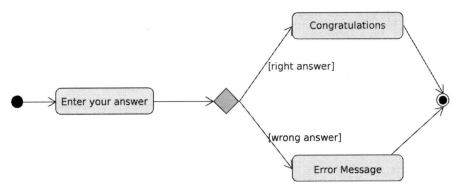

Fig. 23 *Activity diagram for calculation exercise using* `if/else`

10.3   Optional Coding with Only One Statement

FYI, JS allows you to omit the braces in cases where an `if` or `else` branch only contains a single statement. However, we recommend leaving out the braces only when the body is a short statement which can be put on the same line as the `if`. Otherwise, you might run the risk of forgetting to add braces if you later add additional statements to a branch.

Example

```
if (answer === SOLUTION) console.log("42 is correct.");
```

Coding Guidelines

> ➤ Exactly one blank space follows the keyword `if` or `else`.
> ➤ The opening brace `{` of a body is on the same line as the corresponding keyword.
> ➤ A line break follows the opening brace of a body.
> ➤ Each statement within a body is indented using 2 blank spaces.
> ➤ The closing brace `}` of a body appears on a new line and is left-aligned with the corresponding keyword.

Exception:

> ➤ Line breaks and braces may be omitted if a body only contains one statement.

Example:

```
if (answer === SOLUTION) console.log("42 is
correct.");
```

Exercise 21: The Dark Side of JavaScript

else will also come in handy for your JS game. You can use it in code like that for the question of whether the user is ready to play. Instead of adding a second `if`, you can just use `else`.

Replace the `if` statements with an `else` at the appropriate spots in your code:

```
"use strict";

let username = ...
alert(...);

let playerFitness = ...
if (...) {
  let fightOne = prompt(...
  if (...) {
    alert(...
  } else {
    alert(...
```

```
    }
  } else {
    alert(...);
  }
```

Exercise 22: Occurrence of Leap Years

Maybe you're one of those people who gets excited when a leap year occurs. And even if you aren't, you're just going to have to write a program anyway :) Your code must calculate whether or not a given year is a leap year.

Ask the user to enter a year and store this in a variable.

If the year the user entered is a leap year, the console should print out a sentence like "*0000 is a leap year!*", otherwise "*0000 is NOT a leap year*" (of course with the actual year the user entered in place of *0000*).

A year is a leap year if it

➤ is evenly divisible by 400.

➤ is not evenly divisible by 100, but is evenly divisible by 4.

Incidentally, this calculation still isn't 100 percent accurate, but will still work for the next 2000 years.

10.4   For Where Three Gather: The Ternary Operator

We've added books as a new line in our assortment of products. However, the sales tax for books is only 7%. Can you modify your code?

A simple solution to Marty's newest requirement might look something like this, somewhere in the depths of your shop code:

```
1  "use strict";
2
3  let productCategory = "books";
4  let netPrice = 10;
5  let taxRate;
6
7  if (productCategory === "books") {
8      taxRate = 1.07;
9  } else {
10     taxRate = 1.19;
11 }
12
13 let totalPrice = netPrice * taxRate; // => 10.70
```

Listing 22 *accompanying_files/10/examples/totalPrice.js*

Assigning a value to the same variable in both branches of an if statement happens quite regularly. If the if statement (like the one here) has no other purpose than this, you can use the so-called **ternary operator** instead of an **if** statement to improve the readability of your code.

The ternary operator takes three operands (thus the term ternary) and separates these using the characters `?` and `:`. You might also write the code above like this:

```
1  "use strict";
2
3  let productCategory = "books";
4  let netPrice = 10;
5  let taxRate;
6
7  taxRate = productCategory === "books" ? 1.07 : 1.19;
8
9  let totalPrice = netPrice * taxRate; // => 10.70
```

Listing 23 *accompanying_files/10/examples/totalPrice_ternary.js*

The ternary operator in line 7 acts like an `if/else`. First, JS evaluates the boolean expression `productCategory === "books"` which appears before the `?`. If the result is `true`, the overall expression returns the first value, i.e. the value between `?` and `:`: `1.07`. Otherwise, it returns the value following the `:` — `1.19`. This code listing is therefore semantically identical to the one above, but shorter and definitely more readable (once you've become used to this new style).

FYI, the operator is called *ternary* because it takes three operands.

Logical Operators, or the Beginning of Wisdom

> *Logic is the beginning of wisdom, not the end.*
>
> Mr. Spock

11.1 Using Logical Operators to Combine Multiple Conditions

What we feared has come to pass: Marty and Tanya had another meeting. Something like this usually has consequences. But just listen to what Marty has to say:

 We recently implemented a 5% discount for quantities of 3 or more of the same item. We now need the same discount applied to new items, in other words, those which have only come out recently...hmmm, I'd say for the first 30 days of the item. However, the two discounts won't be cumulative. After all, we don't want to give people a 10% discount when they buy more than 3 of a new item — that would be terrible for business!

How can you implement this requirement? One possibility would be to determine the discount using two separate `if` statements.

```
"use strict";

let productAgeInDays = prompt("Product age in days?");
let quantityOfCartItem = prompt("Quantity of the item?");
let discountPercentage = 0;

if (quantityOfCartItem >= 3) {
  discountPercentage = 5;
}

if (productAgeInDays <= 30) {
  discountPercentage = 5;
}

console.log(`Current discount: ${discountPercentage}%`);
```

However, the problem can be solved a lot more easily — just use the ***or operator*** `||` (two vertical lines, so-called "pipes"). You could say:

The discount is applied if

> the cart contains more than 3 of the same item **or**

> the item is not more than 30 days old.

Only one of these two conditions needs to apply — the first **or** the second The following boolean expression in JS describes our situation:

```
quantityOfCartItem >= 3 || productAgeInDays <= 30
```

And so you use the expression in your program:

```
1  "use strict";
2
3  let productAgeInDays = prompt("Product age in days?");
4  let quantityOfCartItem = prompt("Quantity of the item?");
5  let discountPercentage = 0;
6
7  if (quantityOfCartItem >= 3 || productAgeInDays <= 30) {
8    discountPercentage = 5;
9  }
10
11 console.log(`Current discount: ${discountPercentage}%`);
```

Listing 24 accompanying_files/11/examples/or.js

The or operator `||` combines two conditions. As soon as at least one of the two conditions returns `true`, the overall expression of the `if` statement will have a return value of `true` and the `if` statement will react accordingly.

11.2   Or Operator Method of Operation

Exactly how does the or operator work? The operator can be represented as a so-called **truth table**. The result of an or operation is true when either value is `true`.

a	b	a||b
false	false	false
false	true	true
true	false	true
true	true	true

Table 11.1 Truth table for or operator

The first row of the table means: If two variables `a` and `b` each contain `false`, the expression `a || b` must likewise be `false`. This situation can be demonstrated in JS as follows:

```
1 let a = false;
2 let b = false;
3 alert(a || b);
```

Of course you could also examine this expression just by entering `false ||` `false` directly in the console.

11.3   The And Operator

 Oops, I almost forgot. There's also going to be a second type of discount. We're going to apply this 7% discount to everything (!), but only for first-time customers and only if their cart has a total value of at least $100. We're doing this because many new customers only place small trial orders of one or two items. We just want to give them an additional incentive to fill up their cart instead of splitting everything up over several orders.

In this case, both conditions must be satisfied for the discount to be applied. You could say:

The discount is applied if

➤ the total price of the cart is greater than or equal to $100 **and**

➤ the number of prior orders placed is 0 (new customer).

JS provides the ***and operator*** `&&` for just these situations:

```
total >= 100 && numberOfOrders === 0
```

And here's the same expression as used in the actual code:

```
1 "use strict";
2
3 let numberOfOrders = prompt("How many orders has the customer
placed so far?");
4 let cartTotal = prompt("What is the cart's total?");
5 let discountPercentage = 0;
6
7 if (cartTotal >= 100 && numberOfOrders === 0) {
```

```
 8    discountPercentage = 7;
 9  }
10
11  console.log(`Current discount: ${discountPercentage}%`);
```

Listing 25 *accompanying_files/11/examples/and.js*

11.4   And Operator Method of Operation

The and operator works like the or operator but follows its own truth table. The result of an and operation is `true` if**both** variables contain a value of `true`.

a	b	a && b
false	false	false
false	true	false
true	false	false
true	true	true

Table 11.2 *Truth table for and operator*

11.5   The Not Operator

In JS, you're often faced with a situation where you need a `true` but get a `false` or vice versa. A third kind of logical operator proves to be useful in such situations — the **not operator**. This operator is expressed in JavaScript as an exclamation point `!`. You just place it in front of a return value, and it converts any `true` value to a `false`, and vice versa. In other words, it inverts boolean values. For example, try entering `!true` in your console — you'll get back `false`.

a	!a
false	true
true	false

Table 11.3 *Truth table for not operator*

Unlike `&&` and `||`, the `!` operator takes only one operand. Read table 11.3 accordingly. The first row of the table means: If a variable `a` has a value of `false`, the expression `!a` will return the value `true`. There're a number of different situations in which you might use this operator. One example: You want to tell a user he/she entered a number, so you need the function `isNaN`. However, this does exactly the opposite of what you want — it returns `true` when the input is **not** a number. But this isn't a problem when you have the `!` operator:

```
1 "use strict";
2
3 let input = prompt("Please enter a number");
4
5 if (!isNaN(input)) {
6   console.log(`Correct - ${input} is a number`);
7 }
```
Listing 26 *accompanying_files/11/examples/not.js*

11.6   Precedence of Logical Operators

Logical operators have a low precedence, but are still evaluated before assignment operators. The not operator `!` is an exception to this, since it is a ***unary operator*** (i.e. operator with only one operand). Just like all unary operators, it has a very high precedence.

Priority / Precedence	Operator
1	Function call (e.g. `alert()`) Parentheses `()`
2	`!` typeof

3	`*`
	`/`
	`%`

4	`+` `-`

5	`<`
	`>`
	`<=`
	`>=`

6	`===` `!==`
7	**&&**

Table 11.4 *Operators in their order of evaluation*

Priority / Precedence	Operator
8	||
9	= += -= *= /= %=

Table 11.4 Operators in their order of evaluation

11.7   Exercises

Exercise 23: The Dark Side Strikes Back...

At long last, you're resuming your battle against the dark side of JS, so you're creating two new "battle sequences":

> What's the German word for "if"? (multiple possible answers: *wenn, falls*).

> Enter a string with a length between 8 and 15 characters...

Exercise 24: Of Good and Evil Input

1   Input data on a user's first name, last name, gender and age and store these in variables.

2   Then validate this input as follows:

> The first name and last name must each be between 2 and 100 characters long.

> The value input for sex must be *m* (male) or *f* (female).

> Age must be a number less than 150.

Exercise 25: Occurrence of Leap Years — Part 2

Give your leap year tool from lesson 10 a face lift. Use logical operators to eliminate a few `else` statements and make your code simpler, shorter and more readable.

A Veritable String Potpourri   *12*

Mistakes snuck into the text between lines.

Michail Genin

Once again, you get a call from Marty. He sounds a little embarrassed over the phone as he relates his dilemma, in the hopes you can help him out.

> For some time now, customers have been able to subscribe to our newsletter through our current static website. Unfortunately, our programmer who created the site didn't provide separate first name and last name fields in the registration form. So unfortunately, our database isn't very useful in terms of customer service. Of course our designers went back and changed the form, but what do we do with the existing data?

Fortunately, the JS String API provides you with a few functions which can help you solve Marty's problem.

12.1   Searching and Finding using indexOf

The function `indexOf` makes it possible for you to find the position of a specified string within a larger string.

Since you can't access an actual database, create a name as a variable. Instead of storing the corrected string in the database, `log` it to the console.

`indexOf` expects a search string as an argument and returns its position. In this case, the search string will be the blank space separating the customer's first name and last name.

```
1 "use strict";
2
3 let name = "Ladislaus Jones";
4
5 console.log(name.indexOf(" "));
```
Listing 27 accompanying_files/12/examples/indexOf.js

You get back the number `9` indicating the position of the blank space, so now we know where we need to split up the string.

> **More About Index**
>
> ➤ Position numbering begins with 0 — i.e. if the position where the search
>   string was found starts with the first character of the larger string, you'll
>   get back 0.
> ➤ If the `indexOf` function doesn't find the string you're looking for, it
>   returns -1.
> ➤ `indexOf` returns the position of the **first** occurrence it finds.
> ➤ `indexOf` starts its search from the beginning of the string. If you need to
>   start your search from the end of the string, you'll be happy to hear that JS
>   provides a similar function called `lastIndexOf` to find the **last** occur-
>   rence of your search string.

12.2   String Extraction using substr

The function `substr` extracts a substring from a larger string. Its arguments must
include

➤ the position of the first character and

➤ the number of characters you want to extract

For our customer's first name, this means that you would want to extract `9` characters starting from the beginning of the string (position `0`).

```
1  "use strict";
2
3  let name = "Ladislaus Jones";
4  let spacePosition = name.indexOf(" ");
5  let firstName = name.substr(0, spacePosition);
6
7  console.log(firstName);
```

For the customer's last name, you need all letters starting from position `10` (i.e. following the blank space) up to the end of the string. A practical feature of the function is that you can omit the second argument when you want to extract the entire
remaining string starting from your specified position. Don't just write a `10` in your
code, but use the variable `spacePosition` instead. The customer's last name
starts immediately after the position of the blank space, i.e. at `spacePosition +
1`.

```
1  "use strict";
2
3  let name = "Ladislaus Jones";
4  let spacePosition = name.indexOf(" ");
```

```
5 let firstName = name.substr(0, spacePosition);
6 let lastName = name.substr(spacePosition + 1);
7
8 console.log(firstName);
9 console.log(lastName);
```

Listing 28 *accompanying_files/12/examples/substr.js*

Now you have the customer's full name separated out into two different strings, giving you a lot more flexibility when using names.

> ### Exercise 26: When a First Name Just isn't Enough...
>
> You might have noticed that our code to split up a customer's name will only work correctly if the name is in the form `"firstName lastName"`.
>
> If a user previously entered a middle name, our program will also assign this middle name to the last name. So, given the name *Ladislaus Coolio Jones*, we'd get the following incorrect results:
>
> ```
> 1 let firstName = "Ladislaus";
> 2 let lastName = "Coolio Jones";
> ```
>
> Use `lastIndexOf` to correct the output of the following code
>
> ```
> 1 "use strict";
> 2
> 3 let name = "Ladislaus Coolio Jones";
> 4 let spacePosition = name.indexOf(" ");
> 5 let firstName = name.substr(0, spacePosition);
> 6 let lastName = name.substr(spacePosition + 1);
> 7
> 8 console.log(firstName);
> 9 console.log(lastName);
> ```
>
> *accompanying_files/12/exercises/first_name.js*

12.3   Fit and Trim

Marty's impressed, but not yet completely satisfied:

 Hey, this is great! But do you think it'd be possible to clean up our data and remove all the extra blank spaces? Unfortunately, a lot of people don't enter their data cleanly in the form.

It may be hard to believe, but you can almost do this automatically — using the function `trim`. It's so easy to use, you don't even have to specify any parameters.

```
1 let name = " Jones ";
2 console.log(name.trim()); // => "Jones" (without blank spaces)
```

Important: `trim` removes blank spaces from the beginning and from the end of a string, but not from the middle. However, this is generally what you want when you're cleaning up strings in this way.

```
1 "use strict";
2
3 let name = "   Ladislaus Jones     ";
4
5 console.log(name.trim()); // => "Ladislaus Jones" (without space
before and after)
```

Listing 30 *accompanying_files/12/examples/trim.js*

Exercise 27: A Heribert Split

So now satisfying Marty's newest requirement is no problem! You get the following data record:

```
let name = "Heribert  Gold ";
```

1   Split this name up into first name and last name.

2   Remove any superfluous blank spaces.

12.4   Being Choosy with charAt

That's often the way it is with clients – solving their problems in turn awakens their creativity and just encourages them to come up with new problems. So your next task follows quite promptly:

 Now that we can use first names and last names and have a lot more flexibility, we'd really like another way to print out our data records. To be specific, we usually don't need complete first names when we're printing out a simple list. For example, would it be possible to print out the name *Ladislaus Jones* like `"Jones, L."`?

To do this, you need to print out the first letter of the customer's first name. Unfortunately the function `indexOf` won't help you here since you're not searching for a specific string but for a specific position.

Instead, use the function `charAt`. It expects as a parameter the position of the character you want to extract.

```
1  "use strict";
2
3  let firstName = "Ladislaus";
4  let lastName = "Jones";
5
6  console.log(lastName + ", " + firstName.charAt(0) + "."); // =>
   "Jones, L."
```

Listing 31 *accompanying_files/12/examples/charAt.js*

Exercise 28: Ladislaus Transformed

That was a lot of fun, how about another exercise? :)

Store the name "Ladislaus Jones" in a variable and create a printout which follows the pattern `"<lastName>, <first letter of firstName>."`, i.e. `"Jones, L."`.

12.5   Shrinking Strings using toLowerCase

Your solution to our problem with blank spaces was awesome! By the way, I noticed something else while I was looking through our data records . Some names were entered all in lowercase...not only that, sometimes the second letter of a name was accidentally also entered in uppercase. It'd be great if you could fix that data!

You just need two functions to correct this problem:

➤ `toLowerCase` and
➤ `toUpperCase`.

First, let's convert the entire string to lowercase.

```
1  "use strict";
2
3  let firstName = "LAdislaus";
4  firstName = firstName.toLowerCase();
```

```
5
6  let lastName = "JOnes";
7  lastName = lastName.toLowerCase();
8
9  console.log(firstName + " " + lastName);
```

Now our name is completely in lowercase:

```
ladislaus jones
```

However, the two parts of the name should both begin with uppercase letters. To do this, we'll need the new function `toUpperCase`, as well as two other functions you're already familiar with, `substr` and `charAt`.

By using `charAt` and `substr`, you can specify exactly which part of a name should be in uppercase and which part should be in lowercase. Then you can just concatenate both parts together.

```
1  "use strict";
2
3  let firstName = "ladislaus";
4  firstName = firstName.charAt(0).toUpperCase() +
firstName.substr(1).toLowerCase();
5
6  let lastName = "JOnes";
7  lastName = lastName.charAt(0).toUpperCase() +
lastName.substr(1).toLowerCase();
8
9  console.log(firstName + " " + lastName);
```

Listing 32 accompanying_files/12/examples/toLowerCase.js

The console prints out what you expect:

```
Ladislaus Jones
```

Exercise 29: The Dark Side of JavaScript — The Battle Continues

It's time to make some more improvements to our game. Take one of the questions you've already implemented:

"What's the German word for if?" (multiple possible answers: wenn, falls).

Your code already covers three possible solutions. But what happens if a user, instead of `wenn`, enters `Wenn` or `WENN`?

You'll often come across issues related to *uppercase and lowercase* when working with user input. For example, it'd be helpful in our game if players always wrote their answers completely in lowercase. Of course a player would be a little confused if the game considered an answer of `Wenn` as incorrect.

So improve that part of your game's code by converting the answer entered by the player to lowercase (before the if condition test, of course).

12.6   Put in a Substitute using replace

Slowly but surely you're cranking out new functionality. Are you ready for the latest requirement from Marty and company?

Sometimes it turns out that, for marketing reasons, we need to rename products. Doing this by hand would be very error-prone, not to mention it'd also be very tedious. Can you come up with a good solution?

Fig. 24 *Prescription mug, © 2015 ThinkGeek, Inc. All Rights Reserved.*[28]

Of course you can! Just use the function `replace`. `replace` allows you to perform substitutions within a string. The function takes two parameters — the search string and the substitution string.

---

28.   *http://www.thinkgeek.com/product/1a4c/*

```
1  "use strict";
2
3  let productName = "Prescription Mug";
4  let productDescription = "Prescription Mug: Coffee mug which
   looks like a drug bottle. Your Prescription Mug is a great
   conversation starter. Great for the caffeine addict in your life –
   one who doesn't need an intervention. You'll love your Prescription
   Mug.";
5  let newProductName = "Drug Mug";
6
7  console.log(productDescription.replace(productName,
   newProductName));
```

The first thing you'll notice when you run this code is that the function only replaces the first occurrence of the product name.

```
Drug Mug: Coffee mug which looks like a drug bottle.  Your
Prescription Mug is a great conversation starter. Great for the
caffeine addict in your life – one who doesn't need an
intervention. You'll love your Prescription Mug.
```

You can fix this by writing out the first parameter as follows:

```
/searchTerm/g
```

The slashes indicate and delimit a so-called **regular expression**. Regular expressions are extremely useful for text recognition purposes, and open you up to a wide variety of possibilities. At this point, however, all you need to know is that you can use any string as a search term.

The letter `g` stands for *global* and tells the function to make substitutions over the entire text and not just at the first place it finds the search string. Make sure you place your regular expressions within slashes and not within quotation marks!

```
1  "use strict";
2
3  let productName = /Prescription Mug/g;
4  let productDescription = "Prescription Mug: Coffee Mug which
   looks like a drug bottle. Your Prescription Mug is a great
   conversation starter. Great for the caffeine addict in your life –
   one that doesn't need an intervention. You will love your
   Prescription Mug.";
5  let newProductName = "Drug Mug";
6
7  console.log(productDescription.replace(productName,
   newProductName));
```

Listing 33 accompanying_files/12/examples/replace.js

Now `replace` will substitute the new name over the entire item description —
which is just what you want.

```
Drug Mug: Coffee mug which looks like a drug bottle. Your Drug Mug
is a great conversation starter. Great for the caffeine addict in
your life - one who doesn't need an intervention. You'll love your
Drug Mug.
```

12.7   Reference

Function	Purpose	Call Example Based on `let s = "abcde"`	Return Value
charAt	Determines the character at the specified location	`s.charAt(1)`	b
includes	Checks whether a string contains the specified substring	`s.includes("bc")`	true
startsWith	Checks whether a string begins with the specified substring	`s.startsWith("ab")`	true
endsWith	Checks whether a string ends with the specified substring	`s.endsWith("de")`	true
indexOf	Determines the position within a string of the specified substring	`s.indexOf("cd")`	2
lastIndexOf	Determines the position within a string of the specified substring (search begins at the end of the string)	`s.lastIndexOf("de")`	3
repeat	Repeats the string as often as specified	`s.repeat(2)`	abcdeabcde
substr	Extracts a substring from the specified position	`s.substr(1, 3)`	bcd
toLowerCase	Returns the string in lowercase	`"AbCdE".toLowerCase()`	abcde
toUpperCase	Returns the string in uppercase	`"AbCdE".toUpperCase()`	ABCDE
trim	Removes blank spaces at the beginning and end of a string	`" abc ".trim()`	abc

Table 12.1 Overview of String API (based on example `let s = "abcde"`)

12.8   Exercises

Exercise 30: If Someone Could Just Find That Needle in the Haystack...

Most people use this expression only figuratively. But not you! Your new assignment is to actually find that needle!

Fig. 25 Photo: Jannis_V[29], CC Attribution, ShareAlike[30]

Of course we don't mean that you should actually go out and burrow around in some hay. Instead, we're giving you a string which is completely free of (real) hay (this will probably be a lot better for you, especially if you suffer from hay fever):

```
haystack haystack haystack haystack haystack haystack
haystack needle haystack haystack haystack haystack haystack
haystack haystack haystack haystack
```

Now find out what position the needle is at and `log` this out to the console.

(By the way — counting doesn't count!)

29.   https://www.flickr.com/people/52336371@N07/
30.   https://creativecommons.org/licenses/by-sa/2.0/

Exercise 31: Valuable Zeros, Part 1

A while back, NerdWorld changed its item number system. New item numbers now begin with a 0, e.g. 0123. However, many of the old item numbers don't have leading zeros. But unfortunately, you can't just go and add a 0 to all of the old numbers, since quite a few of them already do start with a 0 — in that case, you shouldn't add another 0 at the beginning. Complete the following program fragment so that no matter what value you assign to the variable `itemNumber`, the program prints out the correct number according to the new format. Tip: Use the ternary operator!

```
1 let itemNumber = "123";
2 let correctedItemNumber = …;
3
4 console.log(correctedItemNumber);
```

Examples

➤ 123 => 0123

➤ 7 => 07

➤ 07 => 07

➤ 007 => 007

13 Once More With Function!

13.1   Function is a Function is a Function

I'm now thinking that our new discount could also be a great buy-ing incentive for our existing customers as well. But it often seems like they never notice anything. Could you maybe send out a per-sonalized newsletter which tells our customers about the new dis-count? The personalization part especially is very important to us — we want to address everyone by their first name. Can you do that?

Of course you can!

So that you don't have to make a new copy of the text each time and change each name manually, it's a good idea to define a separate **function**.

You're already well-acquainted with functions, and have been using a number of pre-defined functions in much of your code — functions like `prompt` and `Number`. Taking a closer look "under the hood", a pre-defined function consists of a number of individual statements, and is generally not written in JS. Instead, functions are either part of the JS engine or the environment (e.g. a browser) and are therefore often implemented in C, C++ or Java. Such functions are known as **native** or **built-in** functions.

So now, you're going to define your own functions (don't worry, you won't need to learn C++, it's easy to define your own functions using just JS). A so-called **function definition** (specified here in the form of a **function expression**) consists of

➤ **parameters** in parentheses `()` ,
➤ an arrow `=>` and
➤ a **body** in braces `{}` .

```
() => {
    ...
};
```

Since you won't need any parameters at first, the parentheses will be empty. You can enter any number and any kind of statements in the body (also called a **code block** or just **block**).

Example

```
1 () => {
2   console.log("Dear Customer,\n");
3   console.log(`We're pleased to inform you that NerdWorld is
making a number of new discounts available to you. Please visit
http://www.nerdworld.example/discounts for detailed information.`);
4   console.log("Happy nerding,\nYour NerdWorld Team");
5 };
```

So that you can actually call a function, it's generally a good idea to associate it with a name using `let` or `const` (this is known as `binding` your function to a name). In addition, the name of your function should make it obvious what its task is.

Example

```
1 let showNewsletter = () => {
2   console.log("Dear Customer,\n");
3   console.log(`We're pleased to inform you that NerdWorld is
making a number of new discounts available to you. Please visit
http://www.nerdworld.example/discounts for detailed information.`);
4   console.log("Happy nerding,\nYour NerdWorld Team");
5 };
```

Since a definition of the form `() => {}` is an expression which returns a function (which you then reference through the variable), this form of function definition is also known as a ***function expression***.

Life in the Old Days

In your real life programming work, you'll often come across functions which use the old syntax from ES5 (and even earlier ES versions):

```
function showNewsletter() { }
```

These "old functions" can also be bound to a variable as a ***function expression***:

```
var showNewsletter = function() { };
```

In real life, the names for Marty's newsletter would come from some source like a database and the output wouldn't be sent to the console but through an email client. But that's a story for another chapter which you can safely ignore for now :)

13.2   Let's Function

To actually make use of a self-defined function, you need to call it. The **function call** to a self-defined function is no different than that to a native function — it just consists of the function identifier and parentheses, and of course the statement should be followed by a semicolon as usual.

```
showNewsletter();
```

Here's the code in its entirety:

```
1  "use strict";
2
3  let showNewsletter = () => {
4    console.log("Dear Customer,\n");
5    console.log(`We're pleased to inform you that NerdWorld is
making a number of new discounts available to you. Please visit
http://www.nerdworld.example/discounts for detailed
information.\n`);
6    console.log("Happy nerding,\nYour NerdWorld-Team");
7  };
8
9  showNewsletter();
```

Listing 34 accompanying_files/13/examples/showNewsletter.js

Exercise 32: Logged into the Console, Part 2

1   Write a function which prints your name out to the console.

```
let ... {
  console.log(...);
};
...
```

13.3   Hello ${username},...

Our code is still missing the customer personalization. This brings us to parentheses. You can use these to pass a so-called **parameter** to a function. Rename your function `showNewsletterFor` since this will make it more readable when combined with the parameter.

```
1  "use strict";
2
3  let showNewsletterFor = (username) => {
4    console.log(`Hello ${username},\n`);
5    console.log(`We're pleased to inform you that NerdWorld is
making a number of new discounts available to you. Please visit
http://www.nerdworld.example/discounts for detailed
information.\n`);
6    console.log("Happy nerding,\nYour NerdWorld-Team\n\n");
7  };
8
9  showNewsletterFor("Heribert");
10 showNewsletterFor("Ladislaus");
11 showNewsletterFor("Goldy");
```

Listing 35 *accompanying_files/13/examples/showNewsletterFor.js*

Every time you call the `showNewsletter` function, the console will print out a personalized version of the email.

```
Hello Heribert,

We're pleased to inform you that NerdWorld is making a number of
new discounts available to you. Please visit
http://www.nerdworld.example/discounts for detailed information.

Happy nerding,
- your NerdWorld Team


Hello Ladislaus,

We're pleased to inform you that NerdWorld is making a number of
new discounts available to you. Please visit
http://www.nerdworld.example/discounts for detailed information.

Happy nerding,
- your NerdWorld Team


Hello Goldy,

We're pleased to inform you that NerdWorld is making a number of
new discounts available to you. Please visit
http://www.nerdworld.example/discounts for detailed information.

Happy nerding,
- your NerdWorld Team
```

Let's take a look at the first call: The function takes the name `Heribert` and inserts it in every place it finds the variable `${username}`. In the background, the function is, in a sense, executing the statement `let username = "Heribert"`. A parameter is nothing other than a special variable type which is assigned a value passed to the function.

Argument vs. Parameter

FYI, in the call `showNewsletterFor("Heribert")`, given the definition

```
let showNewsletterFor = (username) => …
```

username is considered a *parameter* and *"Heribert"* (i.e. the value passed to the function) is considered an *argument*. However, the difference between an argument and a parameter is not particularly meaningful. In our everyday programming, we often speak of parameters when we actually mean arguments, and vice versa.

Just a Little Bit Less, Please?

If, as in the last example, your function requires exactly one parameter, you can make your function definition even shorter — in this case, JS allows you to omit the parentheses surrounding your parameters:

```
let showNewsletterFor = username => {
    ...
};
```

This doesn't apply for functions with two or more parameters, nor for functions without any parameters:

```
let myFunction = => { ... } //wrong!
let myFunction = () => { ... } //ok

let myFunction = a, b => { ... } //wrong!
let myFunction = (a, b) => { ... } //ok
```

Coding Guidelines

In principle, you have a number of ways available to you to write function definitions. However, with the goal of establishing a uniform, readable style, we'll observe the following coding guidelines from now on:

Call:

➤ There should be no spaces between the function identifier and the opening parenthesis.

Function Definition:

➤ There should be exactly one blank space between the parentheses and the arrow, and between the arrow and the opening brace.

➤ The statements within the function should each be indented using 2 blank spaces.

➤ The closing brace should be on a new line.

```
1 let showsABrilliantExample = () => {
2   console.log("First brilliant direction");
3   console.log("Second brilliant direction");
4 };
```

Function Identifier:

In addition to our coding guidelines which concern a function's outward appearance, we'll establish some guidelines which specifically concern function identifiers. Of course, function identifiers are subject to the general guidelines for identifiers, but we'll also add some additional guidelines which apply just to functions. In general, it's a good idea to use verbs for function identifiers since each function represents an operation such as printing something out or changing something.

➤ Function identifiers are either verbs or start with a verb. Use the imperative if at all possible!

➤ Function identifiers begin with a lowercase letter (a through z)

For example, write **printOutAwesomeStatement();** instead of **AwesomeStatementPrintout();**

13.4   Signatures: Good Documentation is Already Half the Battle

In fig. 26, you see the definition of the `substr` function as provided by the *Mozilla Developer Network*[31].

The **substr()** method returns the characters in a string beginning at the specified location through the specified number of characters.

Syntax

```
str.substr(start[, length])
```

Parameters

start
: Location at which to begin extracting characters. If a negative number is given, it is treated as `strLength + start` where `strLength` is the length of the string (for example, if `start` is -3 it is treated as `strLength - 3`.)

length
: Optional. The number of characters to extract.

Fig. 26 *Definition of `substr` function by Mozilla Developer Network (MDN)*

The line

```
str.substr(start[, length])
```

describes the so-called ***signature*** of the function. This is the usual procedure in code documentation. A signature consists of the name of the function and its parameters. The brackets `[]` around `length` mean that `length` is an optional parameter which may be omitted. The essential point here is that this documentation is very clear and readable.

13.5 Exercises

Exercise 33: Hello, Mr. ${recipient}... or maybe Ms.?

1 Imagine that you're working for a client who's not entirely reputable. Just like Marty did, this client needs you to send out a mass email:

```
Hello, Mr. Heribert,

We're happy to inform you that you've just won $100,000!
Congratulations! Please write us an email with your
banking information and we will transfer the money.

Sincerely, the Win Team
```

31. *https://developer.mozilla.org/en-US/docs/Web/JavaScript/Reference/Global_Objects/String/substr*

Program a function which handles the job of sending out the newsletter (use console output to simulate this). Instead of *Heribert*, your function should make it possible to use any name.

After you define your function, the following calls will be made from the database:

```
1 showNewsletterFor("Heribert");
2 showNewsletterFor("Goldy");
3 showNewsletterFor("Ladislaus");
```

2 Studies have shown that opening rates are higher when a newsletter uses the correct form of salutation (i.e. *Ms.* or *Mr.*). Pass a second parameter to your function which contains the correct form of salutation. You'll then use this in the first line of your newsletter.

You can specify a second parameter in your function definition within the parentheses, separated from the first parameter by a comma.

Example

```
let showNewsletterFor = (recipient, salutation) => {
  ...
};
```

You can add even more parameters, but here we only need two. As usual, you can use the new parameter as a variable within the body of your function.

After you define your function, the following calls will be made from the database:

```
1 showNewsletterFor("Heribert", "Mr.");
2 showNewsletterFor("Goldy", "Ms.");
3 showNewsletterFor("Ladislaus", "Mr.");
```

3 Tempt email recipients with individualized prizes which you'll differentiate by gender. To do this, you'll need to develop a newsletter which contains the following text:

Male Version

```
We're happy to inform you that you've won an incredible
Ferrari and $20,000!
```

Fig. 27 *Photo:Autoviva[32] (CC)*
Attribution[33]

32. *https://www.flickr.com/photos/autovivacom/*

33. *https://creativecommons.org/licenses/by/2.0/legalcode*

Female Version

> We're happy to inform you that you've won a voucher from
> Tiffany & Co. (worth $50,000), a luxury trip to New York
> and an extra $50,000 for shopping and more!

Fig. 28 Photo: irene.[34](CC)
Attribution-NoDerivs[35]

Fig. 29 Photo: revstan[36](CC) Atttribution[37]

---

34. *https://www.flickr.com/photos/irenetong/*
35. *https://creativecommons.org/licenses/by nd/2.0/legalcode*
36. *https://www.flickr.com/photos/revstan/*
37. *https://creativecommons.org/licenses/by/2.0/*

Exercise 34: Ladislaus Transformed, Part 2

Write a function called `logTransformedName` which takes a first name and last name as parameters and prints out a string in the form

```
<lastName>, <first letter of firstName>.
```

Call example

```
logTransformedName("Ladislaus", "Jones"); // => "Jones, L."
```

Hint: You can reuse parts of your solution from exercise 28.

Functions Give Us So Much...Back

14

What makes life so difficult is that there's no Ctrl + Z.

André M. Hünseler

 Our customers are always complaining that our shipping fees are too high. It looks like from now on we're going to have to calculate shipping costs accurately in advance. But this might be a big problem, especially with our snazzy shipping tubes. Our shipper bills both cartons and rolls by volume. Please make implementing that calculation first on your list.

14.1 When Your Customers are Going Down the Tubes...

You have a talk with Marty's shipping department and now you understand. The dimensions (diameter and height) of the packaging tubes required for shipping are known for most items, so this information can be used to calculate volume. Marty's shipper then charges $ `0.001` per cm³, plus $ `0.70` per unit shipped. As a result, you need the following formulas:

shippingCost formula
shippingCost = volume × costPerCC + costPerUnit

cylindricalVolume formula
cylindricalVolume = π × radius² × height

FYI, you'll find very clear explanations of geometric formulas at*http://www.basic-mathematics.com/volume-of-cylinders.html*[38]

---

38. *http://www.echteinfach.tv/formeln/geometrie/zylinder/volumen/*

Our first attempt at coding this calculation might look something like the listing below. Here, the variables `height` and `diameter` again simulate program input, which in real life would come from a database or at least from a form.

```
1  "use strict";
2
3  const BASE_COST_PER_UNIT = 0.70;
4  const COST_PER_CC = 0.001;
5
6  let height = 80;
7  let diameter = 10;
8
9  let mailingTubeVolume = Math.PI * diameter / 2 * diameter / 2 *
height;
10 let shippingCost = mailingTubeVolume * COST_PER_CC +
BASE_COST_PER_UNIT;
11
12 console.log(shippingCost); // => 6.983185307179587
```

Listing 36 accompanying_files/14/examples/tube.js

14.2   Cartons and Other Reusables...

Things are very similar with a rectangular carton — only the volume calculation is different:

```
cubeVolume = length × width × height;
```

The code for this might look something like:

```
1  "use strict";
2
3  const BASE_COST_PER_UNIT = 0.70;
4  const COST_PER_CC = 0.001;
5
6  let length = 25;
7  let width = 30;
8  let height = 12;
9
10 let cartonVolume = length * width * height;
11 let shippingCost = cartonVolume * COST_PER_CC +
BASE_COST_PER_UNIT;
12
13 console.log(shippingCost); // => 9.7
```

Listing 37 accompanying_files/14/examples/box.js

Unfortunately, these first coding attempts at calculating accurate shipping costs still show some weak areas:

➤ A large part of the code is **redundant**. For example, the calculation of shipping costs from volume is exactly the same in both cases. If any changes are made to that formula, you'll need to implement these in both places and make sure you don't forget anything! Otherwise, your code will result in inconsistencies and bugs.

➤ It's difficult to pick out the original formulas in the code — for example, the formula name *cylinder volume* doesn't even appear anywhere. As a result, you also won't be able to **reuse** these functions if, for example, you need to use the cylinder volume formula in some other place.

➤ The console displays the result. However, in the real world, this wouldn't be enough. In reality, you'd need to be able to pass the shipping costs which were calculated to other functions, to do things like add it to the total cost of the order, etc.

All of these are weaknesses which will eventually make maintaining the code much more difficult. Of course, that's not the end of the world in this small example. But programs grow, and before long you won't be able to see the forest for the trees. Small maintenance problems add up, build up momentum, and before you know it, your programs are mutating into complex monster applications which can only be maintained at the cost of great time and expense.

You're probably thinking there's a way to avoid writing double code and to give formulas clear names and to allow them to be reused.

That's absolutely correct! JS provides **functions** for exactly those reasons! But you're still missing a piece of the puzzle which will allow you to use functions here — you need return values.

14.3   ...Return When Finished

Functions can return values. Consider functions as a whole: A function accepts parameters, processes them (for example in the form of a calculation) and returns the result of this processing.

Basically, you can think of a function as a parking ticket machine. Money goes in at the top of the machine. Processing takes place in the machine itself (it checks the coins you inserted, it prints out your ticket, etc.). Finally, the printed ticket comes out of the bottom of the machine.

So you might consider a function as a small separate program which works according to the so-called ***IPO model*** i.e.:

➤ input

➤ process

➤ output

In the case of cylinder volume calculation, this would translate into: The function accepts radius and height, calculates volume according to the formula, then returns the value. Expressed in JS code, this would be:

```
let cylindricalVolume = (radius, height) => Math.PI * radius *
radius * height;
```

Have you noticed the difference here from the functions above? Right — the braces are missing. If you omit the braces, JS will only allow you to put a single expression in the function body — in other words, this shorthand notation wouldn't work for multi-line functions. On the other hand, the advantage of this is that the function returns the value calculated by the expression. Just imagine that when you call this function, JS is replacing the call with the return value.

So the call `cylindricalVolume(5, 80)` would be replaced with the return value `6283`. (Actually this would be `6283.185307179587`, but we withheld the decimal places for the sake of simplicity. Use a pocket calculator if you don't believe us :) So imagine that the value would appear exactly at the point where the function is called. You can then do something like print out the value:

```
console.log(cylindricalVolume(5, 80));
```

or assign the value to a variable so you can process it further:

```
let volume = cylindricalVolume(5, 80);
```

Again: `radius` (80) and `height` (5) go in, `6283` comes out.

Shipping costs can also be represented as a function:

```
let shippingCost = (volume) => volume * COST_PER_CC +
BASE_COST_PER_UNIT;
```

Of course, you could omit the parentheses around `volume` — these aren't necessary in cases where a function has only one parameter (see lesson 13).

```
let shippingCost = volume => volume * COST_PER_CC +
BASE_COST_PER_UNIT;
```

And now the entire program:

```
1  "use strict";
2
3  const BASE_COST_PER_UNIT = 0.70;
4  const COST_PER_CC = 0.001;
5
6  let shippingCost = volume => volume * COST_PER_CC +
   BASE_COST_PER_UNIT;
7  let cylindricalVolume = (radius, height) => Math.PI * radius *
   radius * height;
8
9  let height = 80;
10 let diameter = 10;
11 let mailingTubeVolume = cylindricalVolume(diameter / 2, height);
12
13 console.log(shippingCost(mailingTubeVolume)); // =>
   6.983185307179587
```

Listing 38 accompanying_files/14/examples/return_values.js

The formulas are now a lot easier to find and maintain — even function calls are much more readable. So when carton volume is calculated in the first step, the only thing that's important is that it's a cylinder volume, which uses radius (half of diameter) and height. Then if you or some other programmer needed the actual details of the calculation, these could be found in the function.

So when you combine the two examples, you only need to code the function for calculating shipping costs once:

```
1  "use strict";
2
3  const BASE_COST_PER_UNIT = 0.70;
4  const COST_PER_CC = 0.001;
5
6  let shippingCost = volume => volume * COST_PER_CC +
   BASE_COST_PER_UNIT;
7  let cubeVolume = (length, width, height) => length * width *
   height;
8  let cylindricalVolume = (radius, height) => Math.PI * radius *
   radius * height;
9
10 let height = 80;
11 let diameter = 10;
12 let mailingTubeVolume = cylindricalVolume(diameter / 2, height);
13
14 let width = 30;
15 let length = 25;
16 let cartonHeight = 12;
17 let cartonVolume = cubeVolume(length, width, cartonHeight);
```

```
18
19 console.log(shippingCost(mailingTubeVolume)); // =>
6.983185307179587
20 console.log(shippingCost(cartonVolume)); // => 9.7
```

Listing 39 accompanying_files/14/examples/return_values_combined.js

Coding Guidelines

Function Definition in Shorthand Notation:

➤ The entire function definition appears on one line.

➤ The arrow is followed by a blank space, with the expression immediately after that.

➤ The function definition must be completed by a semicolon.

➤ For function definitions with a return value, the kind of the returned value can be used as function name instead of a verb. (e.g. `cubeVolume` instead of `calculateCubeVolume`)

```
let cubeVolume = (length, width, height) => length *
width * height;
```

14.4   When You Need More Expression...

The functions above are pretty short; they just consist a single expression. If you need longer functions, you won't be able to omit the braces. In case you still need to specify a return value for these functions, we have a new keyword for you: *return*.

Example

For example, let's say you're writing a function which combines volume calculation and shipping costs.

```
1 "use strict";
2
3 let costForShippingTube = (diameter, height) => {
4   const BASE_COST_PER_UNIT = 0.70;
5   const COST_PER_CC = 0.001;
6
7   let radius = diameter / 2;
8   let volume = Math.PI * radius * radius * height;
9   let cost = volume * COST_PER_CC + BASE_COST_PER_UNIT;
10  return cost;
11 };
```

Listing 40 accompanying_files/14/examples/costForShippingTube.js `return` returns the value calculated by the expression which follows it. In this case, this is just the value stored in the `cost` variable. Since the function consists of more than one expression, you need to make it clear which expression determines the return value.

In general, you could also use the more detailed form which includes `return` to write any one-line function as well.

Example

```
1 "use strict";
2
3 let cylindricalVolume = (radius, height) => Math.PI * radius *
radius * height;
```

Listing 41 *accompanying_files/14/examples/cylindricalVolume1.js*

You could also define this function as follows:

```
1 "use strict";
2
3 let cylindricalVolume = (radius, height) => {
4   return Math.PI * radius * radius * height;
5 };
```

Listing 42 *accompanying_files/14/examples/cylindricalVolume2.js*

or even:

```
1 "use strict";
2
3 let cylindricalVolume = (radius, height) => {
4   let volume = Math.PI * radius * radius * height;
5   return volume;
6 };
```

Listing 43 *accompanying_files/14/examples/cylindricalVolume3.js*

In general, we prefer the shorter form, although it's not possible to express every function on just one line. As soon as a function consists of more than one line, you'll need `return` if you want to return a value.

14.5   Exercises

Exercise 35: Ladislaus Transformed, Part 3

Change your code from exercise 34. Your function now should actually return the transformed name instead of just printing it out directly. However, the output format will remain unchanged:

```
<lastName>, <first letter of firstName>.
```

Call example

```
transformName("Ladislaus", "Jones")
```

Then call your function from `console.log`:

```
console.log(transformName("Ladislaus", "Jones")); // =>
"Jones, L."
```

Hint: Don't forget to rename the function since now it doesn't handle the actual printing.

Exercise 36: Maximum Distance & Consumption, Part 3

Revise *Maximum Distance & Consumption, Part 2* (exercise 18). Create appropriate functions to return the values input by your user.

Exercise 37: Hot, Hot, Hot

Write a function to convert temperature values entered by a user in Celsius to Fahrenheit. Use the following conversion formula:
Fahrenheit = Celsius × 9 / 5 + 32.

One For All and All For One: Arrays 15

NerdWorld just had another innovation meeting, and Marty enthusiastically describes their new concept to you over the phone.

Some of our products are very specialized, and our customers like to talk about them with each other — different ways to use them, tricks, gimmicks, etc.

Up to now, we've been maintaining an externally hosted forum, but of course a forum isn't that interactive and spontaneous. We're thinking that a chat room would be much livelier and more spontaneous, and people would tend to use it a lot more.

We want to maintain a list in our chat room of those customers who are currently online. Although users will be constantly entering and leaving the chat room, the list should of course always be up-to-date. We also need it to be sortable. Finally, it should also show how many customers are currently online.

What's the best way to represent a customer list? One possibility would be to store all customer names in a single string.

```
let customersOnline = "Heribert, Friedlinde, Tusnelda, Oswine,
Ladislaus";
```

However, this would make it difficult to sort names or to find out how many customers are currently online. A so-called *array* is much better suited for requirements like these.

15.1   Creating Arrays

You can picture an array as a list of elements (in this case names). You create a array using square brackets `[]` .

```
let customersOnline = ["Heribert", "Friedlinde", "Tusnelda",
"Oswine", "Ladislaus"];
```

15.2   Determining Length, Part 2

Now it's very easy to find out how many customers are currently online — just ask the array for its length.

```
1 "use strict";
2
3 let customersOnline = ["Heribert", "Friedlinde", "Tusnelda",
"Oswine", "Ladislaus"];
4
5 console.log(customersOnline.length); // => 5
```

Listing 44 *accompanying_files/15/examples/length.js*

15.3   Accessing Arrays Using the Index Operator

The elements within an array are ordered, so you can access a specific element through its position. Picture an array as a numbered list:

0	Heribert
1	Friedlinde
2	Tusnelda
3	Oswine
4	Ladislaus

The numbering is known as the array's *index*, and the names are known as the *values* of the array. If you need to access a specific name, you can use the so-called *index operator*, namely the square brackets [] . Place these immediately after the array, then specify the index of your required element within the brackets.

```
1 "use strict";
2
3 let customersOnline = ["Heribert", "Friedlinde", "Tusnelda",
"Oswine", "Ladislaus"];
4
5 console.log(customersOnline[2]); // => Tusnelda
```

Listing 45 *accompanying_files/15/examples/indexoperator.js*

15.4   Squeeze In a New User Using push

Let's say *Goldy* now logs into the chat room, so you want to show her in the array. You can do this using the function `push` (the idea being you "push" an element into an array).

```
1  "use strict";
2
3  let customersOnline = ["Heribert", "Friedlinde", "Tusnelda",
"Oswine", "Ladislaus"];
4  customersOnline.push("Goldy");
5
6  console.log(customersOnline);
```
Listing 46 *accompanying_files/15/examples/push.js*

You pass the new element to `push` as an argument. This new element will then appear in the last position of the array.

15.5   Show a User the Door Using pop

When Goldy finally leaves the chat room, you'll then need the function `pop`.

```
1  "use strict";
2
3  let customersOnline = ["Heribert", "Friedlinde", "Tusnelda",
"Oswine", "Ladislaus", "Goldy"];
4
5  customersOnline.pop();
6
7  console.log(customersOnline);
```
Listing 47 *accompanying_files/15/examples/pop.js*

`pop` removes the element at the end of the array. In addition, the function also returns the removed element so you can reuse it for some other purpose.

```
1  "use strict";
2
3  let customersOnline = ["Heribert", "Friedlinde", "Tusnelda",
"Oswine", "Ladislaus", "Goldy"];
4  let removedCustomer = customersOnline.pop();
5
6  console.log(`${removedCustomer} just left.`);
```
Listing 48 *accompanying_files/15/examples/pop_return.js*

15.6   Precision Array Manipulation Using splice

Admittedly, the last example was a little unrealistic. `pop` always removes only the last element of an array. However, in our current example, this doesn't make too much sense — you can hardly assume that the last participant in the chat room will always leave first. What do you do with the other people in the chat room?

The function `splice` gives you much more power — it makes it possible to remove an element from any position in the array. For example, let's say Friedlinde is logging out of the chatroom:

```
1  "use strict";
2
3  let customersOnline = ["Heribert", "Friedlinde", "Tusnelda",
   "Oswine", "Ladislaus"];
4  customersOnline.splice(1, 1);
5
6  console.log(customersOnline); // => Array [ "Heribert",
   "Tusnelda", "Oswine", "Ladislaus" ]
```
Listing 49 accompanying_files/15/examples/splice1.js

The first parameter passed to `splice` indicates the position of the element(s) you want to remove. The second parameter specifies the number of elements you want to remove. So in this example, we're removing exactly one element at position `1`. You could have also removed several elements all at once:

```
1  "use strict";
2
3  let customersOnline = ["Heribert", "Friedlinde", "Tusnelda",
   "Oswine", "Ladislaus"];
4  customersOnline.splice(1, 3);
5
6  console.log(customersOnline); // => Array [ "Heribert",
   "Ladislaus" ]
```
Listing 50 accompanying_files/15/examples/splice2.js

`.splice(1,    3)` removes three elements, starting at position `1` (i.e. `Friedlinde`, at the second position in the array).

You can even use `splice` to add new elements:

```
1  "use strict";
2
3  let customersOnline = ["Heribert", "Friedlinde", "Tusnelda",
   "Oswine", "Ladislaus"];
```

```
4  customersOnline.splice(1, 0, "Goldy");
5
6  console.log(customersOnline); // => Array [ "Heribert", "Goldy",
"Friedlinde", "Tusnelda", "Oswine", "Ladislaus" ]
```

Listing 51 accompanying_files/15/examples/splice3.js

And if that weren't enough, you can also remove and add elements at the same time.

```
1  "use strict";
2
3  let customersOnline = ["Heribert", "Friedlinde", "Tusnelda",
"Oswine", "Ladislaus"];
4  customersOnline.splice(1, 1, "Goldy");
5
6  console.log(customersOnline);
7  // => Array [ "Heribert", "Goldy", "Tusnelda", "Oswine",
"Ladislaus" ]
```

Listing 52 accompanying_files/15/examples/splice4.js

15.7   Keeping Things Neat and Tidy Using sort

Marty wants you to print out the names of chat participants in alphabetical order. To do this, you'll first need to sort them alphabetically. Nothing's easier! The JS Array API provides the function `sort` for just that purpose.

```
1  "use strict";
2
3  let customersOnline = ["Heribert", "Friedlinde", "Tusnelda",
"Oswine", "Ladislaus"];
4  customersOnline.sort();
5
6  console.log(customersOnline);
7  // => Array [ "Friedlinde", "Heribert", "Ladislaus", "Oswine",
"Tusnelda" ]
8
```

Listing 53 accompanying_files/15/examples/sort.js

15.8   Making Connections Using join

It would probably be a good idea when printing out current chat room partici-pants to add a line break after each name. You can do exactly that by using `join`. The function `join` converts an array into a string by joining its individual ele-ments together using a specified separator character. If you use the line break `\n` as the separator, you'll then be able to print out the array in the form of a list in which all elements appear one below the other.

```
1 "use strict";
2
3 let customersOnline = ["Heribert", "Friedlinde", "Tusnelda",
"Oswine", "Ladislaus"];
4
5 console.log(customersOnline.join("\n"));
```
Listing 54 *accompanying_files/15/examples/join.js*

```
Heribert
Friedlinde
Tusnelda
Oswine
Ladislaus
```

15.9   Searching and Finding Using indexOf, Part 2

No sooner are your new features online when your favorite never-satisfied client wants something new.

 Every once in a while a bunch of customers are online at the same time, making the list quite confused. Some users have said they'd really like to be able to search directly through the list so they can go straight to their friends. The best way to do this might be for a user to enter the name they're looking for in a search box, then have all results appear in the list highlighted in yellow.

To start off, highlighting names in yellow isn't your problem — that's a job for the designers. Your job is to find out at what position in the list the name you're looking for is. You can do this by using the function `indexOf`:

```
1 "use strict";
2
3 let customersOnline = ["Heribert", "Friedlinde", "Tusnelda",
"Oswine", "Ladislaus"];
4
5 console.log(customersOnline.indexOf("Tusnelda")); // => 2
```
Listing 55 *accompanying_files/15/examples/indexOf1.js*

Note: If the function `indexOf` can't find a name, it'll return `-1` instead.

```
1  "use strict";
2
3  let customersOnline = ["Heribert", "Friedlinde", "Tusnelda",
   "Oswine", "Ladislaus"];
4
5  console.log(customersOnline.indexOf("Goldy")); // => -1
```

Listing 56 *accompanying_files/15/examples/indexOf2.js*

15.10   When Strings Break Up: split

 Since our employees are always forgetting their passwords, we want to standardize them. Our idea is to have each password consist of the employee's first name written *backwards* followed by the length of the name as a number. Can you automate this?

Okay — we already know what you're going to say. The "security policy" concocted by Marty and his team leaves a lot to be desired. Of course you recommend to him that he go back and re-think this requirement a little. (Incidentally, the independent security experts you consulted shared your skepticism — but only after they engaged in a unanimous chorus of facepalms).

But let's assume for the moment that we really are going to implement this "highly secure" feature. To do this, you would need to perform the following steps:

Step 1: Separate the letters of the first name

By now, you've already become acquainted with a function (`join`) which you can use to combine together the individual elements of an array into a string. That function takes your desired separator as a parameter.

Recall:

```
1  let geniusWords = ["Welcome", "to", "NerdWorld"];
2  geniusWords.join(" "); // => Welcome to NerdWorld
```

JS has a function called `split` which does just the opposite. You can use this function to convert a string to an array. Here again, you specify your required separator in parentheses.

```
1  let geniusText = "Welcome to NerdWorld";
2  geniusText.split(" "); // => ["Welcome", "to", "NerdWorld"];
```

Now let's try to implement this first step for Marty's "sophisticated" security policy:

```
1 "use strict";
2
3 let firstName = "Adelgunde";
4 firstName.split(""); // => ["A", "d", "e", "l", "g", "u", "n",
"d", "e"]
```

Listing 57 accompanying_files/15/examples/split_step1.js

By using the empty string `""` as a separator character, you get back an array whose elements are the individual letters of the string. Converting the first name to this format is necessary for our next step.

Step 2: Reverse the order of letters

This next step is incredibly easy, since JS also provides a function which does just that. Use `reverse()` to transpose the order of the elements in an array.

```
1 "use strict";
2
3 let firstName = "Adelgunde";
4 firstName.split("").reverse(); // => ["e", "d", "n", "u", "g",
"l", "e", "d", "A"]
```

Listing 58 accompanying_files/15/examples/split_reverse_step2.js

Step 3: Combine elements of altered array back into a string

You could probably do this next step in your sleep. Since the password is a sting, you just combine the jumble of letters (the array) back into a string.

```
1 "use strict";
2
3 let firstName = "Adelgunde";
4 firstName.split("").reverse().join(""); // => ednugledA
```

Listing 59 accompanying_files/15/examples/split_reverse_join_step3.js

Step 4: Append the length of the name as a number

Finally, you use `length` to calculate the size of the first name, then append this number to the password.

```
1 "use strict";
2
3 let firstName = "Adelgunde";
4 firstName.split("").reverse().join("") + firstName.length; // =>
ednugledA9
```

Listing 60 accompanying_files/15/examples/split_reverse_join_length_step4.js

Of course, you shouldn't write out this code each time you need it. So create a function to generate the corresponding password for each name:

```
let passwordFor = name => name.split("").reverse().join("") +
name.length;
```

Try out your new function:

```
1 "use strict";
2
3 let passwordFor = name => name.split("").reverse().join("") +
name.length;
4 passwordFor("Ladislaus"); // => sualsidaL9
```

Listing 61 accompanying_files/15/examples/passwordFor.js

So far, so good (if you can call that policy good). But at least our client is happy for the time being…

In-Place Mutation vs. Return Value

Array functions come in two forms — those which modify the original array and those which don't. In the first variant, any changes made are effected to the original array itself (so-called *in-place mutation*). In the second variant, the only thing which matters is the return value. Functions which don't make any changes (*mutations*) apart from the return value are also said to be *side-effect free*. `sort`, `splice` or `pop` are examples of functions which make changes to the original array. By contrast, `indexOf`, `join`, `split` and `slice` are side-effect free functions (note that this last function is spelled without a p and should not be confused with `splice`).

Example

```
let someNumbers = [3, 1, 2];
let sortedNumbers = someNumbers.sort();
```

After executing the above code `sortedNumbers` has the value `[1, 2, 3]`. You might expect that `someNumbers` still have their original value `[3, 1, 2]`. But `sort` has also changed `someNumbers`. `someNumbers` now also has the value `[1, 2, 3]`. This is why `sort` is also called a *destructive* function.

If you have a choice, you should always use functions which don't have side effects.

15.11 Reference

Function	Purpose	Call Example	a.join("")	Return Value
push	Adds elements to the end of an array	`a.push("x", "y")`	abcdxy	6 (number)
pop	Removes the element at the end of an array	`a.pop()`	abc	d (string)
unshift	Adds elements to the beginning of an array	`a.unshift("x", "y")`	xyabcd	6 (number)
shift	Removes the element at the beginning of an array	`a.shift()`	bcd	a (string)
slice	Creates a copy of part of an array	`a.slice(2, 4)`	abcd	c,d (array)
splice	Removes and/or adds elements from/to an array	`a.splice(2, 2, "x")`	abx	c,d (array)
sort	Sorts an array	`a.sort()`	abcd	a,b,c,d (array)
reverse	Reverses the order of elements in an array	`a.reverse()`	dcba	d,c,b,a (array)
concat	Joins an array to one or more elements or arrays	`a.concat(["x", "y"])`	abcd	a,b,c,d,x,y (array)
fill	Sets all elements to a specified value	`a.fill("x")`	xxxx	x,x,x,x (array)
includes (*)	Checks whether an element exists in an array	`a.includes("x")`	abcd	false (boolean)
indexOf	Determines the position (index) of an element in an array	`a.indexOf("c")`	abcd	2 (number)
lastIndexOf	Determines the position (index) of an element in an array (starting from the end)	`a.lastIndexOf("c")`	abcd	2 (number)

Table 15.2 *Overview of Array API (based on example* `let a = ["a", "b", "c", "d"]`*)*
* ECMAScript 2016 and higher

Function	Purpose	Call Example	a.join("")	Return Value
split	Splits a string into an array on the basis of a separator character	`("a-b-c-d").split("-")`		a,b,c,d (array)
join	Joins all elements of an array together into a single string	`a.join("==")`	abcd	a==b==c==d (string)
toString	Like `join`, but always uses the comma as the separator character.	`a.toString()`	abcd	a,b,c,d (string)

Table 15.2 *Overview of Array API (based on example* `let a = ["a", "b", "c", "d"])`
* ECMAScript 2016 and higher

15.12 Exercises

Exercise 38: Baking Cookies Using Arrays

Fig. 30 *Rolled oat cookies*

You're writing an online cookbook, and you want to make the ingredients for each recipe available in an array.

1   Your first recipe is rolled oat cookies, so you create an array with the following ingredients:

```
1/4 cup rapeseed oil
1 separated egg
1/2 cup sugar
1 tsp baking powder
```

2   Since the list is missing flour, you'll need to add 1 tbsp flour to the array.

3   As you're reading through the list, you notice that the most important ingredient is also missing. So add 1 cup rolled oats to the list of ingredients and put this at the first position.

4   It's actually better to use butter instead of oil when making cookies. So replace the oil in the list with 1/3 cup butter.

5   Now convert the array to a string and store the string in a variable in a form which will make it possible to print out the ingredients as a list.

6   And in order to make it possible to use these ingredients at all, of course you still need the directions from us. Store these in a variable as well, then print out the complete recipe to the console.

Directions:

Melt the butter in a pan, add the rolled oats and mix everything well.

Remove the mixture from heat and let it cool. Add the sugar to the egg white and beat until stiff. Mix in the yolk, baking powder and flour. Now mix in the cooled oat mixture.

Shape small mounds of batter onto a baking sheet. These mounds should not be too large, since the batter will spread out a little as it is baked. Bake for 15 minutes at 350 °F in a pre-heated oven.

Exercise 39: The Short Trip, or When You Don't Have the Right Change

All that cooking has tired you out, so you decide to take a little bus trip. As luck would have it, you find yourself in Nuremberg, Germany, at the bus stop of the *Nordostbahnhof* train station . Your friends, who are joyfully expecting you (and of course your cookies), live near the *Martha-Maria hospital* stop. Unfortunately, since you only have enough money to pay for a ticket for a short distance, you need to walk the rest of the way. As a result, you'll need the list of stopsfig. 31), but only up to the final stop marked with a white dot (*Hubertusstr.*/Hubert Street).

Note: `slice` and `indexOf` might be good functions to solve this exercise :)

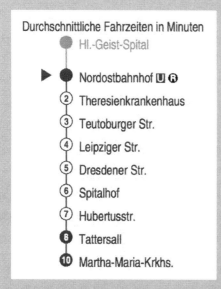

Fig. 31 *Excerpt of bus stops on Nuremberg line 46*

1   Create an array to hold the bus stops on line 46:

```
 1 "use strict";
 2
 3 const LINE_46 = [
 4   "Nordostbahnhof",
 5   "Theresienkrankenhaus",
 6   "Teutoburger Str.",
 7   "Leipziger Str.",
 8   "Dresdener Str.",
 9   "Spitalhof",
10   "Hubertusstr.",
11   "Tattersall",
12   "Martha-Maria-Krkhs."
13 ];
```

accompanying_files/15/exercises/short_trip.js

2   Find the position of your destination stop (*Hubertusstr.*).

3   Remove all bus stops after *Hubertusstr.* from the array.

4   Write a function which takes as a parameter a given destination stop and returns an array with all stops starting from *Nordostbahnhof* up to the destination stop.

5   Extend the function so that it also takes a starting stop as a parameter.

Exercise 40: Old Lists

NerdWorld has another job for you. Up to now, employees have been maintaining products in Excel lists. For purposes of migration, they also just exported these lists to CSV (comma separated value) files. These means all the elements in a list are separated by commas.

```
1 "use strict";
2
3 let productList = "3Doodler 3D Printing Pen, Game of Thrones
Wax Seal Coasters, 10th Doctor Sonic Screwdriver Exclusive
Programmable TV Remote, Electronic Butterfly in a Jar,
Aquafarm: Aquaponics Fish Garden, Cassette Adapter Bluetooth,
Marvel Comics Lightweight Infinity Scarf, Ollie — The App
Controlled Robot, Sound Splash Bluetooth Waterproof Shower
Speaker, PowerCube, Backpack of Holding, Retro Duo Portable NES/
SNES Game System, Universal Gadget Wrist Charger, USB Squirming
Tentacle, USB Fishquarium, Space Bar Keyboard Organizer &amp;
USB Hub Pop, USB Pet Rock, Powerstation 5- E. Maximus Chargus,
Dual Heated Travel Mug, Crosley Collegiate Portable USB
Turntable, Meh Hoodie, Magnetic Accelerator Cannon, 8-Bit
Legendary Hero Heat-Change Mug";
```

accompanying_files/15/exercises/csv_lists.js

Write a function called `handleCsv` which takes a CSV string as a parameter, splits the string into an array and sorts it alphabetically. Finally, print your completely processed array out to the console as a list (one line for each product).

On To New Heights with map, reduce, ...

16.1   Functions as Parameters

You may have heard that JavaScript is an object-oriented language. But you may have also heard that JavaScript is a functional language. And perhaps a colleague spoke of JS disparagingly, describing it as procedural or structured. So which statement is correct?

All of them! Programming languages can often be classified into a so-called **paradigm** (world view) such as *functional* or *object-oriented*. However, JS is a so-called **multi-paradigm language**. This means that JS uses elements from different paradigms. You've already become acquainted with procedural/structural elements, such as branching using `if`. You'll learn about object orientation in a later volume. At this point, we just want to introduce you to a few **functional** elements of JS.

One feature JS inherited from its functional models (e.g. the programming language *Scheme*) was the special concept that functions are just values. Just like you can assign a number to a variable, you can also assign a function to a variable.

```
1 let price = 3;
2 let add = (a, b) => a + b;
```

When you ask JS for the variable's type, you'll get the appropriate answer:

```
1 typeof price; // => number
2 typeof add;   // => function
```

Functional programming refers to such functions as so-called **first-class citizens** or **first class functions** — this means that the given language will treat functions just like any other value. You can reference these with variables and even pass them as arguments. And strangely enough, you can take advantage of this concept to implement Marty's latest stroke of genius.

Tanya, our marketing expert recently had a problem: One of the chat participants was more than just a little rude towards her (but I won't go into the details of that now).

Naturally, I looked into it personally. She would have been happy to report the incident to an admin who was online at that time, but unfortunately, the list of participants was quite sizable and she couldn't find one.

As a result, we'd like in the future for admins to be indicated by having the additional text "*(Admin)*" appended after their name, and also for them to be displayed at the very top of the list. I'll take care of this first requirement myself, and just enter the text along with the name itself. But then you'd need to sort the list so that admins appear at the very top.

Fortunately, the function `sort` does exactly that. But first, we want to show you an even simpler problem — try to sort an array which contains just numbers.

```
[16, 10, 2, 12, 1].sort();
```

You probably want something like this:

```
[1, 2, 10, 12, 16]
```

But you get:

```
[1, 10, 12, 16, 2]
```

So what went wrong here?

By default, the `sort` function performs so-called **lexicographical** sorting, which treats numbers exactly like strings. `sort` considers the number *10* to be smaller than *2* since *10* starts with the digit *1*. Only after `sort` compares the first digit will it compare the second. As a result, *12* is definitely less than *16*, but from a lexicographical point of view, *10* is also less than *2*.

Fortunately, you have the ability to control `sort`'s behavior. You can tell the function which of two values it should consider to be smaller and which it should consider to be larger. To do this, you'll need a second function which takes two parameters and compares them to each other.

`sort` expects the comparison function to return the following values in the following cases:

➤ **0** if a and b are equal

➤ **a positive number** if a is greater than b

➤ **a negative number** if a is less than b

In the case of numbers, you can achieve these return values just by subtracting `b` from `a`.

```
1 let compareNumerical = (a, b) => a - b;
2 [16, 10, 2, 12, 1].sort(compareNumerical); // => [1, 2, 10, 12, 16]
```

In principle, you could also directly define the function without first assigning it to a variable.

```
[16, 10, 2, 12, 1].sort((a, b) => a - b); // => [1, 2, 10, 12, 16]
```

However, in most cases it's a lot easier to read your code if you first assign your function to a variable. The additional variable name *compareNumerical* would make your original intent (numerical comparison) very clear to a maintenance programmer.

Sort — A Look Behind the Scenes

We'll use the sample array `[16, 10, 2, 12, 1]` to illustrate the actual processing which goes on within the `sort` function itself.

`compareNumerical` takes two values and compares them with each other. Pass it the first two values from the sample array:

```
let compareNumerical = (16, 10) => 16 - 10;
```

`16 - 10` returns 6, i.e. a positive number. As a result, the `sort` function knows it needs to exchange the two numbers. Imagine for the moment that the array now looks like this: `[10, 16, 2, 12, 1]`.

The function processes the array from front to back. It exchanges the numbers it's currently processing when the subtraction returns a positive result. On the other hand, if this result is negative, it leaves the numbers alone. The processing next goes through these steps:

10, 2, 16, 12, 1
10, 2, 12, 16, 1
10, 2, 12, 1, 16

`16` has been shifted to the very end of the array. However, the result is not yet complete, and the function again starts from the beginning of the array.

2, 10, 12, 1, 16
2, 10, 1, 12, 16

One more pass:

2, 1, 10, 12, 16

Then finally:

1, 2, 10, 12, 16

This particular sorting algorithm is known as *bubble sort*, though it's an extremely simplified version of the actual process. In reality, `sort` uses variants of other sorting algorithms — quick sort, introsort, merge sort, selection sort and minsort as well as sorting based on AVL trees. The specific sorting variant used is based on the actual JavaScript engine and data types of the values to be sorted. Unfortunately, a detailed explanation of sorting algorithms is beyond the scope of this class.

But back to NerdWorld... To make Marty happy and to protect Tanya from further annoyance, you'll still need one more criterion for your `sort` function — i.e. another comparison function. This new comparison function needs to compare the names of chat room participants to each other and must always indicate that administrators are "smaller". After sorting, the smallest values will be at the very top (i.e. the beginning) of the sorted list.

You'll first need a function which checks whether a given chat room participant is an admin. This means that admins are indicated by the additional text *(Admin)* (putting aside for the moment the question of whether or not Marty's solution is actually a good idea :) Let's write a function called *isAdmin* to do just that:

```
let isAdmin = name => name.endsWith("(Admin)");
```

Next, we'll need the actual comparison function which we'll just call `compareChatParticipants`:

```
1 let compareChatParticipants = (a, b) => {
2     if (isAdmin(a)) return -1;
3     if (isAdmin(b)) return 1;
4 };
```

The function therefore returns `-1` if the first parameter contains the additional wording *(Admin)*. `sort` interprets this as "the first parameter is less than the second". If it's the second parameter instead which has the *(Admin)* tag, the function's return value is `1`. For `sort`, this means: "The second parameter contains the smaller value." However, we're still missing the case where both chat participants are not admins. You can just fall back on standard string comparison to implement this:

```
1 let compareChatParticipants = (a, b) => {
2   if (isAdmin(a)) return -1;
3   if (isAdmin(b)) return 1;
4   return a > b;
5 };
```

If you now pass the new function to `sort` as a parameter, we'll get the behavior we want:

```
1 "use strict";
2
3 let compareChatParticipants = (a, b) => {
4   if (isAdmin(a)) return -1;
5   if (isAdmin(b)) return 1;
6
7   return a > b;
8 };
9
```

```
10 let isAdmin = name => name.endsWith("(Admin)");
11
12 let customersOnline = ["Heribert", "Friedlinde", "Tusnelda",
"Oswine", "Ladislaus (Admin)"];
13
14 console.log(customersOnline.sort(compareChatParticipants).join("\n"));
```

Listing 65 *accompanying_files/16/examples/sort.js*

Output

```
Ladislaus (Admin)
Friedlinde
Herbert
Oswine
Tusnelda
```

The following exercise will allow you to test out your new sorting skills — don't
worry, it'll be a lot more fun than cleaning up your living room :)

Exercise 41: City, Country, River

In the well-known German trivia game "City, Country, River", players have to
come up with words in those categories which begin with a specific letter.
Each player writes these down by himself/herself in silence. As soon as one
player thinks up a word for all three categories, he/she shouts out "Stop!" and
everyone has to stop writing. All words are then compared. Words used by
more than one player are crossed out. All other words get points, the amount
of which depends on the rules of the variant being played.

In one version of the game, points are also awarded based on word length,
with the longest word getting the most points. Of course, nobody wants to
actually count up the letters in words — that's why we have JS :)

So write a function which sorts the words in a category by length. The
longest word should appear at the beginning of the array.

```
1 "use strict";
2
3 let sortByLength = /*? your code here ?*/;
4
5 let city = ["Barcelona", "Basel", "Belgrade", "Berlin",
"Budapest"];
6 let country = ["Belgium", "Bulgaria", "Brazil", "Bolivia",
"Bosnia and Herzegovina"];
7 let river = ["Bode", "Brahmaputra", "Beuvron", "Black
River", "Belaja"];
```

```
 8
 9  console.log(sortByLength(city));
10  console.log(sortByLength(country));
11  console.log(sortByLength(river));
```

accompanying_files/16/exercises/city_country_river.js

16.2   Functions Which Process Functions

Functions such as `sort`, whose parameters themselves are (or could be) functions are called **higher-order functions**. We don't want to overburden you with too much more specific *functional programming* vocabulary this point. But just in case you're itching to learn some more terms and concepts (in order to impress your colleagues or shine out at your next family get-together), we highly recommend you see *Bodil Stoke*'s fantastic talk *What Every Hipster Should Know About Functional Programming*[39]. You'll learn about various things like applicative functors or zygo-histomorphic prepromorphisms.

But now, back to earth. Higher-order functions are quite useful (no kidding!). And hopefully we'll be able to convince you of this in the following sections.

16.3   Arrays in Need of Direction — map

Do you remember Marty's "highly sophisticated security policy" for generating employee passwords from their names?

The principle worked great, but unfortunately it's very likely that NerdWorld has more than just one employee.

Since any respectable programmer is also lazy whenever possible, it's just not an option for a developer to call the function `passwordFor` manually for each employee. This is where the higher-order function `map` comes into play.

You can use `map` to transform an entire array. The function `map` requires a source array and a function as arguments. It creates a result array by using the specified function to transform each element of the source array and assembling the trans-formed elements back into a new array. If that sounds a little too abstract, hope-fully the following example will help you:

---

39.   *https://vimeo.com/68331937*

```
1 "use strict";
2
3 let passwordFor = name => name.split("").reverse().join("") +
name.length;
4
5 let employees = ["Adelgunde", "Heribert", "Mechthild",
"Friedlinde", "Tusnelda", "Oswine", "Ladislaus"];
6 let passwords = employees.map(passwordFor);
7
8 console.log(passwords); // => ["ednugledA9", "trebireH8",
"dlihthceM9", "ednildeirF10", "adlensuT8", "eniwsO6", "sualsidaL9"]
```

Listing 67 *accompanying_files/16/examples/map.js*

If for some reason the function `map` wasn't available in JavaScript but you did have access to a bunch of overzealous programmers instead, you could have them code the example as follows:

```
1 let employees = ["Fritzi", "Heribert", "Berta", "Friedlinde",
"Tusnelda", "Oswine", "Ladislaus"];
2
3 let passwords = [];
4
5 passwords.push(passwordFor(employees[0]));
6 passwords.push(passwordFor(employees[1]));
7 passwords.push(passwordFor(employees[2]));
8 ...
9 passwords.push(passwordFor(employees[6]));
```

As you see, we were even too lazy to write out all the lines. Programming like this is a waste of time and brain power — you even risk allowing errors of concentration or even copy-and-paste errors to creep into your code.

> Use `map` when you want to transform all the elements in an array.

Exercise 42: Fill in the Blanks Using map

We don't plan to throw you off the deep end immediately in our first exercise for `map`. Instead, we prepared a small fill-in-the-blank test. Replace the comments `/* ??? */` with the appropriate code which will achieve the specified results when the entire program is run.

```
1 "use strict";
2
3 let result;
4 let inputs = [1, 2, 3, 4, 5, 6, 7, 8, 9, 10];
5
```

```
 6 //double
 7 result = inputs.map(x => x /* ??? */);
 8 console.log(result); // => [2, 4, 6, 8, 10, 12, 14, 16, 18,
20]
 9
10 //squares
11 result = inputs.map(/* ??? */);
12 console.log(result); // => [1, 4, 9, 16, 25, 36, 49, 64,
81, 100]
```

accompanying_files/16/exercises/koans_map.js

Exercise 43: Ladislaus Transformed, Part 4

Change your `transformName` function exercise 35 so that it has the ability to process any number of first names (as an array).

Call example

```
transformName(["Ladislaus", "Coolio", "Barry"], "Jones"));
// => "L. C. B. Jones"
```

16.4 More About Higher-Order Functions and Callbacks

Take another look at the following simple example:

```
let double = n => 2 * n;
[1, 2, 3].map(double); // => [2, 4, 6]
```

You've already learned the term ***higher-order function***. In this example, `map` is a higher-order function since it takes `double` (itself a function) as a parameter. So what's `double`? Initially, `double` is just a function — or more precisely, a variable in which a function[40] is stored. However, when you pass `double` as an argument to `map`, we now call it a ***callback function***, or just ***callback*** for short. This term is used since `map` actually "calls back" your function. You don't actually call your `double` function yourself, but instead pass `map` the function in its entirety (i.e.

---

40. (or even more precisely, a ***function expression***) instead of a conventional function

the function definition). In turn, `map` then calls (calls back) your function, as if you programmed the following calls:

```
double(1); // => 2
double(2); // => 4
double(3); // => 6
```

```
                          Callback Function
                                |
[1, 2, 3].map(double)
                |
        High-Order Function
```

If you didn't previously save the callback function in a variable, the function would also be called an **anonymous function**:

```
[1, 2, 3].map(n => 2 * n); // => [2, 4, 6]
```

In this example, `n => 2 * n` (in words: *n to two n*) is an anonymous function.

16.5   See Only What You Want to See Using filter

We found out that our customers like to print out our product lists so they can show them to their friends. We'd like these lists to be a little better structured, so we're going to compile them together into a book in index form. In other words, first we'll list a letter as a heading, followed by all products which start with that letter. When can you implement this by?

Notice that Marty is now no longer asking you whether you can do something, but asking you when you can have something done by. You should take that as a compliment — apparently he's gained a lot of trust in your abilities since you first took him on as a client. Okay, that's all well and good, but back to business. What's the best way to approach this newest requirement?

First, write a function which takes a letter and a list of products as arguments. It then needs to return all products which start with that letter. The following function framework might help:

```
let productsStartingWith = (letter, products) => ...
```

Now the function `filter` will help you finish coding the rest of the function. Just like `map`, you can call `filter` on arrays, and `filter` will process each array element separately. Also like `map`, you can pass `filter` a function as an argument, which `filter` will then execute for each element. However, this is where their commonalities end. `filter` expects a function with a boolean return value — in other words, a **condition**.

```
1  let productsStartingWith =
2      (letter, products) => products.filter(
3          product => ...
4      );
```

We still need to answer the question: How should the condition read? Since we're searching for all elements (i.e. products which begin with a specific letter, you could write:

```
product.startsWith(letter)
```

Here it is again as it appears in the complete function:

```
1  let productsStartingWith =
2      (letter, products) => products.filter(
3          product => product.startsWith(letter)
4      );
```

Now try your new function out! Of course, we can only use a small part of the product list in our example — but this should be enough to illustrate the principle.

```
1  "use strict";
2
3  let productsStartingWith = (letter, products) =>
4      products.filter(product => product.startsWith(letter));
5
6  let products = [
7      "Game of Thrones Wax Seal Coasters",
8      "Electronic Butterfly in a Jar",
9      "Aquafarm: Aquaponics Fish Garden",
10     "Cassette Adapter Bluetooth",
11     "Marvel Comics Lightweight Infinity Scarf",
12     "Ollie - The App Controlled Robot",
13     "Sound Splash Bluetooth Waterproof Shower Speaker",
14     "PowerCube",
15     "Backpack of Holding",
16     "Retro Duo Portable NES/SNES Game System",
17     "Universal Gadget Wrist Charger",
18     "USB Squirming Tentacle",
19     "USB Fishquarium",
20     "Space Bar Keyboard Organizer & USB Hub Pop",
21     "USB Pet Rock",
22     "Powerstation 5- E. Maximus Chargus",
23     "Dual Heated Travel Mug",
```

```
24    "Crosley Collegiate Portable USB Turntable",
25    "Meh Hoodie",
26    "Magnetic Accelerator Cannon",
27 ];
28
29 console.log(productsStartingWith("M", products));
```

Listing 69 *accompanying_files/16/examples/filter.js*

You get the following output:

```
["Marvel Comics Lightweight Infinity Scarf", "Meh Hoodie",
 "Magnetic Accelerator Cannon"]
```

16.6   Everybody Gets a Turn with forEach

To get the entire product list, you'll need to repeat your little spiel for all letters, or at least for all relevant letters.

```
1 console.log(productsStartingWith("A", products));
2 console.log(productsStartingWith("B", products));
3 console.log(productsStartingWith("C", products));
4 ...
5 console.log(productsStartingWith("Z", products));
```

But just so you won't have to call the function separately for each letter (as implied in the previous listing), JS provides the function `forEach` for processing arrays. Just like its name implies, `forEach` can call a specific function **for all** elements of an array. And when those elements are the letters of the alphabet, your work is already half done!

To do this, first use `split("")` to split up the string `"ABCDEF…Z"` into an array of individual letters `["A", "B", "C, "D", "E", "F", … "Z"]`. By using the empty string `""` as your separator character, you'll get back each letter as an individual element. You can then call `forEach` on the result array.

```
1 "ABCDEGMO".split("").forEach(letter => {
2   ...
3 });
```

Of course, in reality we should include all letters from A to Z in the string, but to keep our example small, we'll only use a few: `ABCDEGMO`. The function you pass to `forEach` takes a letter as an argument — and in this case, the parameter `letter` takes in that argument. Then, as before, you call

```
console.log(productsStartingWith(letter, products).join("\n"));
```

from within this function. In the process, the current letter replaces the variable
`letter` in the corresponding call to `forEach`.

```
1 "ABCDEGMO".split("").forEach((letter) => {
2   console.log(productsStartingWith(letter, products).join("\n"));
3 });
```

We can touch up our output by adding a small heading which highlights the current letter:

```
1 "ABCDEGMO".split("").forEach((letter) => {
2   console.log("\n==== " + letter + " ====");
3   console.log(productsStartingWith(letter, products).join("\n"));
4 });
```

Here's the code in its entirety:

```
1  "use strict";
2
3  let productsStartingWith = (letter, products) =>
4    products.filter(product => product.startsWith(letter));
5
6  let products = [
7    "Game of Thrones Wax Seal Coasters",
8    "Electronic Butterfly in a Jar",
9    "Aquafarm: Aquaponics Fish Garden",
10   "Cassette Adapter Bluetooth",
11   "Marvel Comics Lightweight Infinity Scarf",
12   "Ollie - The App Controlled Robot",
13   "Sound Splash Bluetooth Waterproof Shower Speaker",
14   "PowerCube",
15   "Backpack of Holding",
16   "Retro Duo Portable NES/SNES Game System",
17   "Universal Gadget Wrist Charger",
18   "USB Squirming Tentacle",
19   "USB Fishquarium",
20   "Space Bar Keyboard Organizer & USB Hub Pop",
21   "USB Pet Rock",
22   "Powerstation 5- E. Maximus Chargus",
23   "Dual Heated Travel Mug",
24   "Crosley Collegiate Portable USB Turntable",
25   "Meh Hoodie",
26   "Magnetic Accelerator Cannon",
27 ];
28
29 "ABCDEGMO".split("").forEach(letter => {
30   console.log(`\n==== ${letter} ====`);
31   console.log(productsStartingWith(letter, products).join("\n"));
32 });
33
```

Listing 70 accompanying_files/16/examples/forEach.js

And when we run the program we get the following output:

```
==== A ====
Aquafarm: Aquaponics Fish Garden

==== B ====
Backpack of Holding

==== C ====
Cassette Adapter Bluetooth
Crosley Collegiate Portable USB Turntable

==== D ====
Dual Heated Travel Mug
```

```
==== E ====
Electronic Butterfly in a Jar

==== G ====
Game of Thrones Wax Seal Coasters

==== M ====
Marvel Comics Lightweight Infinity Scarf
Meh Hoodie
Magnetic Accelerator Cannon

==== O ====
Ollie - The App Controlled Robot
```

Life in the Old Days

Before language version ES5.1 introduced `forEach`, developers who wanted to process arrays had to use conventional `for` loops. Conventional `for` loops have a counter variable which is incremented. Consider the following example which currently uses `forEach`:

```
"ABCDEGMO".split("").forEach(letter =>
console.log(letter));
```

If you use a conventional `for` loop instead of the `forEach`, the code will look like the following:

```
1 let letters = "ABCDEGMO".split("");
2 for (let i = 0; i < letters.length; i += 1) {
3   console.log(letters[i]);
4 }
```

You do need `for`, but not just for processing arrays — the statement has a wide variety of applications. Fortunately, we now have better ways to handle most of these cases, such as the higher-order functions described in this lesson, or recursion, to be discussed in lesson 18.

Beware of the Side Effect

Be a careful with `forEach`. Although it is a higher order function, it has no return value like all other higher order functions presented here. This means that you use `forEach` because of the side effect of the passing function. This makes the function more difficult to understand and should normally be avoided. Prefer the other alternatives, such as `map` or `filter`, if possible.

Exercise 44: Friedemann Friese

Freddy Fitzgerald is a big fan of the board games designed by Friedemann Friese. Take the following list and filter out only those board games which start with *F*.

To do this, replace the comments `/* ??? */` with the appropriate code.

```
1  "use strict";
2
3  let startsWithLetterF = /* ??? */;
4
5  let boardgames = [
6    "Caverna",
7    "Puerto Rico",
8    "Agricola",
9    "Black Friday",
10   "Funny Friends",
11   "Fauna",
12   "Eclipse",
13   "Codenames",
14   "Dominion",
15   "Fast Flowing Forest Fellers",
16   "Fearsome Floors"
17  ];
18  let boardgamesStartingWithF = boardgames./* ??? */;
19
20  console.log(boardgamesStartingWithF); // => [ 'Funny
Friends', 'Fauna', 'Fast Flowing Forest Fellers', 'Fearsome
Floors']
```

accompanying_files/16/exercises/friedemann_friese.js

Exercise 45: Fill in the Blanks Using filter

We also prepared a short fill-in-the-blank exercise for `filter`. Again replace the comments `/* ??? */` with the correct code which will achieve the specified results when the entire program is run.

```
 1 "use strict";
 2
 3 let result;
 4
 5 //even numbers
 6 let inputs = [1, 2, 3, 4, 5, 6, 7, 8, 9, 10];
 7 result = inputs.filter(x => /* ??? */);
 8 console.log(result); // => [2, 4, 6, 8, 10]
 9
10 //names ending with letter 'e' or 'a'
11 let names = ["Heribert", "Friedlinde", "Tusnelda",
"Oswine", "Ladislaus"];
12 result = names.filter(n => /* ??? */);
13 console.log(result); // => [ 'Friedlinde', 'Tusnelda',
'Oswine' ]
14
15 //words with at least three letters
16 let text = "Hi this is a short text";
17 result = text.split(" ")./* ??? */.join(" ");
18 console.log(result); // => "this short text"
```

accompanying_files/16/exercises/koans_filter.js

16.7 Trimming Things Down to their Essentials Using reduce

Before we can activate our new ordering system, the cart still needs to display the total price of the products in it (the so-called cart items).

This isn't too difficult — product prices already exist in an array.

```
let cartItemPrices = [9.99, 19.99, 5.99];
```

We'll need two things in order to total up these prices:

➤ the higher-order function `reduce`

➤ *addition* as a function (instead of the operator itself)

`reduce` reduces an array down to a single value. To do this, it takes as an argument a function which specifies how it should make one value out of two.

So let's first define a separate function `add`:

```
let add = (a, b) => a + b;
```

This function just describes how to add two numbers. If you then apply the function over all the elements in an array, you'll get back the sum total of all the individual values in the array.

Now pass the function `add` to `reduce` as an argument.

```
1  "use strict";
2
3  let add = (a, b) => a + b;
4
5  let cartItemPrices = [9.99, 19.99, 5.99];
6  let sum = cartItemPrices.reduce(add);
7
8  console.log(sum); // => 35.97
```

And that's really all there is to it. You can pass `reduce` any function as long as the function shrinks two values down into one.

Let's look at how `reduce` works behind the scenes. The higher-order function takes the first value from the array (`9.99`) and inserts it in `add` as the first parameter. It then uses the second element from the array (`19.99`) as the second parameter.

`reduce` then calls the function passed in as an argument (`add`) and retains the result.

```
add(9.99, 19.99) // => 29.98
```

This is followed by another call to `add`. The result retained from the last call is now the new first argument. `reduce` takes the third element from the array (`5.99`) and passes this to `add` as the second parameter.

```
add(29.98, 5.99) // => 35.97
```

This completes the calculation, and `reduce` returns `35.97`. If there were more elements in the array, the function would continue to proceed in exactly the same way:

```
add(29.98, /* 4th element */) // => Sum of elements 1 to 4

add(/*Sum of 1st to 4th */, /* 5th element*/) // => Sum of 1st to
5th

add(/*Sum of 1st to 5th */, /* 6th element*/) // => Sum of 1st to
6th

// etc.
```

As a small improvement, you could swap out the sum as a separate function:

```
1  "use strict";
2
3  let sum = numbers => numbers.reduce(add);
4  let add = (a, b) => a + b;
5
6  let cartItemPrices = [9.99, 19.99, 5.99];
7
8
9
10 console.log(sum(cartItemPrices)); // => 35.97
```

Listing 73 accompanying_files/16/examples/reduce.js

Reducing Oddballs

Two rather special cases exist for the function reduce. What do you think will happen if the array to be reduced contains just one element?

Example

```
let add = (a, b) => a + b;
let sum = arr => arr.reduce(add);
sum([3]); // => 3
```

`reduce` can't call the function you passed it (e.g. `add`), since one of its parameters is missing! As a result, `reduce` just returns the one element contained in the array. So in our example, the return value would be just `3`. This actually makes sense — the sum of "all" numbers in the array `[3]` is indeed the number `3`. Reduction successful!

Even more problematic is when there's nothing at all, and the entire array is completely empty.

Example

```
let add = (a, b) => a + b;
let sum = arr => arr.reduce(add);
sum([]); // => ???
```

Instead of returning a value, this code throws an error:

```
[].reduce(add);
 ^

TypeError: Reduce of empty array with no initial value
```

Conveniently enough, the error message itself already shows us the solution to the problem — you can pass `reduce` an *initial value* as a second parameter. In the case of conventional summation, that should be the number `0` .

```
let add = (a, b) => a + b;
let sum = arr => arr.reduce(add, 0);
sum([]) // => 0
```

The first call to the function passed to `reduce` (`add` in this example) uses the initial value as the first parameter — and if the array is empty, `reduce` simply returns that value.

Example

```
let add = (a, b) => a + b;
let sumTo10 = arr => arr.reduce(add, 10);
sumTo10([3, 4]); // => 17
sumTo10([3]);     // => 13
sumTo10([]);      // => 10
```

Using Cool Types in the Initial Value

Another interesting point is that the initial value can have any data type (of course, it should correspond to the function passed in). However, `[]` or `{}` can actually also be used without a problem. As a result you can even use `reduce` to create new objects or arrays (though you won't learn about objects until).

16.8   Some Like it Hot — Using some

Our shop carries a few films which are rated only for customers 18 years of age or older. Although we don't sell these too often, we still need to be able to check the cart appropriately. So if a customer placing an order has one of these products in his/her cart, we need to execute a separate process which checks the customer's age.

This new requirement isn't actually a big problem, since again JS has provided us with something useful for such cases: The function `some`.

The function `some` returns `true` if **some** elements correspond to a specified condition.

The products in the cart have various characteristics. In order to map these, we have one array for product descriptions, one for prices and one for product age ratings.

```
let ageRating = [6, 6, 6, 0, 12, 16, 0, 18, 6, 0, 6];
```

Now we need an appropriate condition. We have to check whether one of the age ratings is `18`. The condition for a given `ageRating` would be:

```
ageRating === 18
```

However, since those age ratings are stored in an array, we could check the first element as follows:

```
1 const AGE_OF_MAJORITY = 18;
2 let ageRating = [6, 6, 6, 0, 12, 16, 0, 18, 6, 0, 6];
3
4 ageRating[0] === AGE_OF_MAJORITY; // => false
```

In this case the return value is `false`, and no further processing needs to be carried out for that film. However, checking the first element is not enough — the cart actually does still contain a film rated only for customers 18 and older. We therefore need to check the entire array.

Fortunately, the function `some` is kind enough to relieve you of the laborsome work of checking all array values individually. `some` applies the condition to all elements of the array.

You can either pass the condition directly to `some` or reference the condition using a variable which you then pass to `some`.

```
1 const AGE_OF_MAJORITY = 18;
2 let ageRatings = [6, 6, 6, 0, 12, 16, 0, 18, 6, 0, 6];
3
4 let isForAdultsOnly = ageRating => ageRating === AGE_OF_MAJORITY;
5 ageRatings.some(isForAdultsOnly); // => true
```

Listing 74 *some with a variable as parameter*

```
1 const AGE_OF_MAJORITY = 18;
2
3 let ageRatings = [6, 6, 6, 0, 12, 16, 0, 18, 6, 0, 6];
4
5 ageRatings.some(ageRating => ageRating === AGE_OF_MAJORITY); //
=> true
```

Listing 75 *some with literal function expression as parameter*

But we're not done yet! The goal is for the shop to show the required age verification in case the array (cart) contains an "18 or older" item (return value: `true`).

Check this using `if`:

```
1 "use strict";
2
3 const AGE_OF_MAJORITY = 18;
4 let ageRatings = [6, 6, 6, 0, 12, 16, 0, 18, 6, 0, 6];
5
6 let isForAdultsOnly = ageRatings =>
7   ageRatings.some(ageRating => ageRating === AGE_OF_MAJORITY);
8
9 if (isForAdultsOnly(ageRatings))
10   console.log("Please verify your age."); // => Please verify
your age.
```

Listing 76 *accompanying_files/16/examples/some.js*

16.9   Reference

Following is an overview of higher-order functions of type array, that we've provided for reference purposes. The examples below are based on the variable `a` which is assigned the following array value:

```
let a = [1, 2, 3, 4, 5]
```

➤ **sort**
Sorts all elements on the basis of a specified compare function.

Example

```
a.sort((x, y) => y - x); // => [5, 4, 3, 2, 1]
```

➤ **map**
Maps one array onto another, transforming each element on the basis of the specified callback.

Example

```
a.map(x => x * x) // => [1, 4, 9, 16, 25]
```

➤ **filter**
Filters elements on the basis of a specified criterion (condition).

Example

```
let even = x => x % 2 === 0;
a.filter(even) // => [2, 4]
```

➤ **reduce**
Reduces an array down to a single value by successively reducing pairs of elements on the basis of the specified callback. An optional initial value may be passed as a second parameter.

Example

```
a.reduce((x, y) => x + y);
// => 1 + 2 + 3 + 4 + 5 => 15

a.reduce((x, y) => x + y, 10);
// => 10 + 1 + 2 + 3 + 4 + 5 => 25
```

➤ **reduceRight**
Like reduce, but starts from the right. An optional initial value can be specified here as well.

Example

```
a.reduceRight((x, y) => x - y);
// => 5 - 4 - 3 - 2 - 1 => -5
```

➤ **every**
Returns `true` if **all** elements correspond to a specified condition.

Example

```
let even = x => x % 2 === 0;
a.every(even); // => false
```

➤ **some**
Returns `true` if **some** elements correspond to a specified condition.

Example

```
let even = x => x % 2 === 0;
a.some(even); // => true
```

➤ **forEach**
Executes a callback for each element.

Example

```
a.forEach(x => console.log(x));
```

➤ **find**
Finds the first element which satisfies a specified condition.

Example

```
let even = x => x % 2 === 0;
a.find(even) // => 2
```

➤ **findIndex**
Returns the index of the first element which satisfies a specified condition.

Example

```
let even = x => x % 2 === 0;
a.findIndex(even) // => 1
```

16.10   Exercises

Exercise 46: Fill-in-the-Blank Exercise for Higher-Order Functions

This is the last fill-in-the-blank exercise for this lesson — promise :) Again, replace the comments `/* ??? */` with the correct code which will achieve the specified results when the entire program is run.

```
 1 "use strict";
 2
 3 let result;
 4 let inputs = [1, 2, 3, 4, 5, 6, 7, 8, 9, 10];
 5 let text = "Hi this is a short text";
 6 let names = ["Heribert", "Friedlinde", "Tusnelda",
"Oswine", "Ladislaus"];
 7
 8 //odd numbers
 9 result = inputs./* ??? */;
10 console.log(result); // => [ 1, 3, 5, 7, 9 ]
11
12 //sum
13 result = inputs./* ??? */;
14 console.log(result); // => 55
15
16 //product
17 result = inputs./* ??? */;
18 console.log(result); // => 3628800
19
20 //longest word length
21 result = text./* ??? */;
22 console.log(result); // => 5
23
24 //longest word
25 result = text./* ??? */;
26 console.log(result); // => short
27
28 //avg word length
29 result = text./* ??? */;
30 console.log(result); // => 3
31
32 //sort by 3rd letter
33 result = names.sort(
34   (a, b) => /* ??? */ > /* ??? */
35 );
36 console.log(result); // => [ "Ladislaus", "Friedlinde",
"Heribert", "Tusnelda", "Oswine" ]
37
```

```
38 // Are there names with more than 8 letters?
39 result = /* ??? */ name.length > 8);
40 console.log(result); // => true
41
42 // Has every name at least 8 letters?
43 result = /* ??? */ name.length > 8);
44 console.log(result); // => false
45
46 // What is the lowest value from the inputs?
47 result = inputs./* ??? */
48 console.log(result); // => 1
```

accompanying_files/16/exercises/koans.js

Exercise 47: Happy Mixing with Arrays — Part 1

Fig. 32 *Didriks / dinnerseries*[41] *(CC) Attribution*[42]

Naturally, you're a little thirsty after reading through all of those dry theories. You open your refrigerator and see a package of passion fruit juice, which you've already opened and need to finish up. You can actually concoct some great cocktails using passion fruit juice — in fact, a friend recommended just the other day that you try a *Honolulu Flip*. Now would be a perfect time, if only that cocktail did contain passion fruit juice…

---

41. *https://www.flickr.com/photos/dinnerseries/*
42. *https://creativecommons.org/licenses/by/2.0/legalcode*

1   Write a function `hasIngredient` which returns `true` if a specified
    ingredient exists in a list of ingredients for a recipe. Call your function
    with *passion fruit juice* and *Honolulu Flip*.

```
1  "use strict";
2
3  let hasIngredient = (listOfIngredients,
searchedIngredient) => /* ??? */;
4
5  let honoluluFlip = ["Maracuja Juice", "Pineapple Juice",
"Lemon Juice", "Grapefruit Juice", "Crushed Ice"];
6
7  console.log(hasIngredient(honoluluFlip, "Maracuja
Juice")); // => true
```

accompanying_files/16/exercises/cocktails1.1.js

2   But your function still isn't all that useful. It'd be a lot better if we had a
    function which takes a list of available ingredients and finds out whether
    we can actually make the cocktail out of these. To do this, you'll need a
    complete   list   of   the   ingredients   you   have   available
    (`ingredientsFromMyBar`). You want to know whether you have on
    hand **all** ingredients which you need to mix the cocktail.

    Hint: Use the array function `every`. You can also make use of
    `hasIngredient` from the last part of this exercise.

```
1  "use strict";
2
3  let isMixableWith = (cocktailRecipe,
availableIngredients) => /* ??? */;
4
5  let hasIngredient = (listOfIngredients,
searchedIngredient) =>
6    listOfIngredients.includes(searchedIngredient);
7
8  let honoluluFlip = [
9    "Maracuja Juice",
10   "Pineapple Juice",
11   "Lemon Juice",
12   "Grapefruit Juice",
13   "Crushed Ice"
14 ];
15 let ingredientsFromMyBar = [
16   "Pineapple",
17   "Maracuja Juice",
18   "Cream",
19   "Lemon Juice",
```

```
20    "Grapefruit Juice",
21    "Crushed Ice",
22    "Milk",
23    "Apple Juice",
24    "Aperol",
25    "Pineapple Juice",
26    "Limes",
27    "Lemons"
28 ];
29
30 //honoluluFlip isMixableWith ingredientsFromMyBar?
31 console.log(isMixableWith(honoluluFlip,
ingredientsFromMyBar)); // => true
```

accompanying_files/16/exercises/cocktails1.2.js

Exercise 48: Sum of its Parts

Write a function `digitSum` which takes a number and returns the sum of its digits.
Tip: Use `charAt` and `length` or `split("")`.

Exercise 49: Assorted Sums

So we've awakened the mathematician in you? Use the function `digitSum` from the last exercise. This time however, use the function to sort an entire array of numbers by their digit sums.

```
1 "use strict";
2
3 let numbers = [99, 5, 8, 12, 111, 123];
4
5 /* your code here */
6
7 console.log(numbers.sort(byDigitSum)); // => [ 12, 111, 5,
123, 8, 99 ]
```

accompanying_files/16/exercises/sort_by_digitSum.js

Exercise 50: Friedemann Friese, Part 2

Freddy Fitzgerald has become even pickier. Take a specified list and filter out
the games whose title words all start with the letter *F* and which consist of at
least two words — i.e. *Fearsome Floors* but not *Fauna* or *Black Friday*.

```
1  "use strict";
2
3  let isFerdinandsBoardgame = /* ??? */;
4  /* more code here */
5
6  let boardgames = [
7    "Caverna",
8    "Puerto Rico",
9    "Agricola",
10   "Black Friday",
11   "Funny Friends",
12   "Fauna",
13   "Eclipse",
14   "Codenames",
15   "Dominion",
16   "Fast Flowing Forest Fellers",
17   "Fearsome Floors"
18 ];
19 let ferdinandsBoardgames =
boardgames.filter(isFerdinandsBoardgame);
20
21 console.log(ferdinandsBoardgames); // => [ 'Funny Friends',
'Fast Flowing Forest Fellers', 'Fearsome Floors' ]
```

accompanying_files/16/exercises/friedemann_friese2.js

17 *Scopes, and Being "strict" with Variables*

> *Any constant has its variables.*
>
> Unknown

You're almost done with the first volume of this course! **Congratulations!**

At this point, we have to confess we've been hiding some sinister secrets about variables from you — but now, we feel you're ready to handle the truth.

17.1   The Whole, Devastating Truth About Scopes

17.1.1   let

A *scope* is the region in a program within which a variable can be accessed. You typically define a variable using `let`. This causes the variable to have *local scope* — i.e. it's available only in the *local region* in which you defined it. Scope in this case is a code block delimited by braces, e.g. a branch in an if statement or even an entire function body.

Example

```
1  "use strict";
2
3  if (true) {
4    let a = 1;
5
6    // Hurry up, we have an "a" here
7    console.log(a); // => 1
8  }
9
10 // a is nowhere to be seen
11 console.log(a);  // => ReferenceError: a is not defined
```

Listing 82 accompanying_files/17/examples/hurry_up.js

In addition, a variable takes effect only from the time it is declared and not before, as demonstrated by the following example.

```
1  "use strict";
2
3  let x = () => {
4    console.log(a); // => ReferenceError: can't access lexical
   declaration "a" before initialization
5    let a = 1;
6  };
7
8  x();
```

Listing 83 *accompanying_files/17/examples/function_x.js*

Life in the Old Days

Variables may only be used after they're initialized?

You might think that sounds logical, but it wasn't always that way. The older keyword `var` always moves variable declarations to the beginning of a function (so-called **hoisting**) and makes variables available over the entire function (**function scope**). This was often very confusing and led to all kinds of errors in practice.

Therefore, you should always use `let` to define variables and make them as local as possible. Try to make sure the scope of a variable is only as large as it needs to be. This will allow you to avoid conflicts and to keep the size of the area in which you're (potentially) looking for errors to a minimum.

17.1.2   const

Constants which you declare using `const` are also available in *local scope* — just like with `let`. You can therefore use `const` and `let` almost equivalently, with the minor difference that constants are just *constant* — in other words, they can no longer be assigned new values after they are initialized. However, this is actually an advantage in most cases. You'll learn more about this soon, in section 17.3.

17.1.3   Parameters

Function parameters behave like variables which you declare at the beginning of a function. This means parameters are available over the entire function. For this reason, you should keep the number of parameters small (Martin 2008) — ideally three or fewer. In addition, functions themselves should not be too long. As a rule of thumb, they should only have a maximum of 10 statements — 5 is better, and 1 is even better than that.

```
1  "use strict";
2
3  let x = a => {
4    // "a" is everywhere in this function
5    console.log(a); // => 1
6  };
7
8  x(1);
```

Listing 84 accompanying_files/17/examples/function_x_everywhere_a.js

Coding Guidelines

➤ Avoid functions which have more than 3 parameters.

➤ Limit functions to 10 statements at the most.

17.1.4   Global Variables

Global variables are variables you define outside of functions, at the top (global) level of a program. These variables can be accessed anywhere in your program.

Example

```
1   "use strict";
2
3   let a = 3;
4
5   let x = () => {
6     console.log(a); // => 3
7   };
8
9   x(); // => 3
10
11  console.log(a);
```

Listing 85 accompanying_files/17/examples/function_x_global_a.js

You should always avoid using global variables! They're one of the most common sources of error. Even worse, the errors they cause are very difficult to find — you need to go back over your entire program to see what variable had what values, and when. Fortunately, you never have to use global variables.

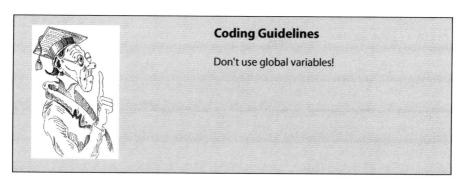

Coding Guidelines

Don't use global variables!

Unfortunately, it's very easy to accidentally create a global variable — namely, if you forget to include a `let`:

```
 1  let x = () => {
 2      a = 3;
 3  };
 4
 5  let y = () => {
 6      console.log(a); // => 3
 7  };
 8
 9  x();
10  y();
11
12  console.log(a); // => 3
```

Listing 86 *accompanying_files/17/examples/function_x_y.js*

In the example above, line 2 produces a global variable, since that statement is missing a `let`. This causes that variable to be available everywhere in the program — even within other functions. The next section will show you how you can guard against this.

17.2 Always Be Strict!

At first, Netscape placed a high importance on making JS friendly to beginners. Unfortunately, this led to a few very questionable design decisions. These in turn resulted in many errors and problems which JS just accepted instead of throwing an error message. Although this made it easy for beginners to get their initial coding efforts up and running, it also made it possible for large applications to hide deep-seated problems. This might mean a programmer could spend hours (or even days) looking for an error whose cause was actually in a completely different place in his/her code.

Starting with language version ES5.1, JS provided an antidote to this: **strict mode**. We already introduced you to this mode very early on in this class (see section 2.7) in order to protect you from pitfalls and dangers in JS (landmines, as these are known to experienced developers).

When running in *strict mode*, JS recognizes many potential problems immediately and flags them as errors. JS encourages you, in a sense, to write your code "cleanly". Although this'll cost you a little time when you're first starting out, it'll save you from hours of searching for errors in the future. For example, take this one-line code listing:

```
price = 10;
```

Do you see the error? The `let` is missing — the statement should actually read `let price = 10`.

As you already know, you enable *strict mode*, by inserting the following code at the beginning of a JS file:

```
"use strict";
```

You've already done this many times in this class — but what does it actually mean?

True, it's really just a string — but that's exactly the trick. An older browser (which doesn't recognize *strict mode*) just sees it as a string literal, one that just wasn't stored in a variable. The browser therefore ignores that code and existing programs just continue to run.

On the other hand, a browser which does recognize *strict mode* understands the string and activates the mode. The following code will result in an error message.

```
"use strict";

price = 10;
```

You get the error message "*ReferenceError: assignment to undeclared variable price*". More specifically, the message says you can't assign a value to a variable which has not yet been declared. It's true that strict mode doesn't prevent you from being able to create global variables, but at least it's no longer possible for these to be created accidentally.

And there're a number of other situations in which `"use strict";` will save you from great disaster. You'll find more information on using this feature on the *MDN page on strict mode*[43].

17.3 Constant for the Future

As a rule, code is difficult to understand and holds a high potential for errors when it contains a large number of "movable" parts. By this we mean a program whose run-time behavior is significantly different from the static code in it — in other words, if you need to first run your code before you're really able to understand what it does. When code is completely "immovable", nothing happens at run time which you couldn't already determine previously from your source code — your code results in no side effects whatsoever. This is typically a characteristic of *functional languages*.

Although JS is not a *purely* functional language, it does provide many functional aspects — features you've already learned about, such as functions as values or array functions like `map`, `reduce` and `filter`. It will therefore benefit you enormously to do without global variables and to always work with `let` — this will greatly reduce the number of movable parts in your code.

Nevertheless, variables themselves are generally movable parts. You can't look at a variable in your source code and see what values it'll take on at run time. To understand the flow of your program, you need to use something like `console.log` or a so-called *debugger* to track what variables had what values at what times. `let` restricts a variable's scope and thus minimizes the overall area you'll need to understand and examine when an error occurs.

The next step is to do away with variables completely. Instead, use constants with `const`. The next time you code, try writing `const` every time you need a `let`. You'll find this actually works in many cases, and you'll only need to make a few minor changes to your code.

Example

Let's go back and look at exercise 34. This exercise involved taking a name in the form "*Ladislaus Coolio Barry Crazy Jones*" and converting it to the form "*L. C. G. C. Jones*" — i.e. abbreviating first and middle names as initials. One possible solution might be the following:

```
1  "use strict";
2
3  let transform = fullName => {
4    let nameParts = fullName.split(" ");
5    let lastName = nameParts.slice(nameParts.length - 1);
6    nameParts = nameParts.slice(0, nameParts.length - 1);
```

---

43. *https://developer.mozilla.org/en-US/docs/Web/JavaScript/Reference/Strict_mode*

```
 7
 8    return nameParts
 9       .map(firstName => firstName.charAt(0) + ".")
10       .join(" ") + " " + lastName;
11  }
12
13  let aLongName = "Ladislaus Coolio Barry Crazy Jones";
14  console.log(transform(aLongName));
```

Listing 87 *One solution (which still requires improvement) to "Ladislaus Transformed"*

The solution above in doesn't necessarily represent the best solution. Do you see the problem?

Line 6 overwrites the variable `nameParts`. When you run your program, this would make it difficult to track what value is assigned to the variable at what time. If `nameParts` received an invalid value at some point, you couldn't necessarily conclude that the error must be in line 6 — it could just as well have been an error caused by a previous line.

The code is also misleading — after line 6, `nameParts` just contains first names as name parts. Previously the string also contained the last name. This makes the code very difficult to understand. The following solution is a little better:

```
 1  "use strict";
 2
 3  let transform = fullName => {
 4    let nameParts = fullName.split(" ");
 5    let positionOfLastName = nameParts.length - 1;
 6    let firstNames = nameParts.slice(0, positionOfLastName);
 7    let lastName = nameParts.slice(positionOfLastName);
 8
 9    return firstNames
10       .map(firstName => firstName.charAt(0) + ".")
11       .join(" ") + " " + lastName;
12  };
13
14  let aLongName = "Ladislaus Coolio Barry Crazy Jones";
15
16  console.log(transform(aLongName));
```

All information in this new listing is stored separately in variables whose names reflect their content as precisely as possible. There is never any uncertainty about the contents of these variables since none of them are overwritten, and the names selected for them accurately describe their contents.

In this first solution, it wasn't possible to replace `let` statements with `const` since constants may not be overwritten. On the other hand, this is no problem in the last solution:

```
1  "use strict";
2
3  let transform = fullName => {
4    const nameParts = fullName.split(" ");
5    const positionOfLastName = nameParts.length - 1;
6    const firstNames = nameParts.slice(0, positionOfLastName);
7    const lastName = nameParts.slice(positionOfLastName);
8
9    return firstNames
10     .map(firstName => firstName.charAt(0) + ".")
11     .join(" ") + " " + lastName;
12 };
13
14 const aLongName = "Ladislaus Coolio Barry Crazy Jones";
15
16 console.log(transform(aLongName));
```

Listing 88 *accompanying_files/17/examples/nameParts_of_Ladislaus.js*

Constants are, in a sense, insurance against accidentally overwriting variables. An even better solution would be to use functions instead of variables or constants. Of course, you would then store these functions in constants:

```
1  "use strict";
2
3  const transform = name =>
4    firstNames(name).map(initial).join(" ")
5    + " "
6    + lastName(name);
7
8  const initial = name => name.charAt(0) + ".";
9
10 const lastName = fullName =>
11   nameParts(fullName).slice(positionOfLastName(fullName));
12
13 const firstNames = fullName =>
14   nameParts(fullName).slice(0, positionOfLastName(fullName));
15
16 const positionOfLastName = fullName =>
nameParts(fullName).length - 1;
17
18 const nameParts = fullName => fullName.split(" ");
19
20 const aLongName = "Ladislaus Coolio Barry Crazy Jones";
21
22 console.log(transform(aLongName));
```

Listing 89 *accompanying_files/17/examples/nameParts_of_Ladislaus2.js*

This gives you an unbeatable advantage: Every single concept in the solution (e.g. determining a last name) can now be reused in other contexts — in other words, independently of the `transform` function. In addition, this approach makes searching for errors enormously easier — you can now test each function in isolation. For example, if a bug somehow snuck into the function `firstNames`, you could rule out the error being caused by a different function.

FYI, this new style is fast gaining in popularity as ES 2015 is becoming more widespread, and is being found more and more in coding guidelines, e.g. those established by *AirBnB*[44].

Coding Guidelines

➤ Avoid variables (`let`) — try to work with constants (`const`) instead.

➤ Write variable and constant identifiers in CamelCase.
Exception: Continue to write constants which serve to configure your program (e.g. `const HOURS_PER_DAY = 24`), i.e. those whose values are already defined before your program runs, in SCREAMING_SNAKE_CASE.

44. *https://github.com/airbnb/javascript*

Once More From the Top with Recursion 18

> With each new beginning, you should keep in
> mind that you drag around your experiences as
> intellectual baggage.
>
> Prof. Hermann Simon

18.1 Reps Don't Have to Be Exhausting

 Stephanie, our product manager, is always complaining that our system for entering new products is impractical — especially the part where you enter product prices. If you make a typo, you have to cancel the entire process and start again from scratch. Isn't it possible just to ask the user for the product price again without having to repeat the entire process?

Actually, in the real world, forms are usually used for input of that kind . For didactic reasons, however, we only cover forms in a later class and for the time being will continue to work with console and **prompt**.

Let's look at a program excerpt for inputting a product price:

```
const productPrice = Number(prompt("Please enter the product
price."));
```

A number of different errors could occur here. For example, Stephanie could accidentally type in a space, or even worse, another employee could enter a negative price (of course that wouldn't happen to Stephanie). Customers might even be happy in the latter case, and the item would become a real hit — but it could be a little awkward for the company if that kept up…

Ideally, the program would detect such an error then ask for the price again. The program should continue to ask for price **until** the input is in the correct format.

So first, wrap the price prompt up into a function:

```
1 const getProductPrice = () =>
2   Number(prompt("Please enter the product price."));
3
4 console.log("$" + productPrice());
```

Of course, the prompt asks for price just once. What we really want might be described as follows:

"Repeat the question until the response is a valid number."

The function needs to find out whether the user's input makes it necessary to repeat the prompt. How can it find this out? Right! By using a condition. Add the following `if` statement to the function:

```
1 if (productPrice < 0) {
2       console.log("A negative price could be disastrous for your
company's health.");
3 }
```

The body of the `if` statement is only executed if `productPrice` is negative. Here's the complete code:

```
1 "use strict";
2
3 const getProductPrice = () => {
4       const productPrice = Number(prompt("Please insert the
product price."));
5       if (productPrice < 0) {
6             console.log("A negative price could be disastrous for
your company's health.");
7       }
8       return productPrice;
9 };
10
11 console.log("$" + getProductPrice());
```

If we now enter `-12.95`, we'll get the following output:

```
A negative price could be disastrous for your company's health
$-12.95
```

Although we are getting an error message as expected, the price is still negative. The repeated prompt is still missing.

To repeat the prompt, all you need to do is call the function again (and of course, only if the input was negative).

```
1  "use strict";
2
3  const getProductPrice = () => {
4    const productPrice = Number(prompt("Please insert the product
price."));
5    if (productPrice < 0) {
6      console.log("A negative price could be disastrous for your
company's health.");
7      return getProductPrice();
8    }
9    return productPrice;
10 };
11
12 console.log("$" + getProductPrice());
```

Listing 90 *accompanying_files/18/examples/product_price.js*

Now, you can enter as many negative numbers as you like: The program never gets tired of patiently sending you prompt after prompt after prompt...until you finally do manage to enter a valid positive number.

18.2   Calling...Itself

So is it a simple concept that a function can call itself, or does it seem like this would take a little getting used to, or...? Just imagine you could clone yourself and that you could delegate work to your clone at any time. Sound crazy?

But that's exactly what functions can do. This principle has a long tradition in programming and there's much more behind it than first meets the eye (but more on that later). FYI, programmers refer to this principle as **recursion**.

18.3   Exercises

Exercise 51: Maximum Distance & Consumption, Part 4

Those users just keep making typos. Now that you've finally put an end to the flood of complaints, perhaps you should go back and polish up your gas calculator a little. The code comes from the solution to exercise 36: *Maximum Distance & Consumption, Part 3*:

```
"use strict";

let askForFuelLoad = () => prompt("How much fuel did you
consume?");
```

```
let askForDistance = () => prompt("How many km did you
travel?");
let askForTankSize = () => prompt("How many liters of
gasoline fits in your tank?");

let fuelLoad = askForFuelLoad();
let distance = askForDistance();
let tankSize = askForTankSize();

let consumption = () => Math.floor(fuelLoad / distance * 100);
let fuelRange = () => Math.floor(tankSize * distance /
fuelLoad);

console.log(`Your car has a consumption of ${consumption()}
liter per 100 kilometers .\nYou can travel ${fuelRange()} km
with a full tank.`);
```

accompanying_files/14/solutions/gasoline.js

Actually, the program will just carry on regardless and do the calculations even if you do give it invalid input. However, only positive numbers make any sense in the case of distance and fuel quantity. So give your user the opportunity to re-enter his/her input if it contains an error (e.g. letters only).

Exercise 52: I'm Thinking of a Number

Program a guessing game which has the following rules. JS "thinks up" a number between 1 and 10 which the user must guess. The user enters his/her guess in a prompt box, then an alert box tells the user whether

➤ the guess was too high,

➤ the guess was too low,

➤ the number is correct.

The user wins the game and the game ends if he/she correctly guesses the number. Otherwise, the program continues to ask for a new guess.

Designing Wallpaper using Recursion — Part 2

19

19.1   Under the Sign of the Line

Today you wait for a call from Marty, but in vain. Actually, your phone has been completely quiet all day — none of your clients want anything! So you take advantage of the situation and abandon yourself to releasing your creative talents.

Have you heard of ASCII art? Such images used to be very popular, e.g. in chat rooms.

Fig. 34 *ASCII Art by SSt*[45]

In this section, we'll use recursion to construct a rectangle using any character and any number of characters. Since even Rome wasn't built in a day, we'll start off with just a line. Multiple lines placed one under the other will eventually form a rectangle.

---

45.   *http://www.ascii-art.surfhome.de*

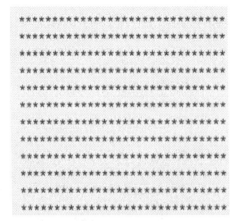

Fig. 35 Character rectangle

First, let's write the following (admittedly somewhat useless) function that returns a specified character. You then print out the character it returns to the console:

```
1 const line = character => {
2   return character;
3 };
4
5 console.log(line("*"));
```

My personal **tip**: Don't be afraid of a function which may seem useless or silly at first. If you're like me, you'll find out that your next step becomes much easier once that evil "blank slate" is no longer blank.

Just as we want, this function returns a single character. For the next step, we'll need a parameter which specifies the number of characters. In the case of our line, you might say that the number of characters is the `length` of the line. And if length is 0, you can return an empty string as a line:

```
1 "use strict";
2
3 const line = (length, character) => {
4   if (length === 0) return "";
5   return character;
6 };
7
8 console.log(line(10, "*"));
```

But what should the function do otherwise (i.e. for a length greater than 0)? By using recursion, you can pretend as if the line already exists. For example, to display a line of 10 characters, you'll first need a line which consists of 9 characters, then add a character: `line(9, character) + character`. The 9 here is nothing other than the current length minus 1. So you could also write `line(length - 1, character) + character`.

```
1 "use strict";
2
3 const line = (length, character) => {
4   if (length === 0) return "";
5   return line(length - 1, character) + character;
6 };
7
8 console.log(line(10, "*"));
```

We've crossed the first hurdle, and programmed a line. As your reward, not only do you get to keep it, you also get to play a little with characters and lengths.

Also, a little refactoring will tighten up our code:

```
1 "use strict";
2
3 const line = (length, character) =>
4   length === 0
5     ? ""
6     : line(length - 1, character) + character;
7
8 console.log(line(10, "*"));
```

Listing 92 accompanying_files/19/examples/line.js

> **Careful!**
>
> If you make a mistake here, it's possible your program will get into an infinite loop and "hang" as a result. Firefox is often able to detect such a situation; if so, it'll display a message box allowing you to stop your program. However, this may not always be the case depending on your specific browser and situation. If you do notice that your browser is no longer responding, you should try to restart it.
>
> Even better, don't get into this situation at all — make sure your exit condition is satisfied.
>
> Strictly speaking, this means that the variable (in this case `length`) must be incremented or decremented appropriately (in this case decrement, or `length - 1`) so that the condition (in this case `length === 0`) is eventually fulfilled.

19.2   Rectangle: When Lines Get Together

Let's keep going and try some bigger and better building projects. With lines, we now have a foundation for some even greater marvels of construction.

So now, let's write another function which makes use of our line. In addition to its width (the length of the line), a rectangle also needs a height. In our case, this height is just the number of lines printed under each other to form the rectangle. We'll essentially need the same components for our new function, only this time we'll print out entire lines instead of just individual characters. Our new `line` function will provide our lines, then we'll use `\n` to have these lines printed out under each other. Then instead of width, we'll use the height of the rectangle as our counter and for our exit condition.

```
1  "use strict";
2
3  const rectangle = (width, height, character) =>
4     height === 0
5        ? ""
6        : rectangle(width, height - 1, character) + "\n" +
   line(width, character);
7
8  const line = (length, character) =>
9     length === 0
10       ? ""
11       : line(length - 1, character) + character;
12
13 console.log(rectangle(50, 12, "*"));
```

Listing 93 *accompanying_files/19/examples/rectangle.js*

If you find this result a little boring, just trying using a different character in place of the `*` — unleash your creativity!

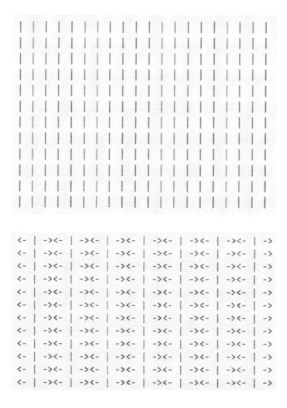

And for you emoticon addicts:

With this small program, you're already well on your way to becoming a wallpaper designer ;)

19.3   Exercises

Exercise 53: It Should Have Three Sides...

Now that you're a master designer, here's your next question — how can we program a triangle?

```
Console

*
**
***
****
*****
******
*******
********
*********
**********
***********
************
*************
**************
***************
```

Fig. 36 Example of a triangle generated using recursion.

Whether you do this from top to bottom or from bottom to top is completely up to you. And if you develop code for both cases, we'll personally paste a gold star in your homework book :)

The function `triangle` should only have one parameter, which specifies both the height and the width of the triangle. For example, `triangle(10)` should generate a triangle with a height and width of 10 characters.

Tip: Lines again will serve as the foundation for generating this shape.

```
1  "use strict";
2
3  /* your code here */
4
5  const line = (length, character) =>
6    length === 0
7      ? ""
8      : character + line(length - 1, character);
9
10 console.log(triangle(10));
```

accompanying_files/19/exercises/triangle.js

Exercise 54: I'm Thinking of a Number, Part 2

Add a new feature to your guessing game from exercise 52. Also include in each question prompt the number of the current round (in other words, the number of previous guesses).

Exercise 55: Everything in Its Place? ["Brainteaser"]

The list display of NerdWorld chat room participants currently online must now be optimized for performance. The list should now only be re-sorted if it hasn't yet been sorted.

```
let customersOnline = ["Heribert", "Friedlinde", "Tusnelda",
"Oswine", "Ladislaus", "Goldy"];
```

To do this, write a function called `isSorted` which checks whether an array of participant names is already sorted alphabetically and if so, returns `true`, otherwise returns `false`. You may not use the function `sort`, otherwise you'd lose the performance advantage right away.

Tip: An array is properly sorted when the first two elements of the list are in the correct order and the rest of the list is sorted. An array which contains only one element is always sorted.

20 Lost in Space and Time? Times & Range

To be honest, the way we constructed the wallpaper in the last lesson was actually more complicated than it had to be. Let's take another look at the code in the `line` function:

```
1 "use strict";
2
3 const line = (length, character) =>
4   length === 0
5     ? ""
6     : line(length - 1, character) + character;
7
8 console.log(line(10, "*"));
```

Listing 96 *Recursive implementation of the line function*

The function in listing 96 for generating a line does work, but is actually quite involved.

Wouldn't it be simpler just to say: *Print out the character "*" 10 times?*

This could be expressed in JS code as something like the following:

```
times(10, () => console.log("*"));
```

Did you try it out?

Yep, unfortunately it doesn't work. Although many functional languages do provide a `times` function for just this purpose, JS isn't one of them — at least not yet. Fortunately, you can easily write the code to do this yourself.

20.1   For the nth Time! — times

Unfortunately, you need to fall back on conventional for loops for the implementation. Not to worry, once the `times` function does become available, you can just reuse it (for once, copy & paste is your friend) — and after that, you no longer have to write loops.

```
1  "use strict";
2
3  const line = (length, character) =>
4    times(length, () => console.log(character));
5
6  const times = (n, fn) => {
7    for (let i = 0; i < n; i += 1) fn();
8  };
9
10 line(10, "*");
```

Listing 97 *accompanying_files/20/examples/line_times.js*

The `for` in `times` here stands for a so-called `for` loop. The code `for (let i = 0; i < n; i += 1)` means: Count from `0` to `n` (exclusive), incrementing the **counter variable** `i` by `1` each time. This code is followed by a call to the function `fn`. In each pass through the loop, `fn()` calls the function which you passed to the parameter `fn` — in our case, the function `() =>` `console.log(character)`)

The `line` function therefore calls `console.log("*")` ten times and you get the following output:

```
*
*
*
*
*
*
*
*
*
*
```

Unfortunately, this output isn't exactly what we want: The asterisks have been printed one under the other instead of next to one another. The reason for this is that `console.log` generates a line break after each printout. In addition, this is bad style, since the printout here constitutes a side effect and the string can't be processed further — we can't even begin thinking about constructing rectangles or even wallpaper.

You actually want the asterisks separate so the `line` function can combine them together without line breaks. Finally, `line` could also return the string for further processing (like for rectangles, wallpaper, etc.).

To do this, you just need to jazz up the `times` function a little. It would be awesome if the `times` function could store the results of individual calls. But we do have something that can do that — arrays!

In each loop pass, `times` can push the value into an array and return the `result`. `line` can then use `join` to assemble the array back into a string which `console.log` can print out at the very end. Fortunately, you don't need to do any printing before that.

```
 1  "use strict";
 2
 3  const line = (length, character) =>
 4    times(length, () => character).join("");
 5
 6  const times = (n, fn) => {
 7    const result = [];
 8    for (let i = 0; i < n; i += 1) result.push(fn());
 9    return result;
10  };
11
12  console.log(line(10, "*"));
```

Listing 98 accompanying_files/20/examples/line_times2.js

And finally we get the desired result:

```
**********
```

20.2   times Optimized Times Times

However, we still need to implement two small improvements to the `times` function.

Because of the `push` within the loop, JS needs to dynamically increase the size of the array in each loop pass. This takes time and slows the function down.

Because of the parameter `n`, `times` already knows from the start how many elements the final result array will contain. We can take advantage of this. By using `new Array(n)`, you can create a so-called sparse array of size `n`.

```
const result = new Array(n);
```

Sparse here means that the array doesn't hold any actual values, but rather "holes" (just like my socks). So although you couldn't apply higher-order functions (e.g. `map`) to such an array without a problem, at least the array `result` already has the correct size from the outset. Instead of adding elements using `push`, you now mend holes at the required locations using the index operator `[]`. This would work as follows:

```
for (let i = 0; i < n; i += 1) result[i] = fn();
```

Finally, you still pass the variable `i` as an argument to the `fn` call in the loop. The counter variable `i` contains the current number of the loop pass (0, 1, 2, etc.).

```
for (let i = 0; i < n; i += 1) result[i] = fn(i);
```

This isn't necessary when generating a line, but it does give you the option at some later time to access the value of the counter variable, which may prove to be very useful. Here's the complete function:

```
1 "use strict";
2
3 const times = (n, fn) => {
4   const result = new Array(n);
5   for (let i = 0; i < n; i += 1) result[i] = fn(i);
6   return result;
7 };
```

Listing 99 *accompanying_files/20/examples/times_optimized.js*

Examples

```
times(3, i => i + 2) // => [2, 3, 4]
times(5, () => "") // => ['', '', '', '', '']
```

But Why Not Use Recursion?

Normally we would just write the `times` function using recursion:

```
1  "use strict";
2
3  const times = (n, fn) =>
4    n === 0
5      ? []
6      : times(n - 1, fn).concat(fn(n - 1));
```

Listing 100 *Recursive version of times*

`times` is a very basic function which you'll probably use very often over the course of your programming career, in a wide variety of scenarios. Some application cases require better performance than is possible using recursion. The solution to this is a concept known as ***tail call optimization***. This just requires us to make sure that at the point where the function returns a value, nothing occurs apart from the recursive function call:

```
1  "use strict";
2
3  const times = (n, fn, result = []) =>
4    n === 0
5      ? result
6      : times(n - 1, fn, [].concat(fn(n - 1), result));
```

Listing 101 *Optimized tail-recursive version of times*

Unfortunately, many JS environments (especially those of most browsers) are not yet able to support *tail call optimization*. As a result, our recursive implementation in listing 101 would be rather slow. In addition, you can only use it to a very limited extent — i.e. up to a certain number of recursive calls (depending on how much RAM you have). A technique known as **trampolining** would provide a solution, but it's quite complicated and also doesn't contribute to performance.

Using Ready-Made Functions

Actually, I'm not a very big fan of using copy & paste to integrate outside functions into one's code. Better techniques exist for reusing code, like loading functions from so-called **function libraries**. For example, in the case of security updates, there're ways of installing these with little effort. But if you used copy & paste instead to integrate a large number of functions, then you yourself are responsible for manually maintaining those functions. This can translate into significant effort if you have a large amount of code.

On the other hand, I do feel that this is acceptable with two functions or less. If you find you later want to make use of an external library, here are two which already provide the `times` function:

> ➤ *Ramda*[46]
> ➤ *lodash*[47]

Exercise 56: The Most Wonderful Time of the Year

Since it's snowing outside, you could write a small program which prints out the word `Ho!` to the console three times. Use the `times` function to do this.

When you get some warmer weather, of course you could turn this into a pirate version and print out `Arrrr!` three times instead.

Exercise 57: Wallpaper Time

Now that you know how to use `times` to draw lines, it's now high time you turned back to wallpaper (rectangles). Write a function `rectangle` (listing 102), using `times` so that you don't need recursion.

---

46. *http://ramdajs.com/*
47. *https://lodash.com*

```
const rectangle = (width, height, character) =>
  height === 0
  ? ""
  : rectangle(width, height - 1, character)
    + "\n" + line(width, character);
```

Listing 102 Recursive version of rectangle function

Exercise 58: Valuable Zeros, Part 2

NerdWorld has changed its item number system yet again. They're now always going to use 7-digit item numbers. Numbers with fewer than 7 digits (e.g. 123) should be expanded to 7 digits using leading zeros. For example, 123 would be corrected to 0000123. Write a function which takes an item number and returns the corrected version as a string.

Experiment: Try solving the exercise using `times`, then using recursion, and finally without using either recursion or `times` at all.

20.3   From Start to End with range

The "sister" function to `times` is `range`, and you can likewise just copy and reuse this function as well. Unfortunately, the following code isn't very easy to understand since it also contains a few optimizations. In addition, we're using a so-called **default parameter** for the function `rangeFromStartToEnd` (you'll learn more about default parameters in section 21.2).

```
 1 "use strict";
 2
 3 const range = (startOrEnd, end, step) =>
 4   end
 5     ? rangeFromStartToEnd(startOrEnd, end, step)
 6     : rangeFromStartToEnd(0, startOrEnd);
 7
 8 const rangeFromStartToEnd = (start, end, step = 1) => {
 9   const length = Math.max(Math.ceil((end - start) / step), 0);
10   const result = Array(length);
11   const sign = step / Math.abs(step);
12   let index = 0;
13   for (let value = start; value * sign < end * sign; value +=
```

```
step)
14      result[index++] = value;
15    return result;
16 };
```

Listing 103 *accompanying_files/20/examples/range.js*

Even though the implementation is somewhat more complex, you can still use the function very easily. Just like `times`, `range` generates an array. Unlike `times` however, the array always contains sequence numbers as elements. In addition, you can specify any numbers for the start and end values.

```
console.log(range(9)); // => [ 0, 1, 2, 3, 4, 5, 6, 7, 8 ]

console.log(range(5, 9)); // => [ 5, 6, 7, 8 ]
```

Note that `range` starts with `0` if you don't specify a starting value. In addition, the last value (`9` in this case) no longer appears in the array (***exclusive range of values***).

If you like, you can even specify an increment:

```
console.log(range(3, 9, 2)); // => [ 3, 5, 7 ]
```

This increment is `2` in the example. However, you can also specify any positive integer or even a negative integer as an increment.

What's Wrong with Loops?

Have you had a chat with your neighbor — that guy who's been programming for 20 years? And did you mention to him our recommendation of doing away with conventional loops? How did he react? Was he totally appalled?

No? Well, at least something like that might have happened to you if you did have a neighbor who's been working in software development for 20 years.

Loops are actually a very common language construct — practically every experienced programmer you meet will have used them. For many traditionalists, life without loops is hardly imaginable.

So why in the world are we recommending that you don't use loops?

Imperative vs. Declarative

JS is a language which supports both *imperative* as well as *declarative* constructs. Imperative means that you need to formulate **how** things work — in other words, you must describe a process. Declarative means that you only need to describe the **what**.

For example, it's a laborious task to describe in detail the process of looping through an array and using `if` to filter out specific elements. Instead, just say you want a filtered array. Declarative solutions are generally shorter, clearer and simpler.

Example: Even Numbers

```
// imperative
let numbers = range(10);
let evenNumbers = [];
for (let i = 0; i < numbers.length; i += 1) {
  if (numbers[i] % 2 === 0) {
    evenNumbers.push(numbers[i]);
  }
}
console.log(evenNumbers); // => [0, 2, 4, 6, 8]

// declarative
range(10).filter(v => v % 2 === 0) // => [0, 2, 4, 6, 8]
```

Loops are a conventional imperative concept and as a result are better avoided. This was hardly possible in JS up to now, but modern language constructs provided in ES5/6 paired with a few small enhancements like `range` and `time` have made doing without loops (in one's own code) a reality.

Here're a few arguments if you still want to discuss loops with your neighbor over the garden fence:

➤ When you need to run through an array, it's better to work with higher-order functions since you don't need a counter variable. In addition, you see immediately in the higher-order function why you're going through the array, e.g. is it being filtered or mapped or...?

➤ Loops always hold the risk of an index error (one of the most popular is the classic +/- 1 error, in which the number of loop passes differs by exactly one). This cannot occur in higher-order functions like `map`, `reduce` and `filter`.

➤ You can use the functions `times` and `range` in place of loops if, instead of running through arrays, you need to process a fixed value range — an item number with a fixed length, 6 matching numbers in lotto, etc. Just like loops, the two functions are susceptible to index errors, but even when an error does occur, at least it doesn't result in an infinite loop which causes your program to crash.

➤ In addition, `times` and `range` require less "fine-tuning" than a `for` loop. For example, in `times`, you only need to specify the number of repetitions, but no loop condition or update operation. Less fine-tuning also means less possibility for errors.

➤ There are a number of programming problems which are easier to solve with recursion than with loops, such as the question from one of the last exercises of whether a list is sorted.

20.4   Exercises

Exercise 59: Learning How to Count

1   Print out the numbers from 70 to 130 to the console.

2   Now, let JS count backwards from 200 to 20.

3   Print out all even numbers from 10 to 50 to the console.

Exercise 60: 6 Correct?

1   Make some additions to your lotto generator from exercise 17. Have your generator print out six random lotto numbers. (Repeated numbers will be allowed at first.)

2   Write a new lotto generator which doesn't produce repeated numbers.

Hint: One way you could solve this would be to imitate an actual lottery, by first casting 49 numbers into one container, shaking it up, then drawing out the first 6 numbers.

Exercise 61: Prime Numbers

Write a program which will calculate all prime numbers and print these out to the browser. A prime number is an integer greater than 1 which is evenly divisible only by itself or by 1.

1   Print out the prime numbers from 1 to 97 (inclusive). You should get the following result:

```
[2, 3, 5, 7, 11, 13, 17, 19, 23, 29, 31, 37, 41, 43, 47,
53, 59, 61,67, 71, 73, 79, 83, 89, 97]
```

2   Now, print out all prime numbers up to 1000.

Exercise 62: Lotto Statistics ["Brainteaser"]

Now we want to know — how often does someone actually get 6 correct numbers? Write a program which holds 10000 lotto drawings — always with the same numbers. Then print out statistics on how often someone got 6 correct numbers, 5 correct numbers, etc.

Special Features of Function Definitions at Call Time

I know, I know — we've already covered functions in a lot of detail. However, we still kept you in the dark about a couple of things. We didn't do this with any bad intentions — we just wanted to keep things easy at first. But now we want to break things wide open and reveal to you all the small, ugly details that you've always wanted to know about functions and their parameters.

21.1 Function Parameters — Sometimes Too Many, Sometimes Not Enough

One special feature of JS is that when you call a function, you can pass it more (or even fewer) arguments than are specified in the function definition. Let's go back to our `cylindricalVolume` function from lesson 14:

```
const cylindricalVolume = (radius, height) => Math.PI * radius *
radius * height;
```

What happens if you call the function and pass it three arguments instead of two?

```
cylindricalVolume(10, 80, 27)
```

The answer is, nothing special. The result is `25132.741228718347`, the same as it would be with the call `cylindricalVolume(10, 80)`. The function just ignores the third argument. This doesn't sound too alarming, but unfortunately it is a common source of errors. Maybe you did want to add a third parameter but forgot to update your function definition. Now, instead of getting back a meaningful error message, your code produces incorrect results, and you need to take off hunting for errors.

Even worse is when you call a function and you pass it fewer arguments than it needs.

```
cylindricalVolume(10)
```

Instead of an error message, you get `NaN`.

On the plus side, this behavior makes refactoring easier, for example when you add a new parameter to a function and then have to go back and modify some or even all of the corresponding calls. In addition, JS provides a trick for higher-order functions which takes advantage of this relaxed parameter handling (but more on that later …)

On the other hand, a big drawback of this behavior is its high error potential — so you should always try to avoid such discrepancies!

My Recommendation

Make sure that the

➤ **number of parameters** in the function definition and the
➤ **number of arguments** in the function call

are always the same!

There're a couple of exceptions to this rule, but we'll get to these shortly.

21.2   Taking Care of Standard Cases Using Default Parameters

Let's assume that Marty's packaging tubes have a standard height of 80 cm. There're only a few special cases where this tube height is different. So it'd be very practical here if you could call the function with just radius, and the standard value were automatically used for the height.

```
cylindricalVolume(10) // => 25132.741228718347
```

There's good news — you can do this! You just need a so-called **default parameter**.

All you need to do to implement this is to use `=` in the parameter definition to assign your required default value.

```
1 const cylindricalVolume = (radius, height = 80) => Math.PI *
radius * radius * height;
```

If you now call the function with just radius, the `height` parameter will automatically be assigned a value of `80`. In special cases, e.g. if Marty has a special short tube, you can still specify all the arguments in the call:

```
cylindricalVolume(10, 60) // => 18849.55592153876
```

In this case, the call will just ignore the default value of `80`.

Life in the Old Days

One of the reasons JS doesn't check the number of parameters is that earlier versions of JS also supported the use of default parameters, even before ES2015 introduced the feature officially.

Example

```
1  const cylindricalVolume = (radius, height) =>
2    Math.PI * radius * radius * height;
```

If the function call only specifies one argument (e.g. `cylindricalVolume(10)`), the second parameter (`height`) will get a value of `undefined`.

Although this isn't terribly elegant, it's still possible to test the parameter (`typeof height === "undefined"`), and if necessary a default value can be assigned.

```
1  const cylindricalVolume = (radius, height) => {
2    if (typeof height === "undefined") height = 80;
3    return Math.PI * radius * radius * height;
4  }
```

This made it possible for default parameters to be emulated in earlier versions of JS as well. These days it's much easier — "real" default parameters make code much more readable.

21.3 Taking What They're Given: Rest Parameters

Sometimes it's useful for a function to be able to take in any number of parameters. The function `console.log` (with which you're very familiar by now) is one such function.

```
const a = 1;
const b = 2;

console.log("a: ", a , " ", "b: ", b);
```

But his option isn't just available for functions in the standard JS library — you can also write such functions yourself. ECMAScript2015 provides so called rest parameters for just this purpose.

Here's a small example:

```
greetWith("HeyHo", "Goldy", "Ladislaus", "Heribert");
```

The function `greetWith` takes a series of names as arguments (starting with the second). The function then addresses these names in order, each time using the greeting specified in the first argument:

```
HeyHo Goldy
HeyHo Ladislaus
HeyHo Heribert
```

The function doesn't set any limit on the number of names you can pass it — everybody gets a friendly greeting. How is this done?

Declare the last parameter of the function as a rest parameter, by preceding it with three dots (`...`):

```
const greetWith = (greeting, ...names) =>
```

The function call `greetWith("HeyHo", "Goldy", "Ladislaus", "Heribert");` moves the first argument (in this case `HeyHo`) into the first parameter. All "normal" parameters must appear before the rest parameter, and are assigned as usual. The rest parameter `...names` then swallows up all the remaining arguments (`"Goldy", "Ladislaus", "Heribert"`).

A rest parameter is an array which contains the remaining arguments as elements (in this case `["Goldy", "Ladislaus", "Heribert"]`). Now you can use a `forEach` to print out a greeting for each name:

```
1  "use strict";
2
3  const greetWith = (greeting, ...names) =>
4    names.forEach(name => console.log(greeting + " " + name));
5
6  greetWith("HeyHo", "Goldy", "Ladislaus", "Heribert");
```

Listing 104 *accompanying_files/21/examples/rest.js*

21.4   Higher-Order Functions Can Swallow Up More Than Just Elements

We want to implement a small contest game on our website and we need to be able to print out a list of the winners. The first three winners will get special prizes, so we want to add the text *Winner 1*, *Winner 2* and *Winner 3* before those names.

```
let winners = ["Heribert", "Friedlinde", "Tusnelda", "Oswine",
"Ladislaus"];
```

The winners already exist in the form of an array, sorted by their place in the drawing. Your job is to append the prefix `"Winner 1:"` etc. to the strings. Basically, you can just execute a `map` over the array `winners`. First, add just the prefix `"Winner:"` without the number.

```
winners.map(winner => `Winner: ${winner}`);
```

You get:

```
[ 'Winner: Heribert',
  'Winner: Friedlinde',
  'Winner: Tusnelda',
  'Winner: Oswine',
  'Winner: Ladislaus' ]
```

The tough part now is to deal with the place number. This isn't provided in the parameter `winner`, and you don't have much more information than that. So what do we do?

A special feature of higher-order functions will meet our needs very nicely here. As you know, `map` takes a function as an argument — a so-called callback function. What parameters should this callback function have? `map` and the callback function passed to it have, in a sense, a contract:

One by one, `map` passes the function an element of its array as the first argument. The callback function takes in the argument as its first parameter, processes it and produces a return value.

But in reality, `map` passes the function more than just the current element — `map` also passes it the index of the array element. So all you need to do is to implement a second parameter which will take in this value. This parameter is typically named `i` (for index).

```
winners.map((winner, i) => `Winner ${i}: ${winner}`);
```

You get:

```
[ 'Winner 0: Heribert',
  'Winner 1: Friedlinde',
  'Winner 2: Tusnelda',
  'Winner 3: Oswine',
  'Winner 4: Ladislaus' ]
```

As is usual with arrays, the index begins at `0`, — or as we programmers say, `i` is **0-indexed**. So in order to get the correct placing we just need to add a 1.

```
winners.map((winner, i) => `Winner ${i + 1}: ${winner}`);
```

Result:

```
[ 'Winner 1: Heribert',
  'Winner 2: Friedlinde',
  'Winner 3: Tusnelda',
  'Winner 4: Oswine',
  'Winner 5: Ladislaus' ]
```

Awesome! This is coming along very nicely. Still, Marty wanted the text to be displayed for just the first three winners. Thanks to the index parameter, that's also easy to implement:

```
1 winners.map((winner, i) =>
2   i < 3
3     ? `Winner ${i + 1}: ${winner}`
4     : winner );
```

Turn this into a function called `withPlace`, and the program is finished:

```
1 "use strict";
2
3 const winners = ["Heribert", "Friedlinde", "Tusnelda", "Oswine",
"Ladislaus"];
4
5 const withPlace = winners =>
6   winners.map((winner, i) =>
7     i < 3
8       ? `Winner ${i + 1}: ${winner}`
```

```
 9       : winner
10    );
11
12  console.log(withPlace(winners));
```

Listing 105 *accompanying_files/21/examples/winners.js*

The return value of `withPlace` is in the form we want and can now be reused for any other appropriate task:

```
[ 'Winner 1: Heribert',
  'Winner 2: Friedlinde',
  'Winner 3: Tusnelda',
  'Oswine',
  'Ladislaus' ]
```

Exercise 63: True Winners

The printout of the winners in the last example (listing 105) still leaves a little to be desired. The following result array would be perfect:

```
[ '1st place: Heribert',
  '2nd place: Friedlinde',
  '3rd place: Tusnelda',
  'Oswine',
  'Ladislaus' ]
```

Improve the code accordingly.

A Third Mystery Uncovered — Callback Parameters

In addition to the index operator (second parameter) and the current array value (first parameter), you can even tap into a third parameter. The callback function passed to `map` again receives the complete source array as a third parameter. Admittedly, real world situations in which you would actually need this third parameter are rare.

Example

```
1 "use strict";
2
3 ["Heribert", "Friedlinde", "Tusnelda", "Oswine",
"Ladislaus"].forEach(
4   (v, i, a) => console.log(`v: ${v}, i: ${i}, a: ${a}`)
5 );
```

Listing 106 *accompanying_files/21/examples/three_callback_params.js*

Output:

```
v: Heribert, i: 0, a: Heribert,Friedlinde,Tusnelda,Oswine,Ladislaus
v: Friedlinde, i: 1, a:
Heribert,Friedlinde,Tusnelda,Oswine,Ladislaus
v: Tusnelda, i: 2, a: Heribert,Friedlinde,Tusnelda,Oswine,Ladislaus
v: Oswine, i: 3, a: Heribert,Friedlinde,Tusnelda,Oswine,Ladislaus
v: Ladislaus, i: 4, a:
Heribert,Friedlinde,Tusnelda,Oswine,Ladislaus
```

Other Array Callback Functions

Conveniently enough, these optional callback parameters don't just work with `map`, but also with many other array functions such as:

> filter

> reduce

> reduceRight

> every

> some

> find

> findIndex

> forEach

21.5   Reference

Name	Callback Function Parameters
map, filter, every, some, find, findIndex, forEach	1. **Value**: The value of the array element currently being processed. 2. **index**: A running index value, starting from 0. 3. **Array**: The entire array on which `map` is called.
reduce, reduceRight	1. **previousValue**: Result from the last time the callback was executed, or initial argument to `reduce` in the case of the first call. If no initial argument exists, `reduce` uses the first array value instead. 2. **Value**: The value of the array element currently being processed. 3. **index**: A running index value, starting from 0. 4. **Array**: The entire array on which `reduce` is called.

Table 21.1 Callback parameters of higher-order array functions

21.6   Exercises

Exercise 64: Letter Thief

In the German children's song *Auf der Mauer, auf der Lauer*[48], you sing the words *Wanze* (bug) and *tanzen* (dance), but in each new verse you drop a letter of each word until no more of the word remains.

Write a function which will take any word as an argument. It should return an array in which each element is a substring of the original word, such that a letter is always dropped from element to element. The last element in the array must always be an empty string.

Example

```
letterThief("dance") //=> ["danc", "dan", "da", "d", ""];
```

Exercise 65: ISBNx — The Secret of Checksums ["Brainteaser"]

Do you know how books are identified worldwide? This is done using an **ISBN** (**International Standard Book Number**).

Just take a book from your bookshelf and turn it over, and on the back, you'll see the ISBN.

The ISBN-13 (an ISBN which consists of 13 digits) has been used exclusively since 2007. But what's really of interest to people like programmers is that the last digit is a so-called checksum — it's calculated from the other 12 digits of the ISBN. This lets you easily determine whether or not a 13-digit number is actually a valid ISBN or not.

1   Write a function which will take a 12-digit number (e.g. `978151705411`) and calculate the ISBN checksum (`3` in this case).

Exactly how is the checksum calculated? Here's the algorithm:

> Calculate the sum of the individual digits in the number, multiplying every second digit by 3. **Example based on 4-digit number 4567:**

```
4567 => 4 + 5 * 3 + 6 + 7 * 3 => 46
```

> Take just the last digit of the result of that calculation, and subtract it from 10. **Example:**

```
4567 => 46 => 6 => 10 - 6 => 4
```

> If the result is 10, you replace it with 0.

2   Make sure that your program is capable of handling any number of digits (not just exactly 12).

3   Also make it possible for your program to accept an ISBN which includes hyphens, e.g. `978-3-86680-192-9`

4   Grab a couple of books from your shelf, blow off the dust and turn them to the back cover. Now test your program using the ISBNs from these books.

Thinking in Higher Dimensions: Multi-Dimensional Arrays

22.1   Checkmate with 2D Arrays

We're planning a "chess special" for the summer. To be specific, we're going to sell chess piece ice cube trays. These cubes will go great in your Kasparov and DeepBlue cocktails. And if you're fast enough, you can even use them to play a game of chess.

As part of our advertising campaign, we plan to show famous chess games — move for move! Our front end developer will take care of the visuals. But your job as developer is to design an appropriate data structure and core logic. Of course, a small text printout would also be nice ...

Fig. 37 © 2015 ThinkGeek, Inc. All Rights Reserved.

The basic problem is the fact that a chessboard is a two-dimensional structure — it consists of 8x8 squares. These squares form a checked pattern in which white and black squares alternate. You could use letters to represent the chess pieces (e.g. K for *king*, etc.), or perhaps you'd like to try something a little fancier: Use the matching UTF8 characters. UTF-8 provides characters for all chess pieces, in both black and white.

The first row of our chessboard might look something like the following:

♜♞♝♛♚♝♞♜

So that you can later read out and change each individual square separately, it'll be helpful to use an array:

```
const firstRow = ["♜", "♞", "♝", "♛", "♚", "♝", "♞", "♜"];
```

Now comes the interesting part: There's more than just one row. As a result, the array needs to be two-dimensional. However, "true" 2D arrays don't exist in JS. So the trick will be to nest arrays inside one another. The elements in an array don't necessarily have to be `strings` or `numbers` — they can also be arrays them-selves. So the complete board could be represented as follows:

```
1  "use strict";
2
3  const boardInStartPosition = [
4    ["♜", "♞", "♝", "♛", "♚", "♝", "♞", "♜"],
5    ["♟", "♟", "♟", "♟", "♟", "♟", "♟", "♟"],
6    ["□", "■", "□", "■", "□", "■", "□", "■"],
7    ["■", "□", "■", "□", "■", "□", "■", "□"],
8    ["□", "■", "□", "■", "□", "■", "□", "■"],
9    ["■", "□", "■", "□", "■", "□", "■", "□"],
10   ["♙", "♙", "♙", "♙", "♙", "♙", "♙", "♙"],
11   ["♖", "♘", "♗", "♕", "♔", "♗", "♘", "♖"]
12 ];
```

Listing 107 accompanying_files/22/examples/chessboard.js

In case of those squares which don't hold any pieces, you can use the characters UTF8 provides for checked patterns (empty and filled-in squares). So now, if you access the array with an index (e.g. `boardInStartPosition[7]`), you'll get back a complete line.

```
boardInStartPosition[7] // => ["♖", "♘", "♗", "♕", "♔", "♗", "♘",
"♖"]
```

Since this line is in turn itself an array, you can use another index to access a specific character, e.g. the white queen is the element at position three in row 7.

```
1  const lastRow = boardInStartPosition[7];
2  lastRow[3] // => "♕"
```

You don't even need an intermediate variable, you can access the piece directly!

```
boardInStartPosition[7][3] // => "♕"
```

Of course, you can also change the value at this position — for example, if the queen is captured by a black pawn, you could write:

```
boardInStartPosition[7][3] = "♟";
```

We don't need anything new for the rest of the functionality required. We can use a function `board2string` to print out the chessboard.

```
1 const board2string = board =>
2   board.map(row => row.join("")).join("\n");
```

We get the following console printout for the game's starting position (`board2string(boardInStartPosition)`):

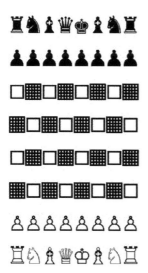

We'll use the following functions to execute a move such as `"e2e4"`.

```
1 const originSquare = move => move.slice(0, 2);
2 const targetSquare = move => move.slice(2);
```

The functions `originSquare` and `targetSquare` respectively extract the starting square and target square of a move — e.g. `targetSquare("e2e4")` returns the target square `"e4"`.

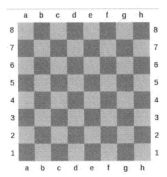

Fig. 38 *Chessboard with column positions a-h and row positions 1-8*
Source: wikipedia.org

```
1 const squareToXPosition = square => letterToChessIndex(square[0]);
2 const squareToYPosition = square => numberToChessIndex(square[1]);
3 const letterToChessIndex = letter => "abcdefgh".indexOf(letter);
4 const numberToChessIndex = num => 8 - num;
```

By using `squareToXPosition` and `squareToYPosition`, you can respectively extract the X and Y positions for the array.

Convert the letters of the chessboard (*a-h*) to the corresponding array index, using `letterToChessIndex`. In addition, the numbering of the Y-axis of the chessboard runs opposite to that of an array. The first row in an array begins with index 0, and the last has index 7. The chessboard begins at the top with row 8 and ends at the bottom with row 1. The conversion is therefore carried out by using `num => 8 - num`.

22.2   Move By Move

Now we can write the function `execMove` which will execute a move.

```
 1 "use strict";
 2
 3 const board2string = board =>
 4   board.map(row => row.join("")).join("\n");
 5
 6 const execMove = (board, move) => {
 7   const originX = fieldToXPosition(originField(move));
 8   const originY = fieldToYPosition(originField(move));
 9   const targetX = fieldToXPosition(targetField(move));
10   const targetY = fieldToYPosition(targetField(move));
11
12   board[targetY][targetX] = board[originY][originX];
13   return board;
14 };
```

```
15
16 const originField = move => move.slice(0, 2);
17 const targetField = move => move.slice(2);
18
19 const fieldToXPosition = field => letterToChessIndex(field[0]);
20 const fieldToYPosition = field => numberToChessIndex(field[1]);
21 const letterToChessIndex = letter => "abcdefgh".indexOf(letter);
22 const numberToChessIndex = num => 8 - num;
23
24 const boardInStartPosition = [
25     ["♜", "♞", "♝", "♛", "♚", "♝", "♞", "♜"],
26     ["♟", "♟", "♟", "♟", "♟", "♟", "♟", "♟"],
27     ["□", "■", "□", "■", "□", "■", "□", "■"],
28     ["■", "□", "■", "□", "■", "□", "■", "□"],
29     ["□", "■", "□", "■", "□", "■", "□", "■"],
30     ["■", "□", "■", "□", "■", "□", "■", "□"],
31     ["♙", "♙", "♙", "♙", "♙", "♙", "♙", "♙"],
32     ["♖", "♘", "♗", "♕", "♔", "♗", "♘", "♖"]
33 ];
34
35 console.log(board2string(boardInStartPosition));
36
37 console.log("\n");
38
39 console.log(board2string(
40     execMove(boardInStartPosition, "e2e4")
41 ));
```

Listing 108 *accompanying_files/22/examples/chess1.js*

`execMove` copies a figure from its original position `board[originY][originX]` to the target square `board[targetY][targetX]`. Unfortunately, that's not all we need. The figure now appears twice on the board. So now we also need to remove the figure from the original square. To do this, copy the appropriate square back from an empty chessboard (`emptyBoard`):

```
board[originY][originX] = emptyBoard[originY][originX];
```

You overwrite the double figure with the appropriate square (black or white character square) from the empty chessboard. Of course, we first need to create the empty chessboard:

```
1 "use strict";
2
3 const emptyBoard = [
4     ["□", "■", "□", "■", "□", "■", "□", "■"],
5     ["■", "□", "■", "□", "■", "□", "■", "□"],
6     ["□", "■", "□", "■", "□", "■", "□", "■"],
7     ["■", "□", "■", "□", "■", "□", "■", "□"],
```

```
 8      ["□", "■", "□", "■", "□", "■", "□", "■"],
 9      ["■", "□", "■", "□", "■", "□", "■", "□"],
10      ["□", "■", "□", "■", "□", "■", "□", "■"],
11      ["■", "□", "■", "□", "■", "□", "■", "□"]
12 ];
```

Listing 109 accompanying_files/22/examples/emptyBoard.js

Small Improvement: Unchangeable Chessboard

In order to ensure that you don't wind up modifying an array when you access the empty chessboard (`emptyBoard`) or starting position (`boardInStartPosition`), it's a good idea to return arrays via functions. Instead of `const emptyBoard = [...]`, write `const emptyBoard = () => [...]`.

Here's the complete code:

```
 1 "use strict";
 2
 3 const board2string = board =>
 4   board.map( row => row.join("")).join("\n");
 5
 6 const execMove = (board, move) => {
 7   const originX = fieldToXPosition(originField(move));
 8   const originY = fieldToYPosition(originField(move));
 9   const targetX = fieldToXPosition(targetField(move));
10   const targetY = fieldToYPosition(targetField(move));
11
12   board[targetY][targetX] = board[originY][originX];
13   board[originY][originX] = emptyBoard()[originY][originX];
14   return board;
15 };
16
17 const boardInStartPosition = () => [
18   ["♜", "♞", "♝", "♛", "♚", "♝", "♞", "♜"],
19   ["♟", "♟", "♟", "♟", "♟", "♟", "♟", "♟"],
20   ["□", "■", "□", "■", "□", "■", "□", "■"],
21   ["■", "□", "■", "□", "■", "□", "■", "□"],
22   ["□", "■", "□", "■", "□", "■", "□", "■"],
23   ["■", "□", "■", "□", "■", "□", "■", "□"],
24   ["♙", "♙", "♙", "♙", "♙", "♙", "♙", "♙"],
25   ["♖", "♘", "♗", "♕", "♔", "♗", "♘", "♖"]
26 ];
27
28 const emptyBoard = () => [
29   ["□", "■", "□", "■", "□", "■", "□", "■"],
30   ["■", "□", "■", "□", "■", "□", "■", "□"],
31   ["□", "■", "□", "■", "□", "■", "□", "■"],
32   ["■", "□", "■", "□", "■", "□", "■", "□"],
33   ["□", "■", "□", "■", "□", "■", "□", "■"],
```

```
34    ["■", "□", "■", "□", "■", "□", "■", "□"],
35    ["□", "■", "□", "■", "□", "■", "□", "■"],
36    ["■", "□", "■", "□", "■", "□", "■", "□"]
37 ];
38
39 const originField = move => move.slice(0, 2);
40 const targetField = move => move.slice(2);
41
42 const fieldToXPosition = field => letterToChessIndex(field[0]);
43 const fieldToYPosition = field => numberToChessIndex(field[1]);
44 const letterToChessIndex = letter => "abcdefgh".indexOf(letter);
45 const numberToChessIndex = num => 8 - num;
46
47 console.log(board2string(boardInStartPosition()));
48
49 console.log("\n");
50
51 console.log(board2string(
52    execMove(boardInStartPosition(), "e2e4")
53 ));
```

Listing 110 accompanying_files/22/examples/chess2.js

22.3   Determined by Position

Actually, we haven't completely satisfied Marty's requirements yet. Right now, we're always only executing a single move. So that our front end developer can display a master game, we need to be able to execute multiple moves in succession! Try the following short exercise:

Exercise 66: Chess: Different Positions

Add another function to your chess program: `execMoves(moves)`. This function should take in multiple moves (in the form of an array) then execute these in succession, e.g.

```
execMoves(["e2e4", "e7e5", "f2f4"])
```

It's enough here to just print out the final position (after all moves have been executed).

Did you manage to do it? Don't worry, we'll solve it right now. Ideally you used a `reduce` function to reduce a series of moves down to a single final position.

This is actually not too different from a summation:

```
1 const add = (a, b) => a + b;
2 const sum = numbers => numbers.reduce(add, 0);
```

The function `sum` starts with an initial value of 0 and adds the next number from the array in turn in each step. The result of each step is a new sum, until finally the sum total of all numbers in the array `numbers` can be returned as a final result. In exactly the same way, you can begin with a starting position on the chessboard and call `execMove` (instead of the function `add`) so that you get a new intermediate position every time a move is executed, until `reduce` finally returns the last position at the end (after executing all moves).

Calculating a sum using `reduce` and calculating final position are astonishingly similar. `reduce` "reduces" all elements of an array down into a single value. In this respect, `reduce` might be considered to be more of an abstract function. How this reduction is executed can be completely different in different situations. You always give `reduce` a rule specifying how it should process two elements, and `reduce` handles the rest. In the case of summation, this rule is just addition. You might also say: Summation is the "reduction" of an array of numbers through **addition**, and the final position in a chess game is the reduction of an array of moves through the **execution of each individual move**.

So you might implement the function `execMoves` as follows:

```
const execMoves = moves =>
  moves.reduce(execMove, boardInStartPosition());
```

And here's an example of a call:

```
1 console.log(board2string(
2   execMoves(["e2e4", "e7e5", "f2f4"])
3 ));
```

And here's the example again in its entirety:

```
1 "use strict";
2
3 const board2string = board =>
4   board.map(row => row.join("")).join("\n");
5
6 const execMoves = moves => moves.reduce(execMove,
boardInStartPosition());
7
8 const execMove = (board, move) => {
9   const originX = fieldToXPosition(originField(move));
10  const originY = fieldToYPosition(originField(move));
11  const targetX = fieldToXPosition(targetField(move));
12  const targetY = fieldToYPosition(targetField(move));
13
```

```
14   board[targetY][targetX] = board[originY][originX];
15   board[originY][originX] = emptyBoard()[originY][originX];
16   return board;
17 };
18
19 const boardInStartPosition = () => [
20   ["♜", "♞", "♝", "♛", "♚", "♝", "♞", "♜"],
21   ["♟", "♟", "♟", "♟", "♟", "♟", "♟", "♟"],
22   ["□", "■", "□", "■", "□", "■", "□", "■"],
23   ["■", "□", "■", "□", "■", "□", "■", "□"],
24   ["□", "■", "□", "■", "□", "■", "□", "■"],
25   ["■", "□", "■", "□", "■", "□", "■", "□"],
26   ["♙", "♙", "♙", "♙", "♙", "♙", "♙", "♙"],
27   ["♖", "♘", "♗", "♕", "♔", "♗", "♘", "♖"]
28 ];
29
30 const emptyBoard = () => [
31   ["□", "■", "□", "■", "□", "■", "□", "■"],
32   ["■", "□", "■", "□", "■", "□", "■", "□"],
33   ["□", "■", "□", "■", "□", "■", "□", "■"],
34   ["■", "□", "■", "□", "■", "□", "■", "□"],
35   ["□", "■", "□", "■", "□", "■", "□", "■"],
36   ["■", "□", "■", "□", "■", "□", "■", "□"],
37   ["□", "■", "□", "■", "□", "■", "□", "■"],
38   ["■", "□", "■", "□", "■", "□", "■", "□"]
39 ];
40
41 const originField = move => move.slice(0, 2);
42 const targetField = move => move.slice(2);
43
44 const fieldToXPosition = field => letterToChessIndex(field[0]);
45 const fieldToYPosition = field => numberToChessIndex(field[1]);
46 const letterToChessIndex = letter => "abcdefgh".indexOf(letter);
47 const numberToChessIndex = num => 8 - num;
48
49 console.log(board2string(boardInStartPosition()));
50
51 console.log("\n");
52
53 console.log(board2string(
54   execMove(boardInStartPosition(), "e2e4")
55 ));
56
57 console.log("\n");
58
59 console.log(board2string(
60   execMoves(["e2e4", "e7e5", "f2f4"])
61 ));
```

Listing 111 accompanying_files/22/examples/chess3.js

22.4 ...And Now in 3D!

So are we finished? Can you go home and pocket a fat bonus for a quick solution?

Not yet, unfortunately. For the visualization to work, the front end developer needs each intermediate position after every single move!

Right now we're only providing the final position after a series of moves. How can intermediate positions be stored?

Yes, you may have already suspected the answer after seeing our spoiler in the section heading...you need another dimension!

Basically, you need an array in which every element is a position. In principle, this would be something like:

```
[startPosition, positionAfterMove1, positionAfterMove2, ...]
```

Note that every single position is itself a 2D array. As a result, the overall history of positions must be a **3D array**. For example, let's take a look at the sequence of moves `["e2e4", "e7e5", "f2f4"]` (not an especially clever play, we agree). The following position history is associated with this sequence of moves:

Fig. 39 Starting position

Fig. 40 e2e4

Fig. 41 e7e5

Fig. 42 f2f4

When represented as a three-dimensional JS array, the position history would look like:

```
 1  [
 2    [
 3      [ '♜', '♞', '♝', '♛', '♚', '♝', '♞', '♜' ],
 4      [ '♟', '♟', '♟', '♟', '♟', '♟', '♟', '♟' ],
 5      [ '□', '■', '□', '■', '□', '■', '□', '■' ],
 6      [ '■', '□', '■', '□', '■', '□', '■', '□' ],
 7      [ '□', '■', '□', '■', '♙', '■', '□', '■' ],
 8      [ '■', '□', '■', '□', '■', '□', '■', '□' ],
 9      [ '♙', '♙', '♙', '♙', '□', '♙', '♙', '♙' ],
10      [ '♖', '♘', '♗', '♕', '♔', '♗', '♘', '♖' ]
11    ],
12    [
13      [ '♜', '♞', '♝', '♛', '♚', '♝', '♞', '♜' ],
14      [ '♟', '♟', '♟', '♟', '■', '♟', '♟', '♟' ],
15      [ '□', '■', '□', '■', '□', '■', '□', '■' ],
16      [ '■', '□', '■', '□', '♟', '□', '■', '□' ],
17      [ '□', '■', '□', '■', '♙', '■', '□', '■' ],
18      [ '■', '□', '■', '□', '■', '□', '■', '□' ],
19      [ '♙', '♙', '♙', '♙', '□', '♙', '♙', '♙' ],
20      [ '♖', '♘', '♗', '♕', '♔', '♗', '♘', '♖' ]
21    ],
22    [
23      [ '♜', '♞', '♝', '♛', '♚', '♝', '♞', '♜' ],
24      [ '♟', '♟', '♟', '♟', '■', '♟', '♟', '♟' ],
25      [ '□', '■', '□', '■', '□', '■', '□', '■' ],
26      [ '■', '□', '■', '□', '♟', '□', '■', '□' ],
27      [ '□', '■', '□', '■', '♙', '♙', '□', '■' ],
28      [ '■', '□', '■', '□', '■', '□', '■', '□' ],
29      [ '♙', '♙', '♙', '♙', '□', '■', '♙', '♙' ],
30      [ '♖', '♘', '♗', '♕', '♔', '♗', '♘', '♖' ]
31    ]
32  ]
```

This history array contains 3 elements, each of which represents the board's position after a move. Every position here is a complete chessboard with 8x8 squares in the form of a 2D array.

Now we just need one more function (we'll call it `positionHistoryForMoves`) which will return the complete history for a sequence of moves.

The first step involves generating a 2D array out of a simple sequence of moves such as `["e2e4", "e7e5", "f2f4"]`. Each element in this 2D array describes all moves from the beginning of the game up to the current move. So in this case this would be:

```
[["e2e4"], ["e2e4", "e7e5"], ["e2e4", "e7e5", "f2f4"]]
```

This is actually much easier to implement than you might imagine:

```
1  ["e2e4", "e7e5", "f2f4"].map((move, i) => moves.slice(0, i + 1))
```

You map individual moves onto a sub-array (`slice`) which contains all moves from the original array `moves` from the beginning (0) up to the current position (`i + 1`).

The result is an array with "move paths". You pass each individual path to the function `execMoves` and get back the current position.

```
1  const positionHistoryForMoves = moves =>
2    moves
3      .map((move, i) => moves.slice(0, i + 1))
4      .map(execMoves);
```

As usual, here's the code again in its entirety:

```
1  "use strict";
2
3  const board2string = board =>
4    board.map(row => row.join("")).join("\n");
5
6  const positionHistoryForMoves = moves =>
7    moves
8      .map((move, i) => moves.slice(0, i + 1))
9      .map(execMoves);
10
11 const execMoves = moves => moves.reduce(execMove,
   boardInStartPosition());
12
13 const execMove = (board, move) => {
14   const originX = fieldToXPosition(originField(move));
15   const originY = fieldToYPosition(originField(move));
16   const targetX = fieldToXPosition(targetField(move));
17   const targetY = fieldToYPosition(targetField(move));
18
19   board[targetY][targetX] = board[originY][originX];
20   board[originY][originX] = emptyBoard()[originY][originX];
21   return board;
22 };
23
24 const boardInStartPosition = () => [
25   ["♜", "♞", "♝", "♛", "♚", "♝", "♞", "♜"],
26   ["♟", "♟", "♟", "♟", "♟", "♟", "♟", "♟"],
27   ["□", "■", "□", "■", "□", "■", "□", "■"],
28   ["■", "□", "■", "□", "■", "□", "■", "□"],
29   ["□", "■", "□", "■", "□", "■", "□", "■"],
30   ["■", "□", "■", "□", "■", "□", "■", "□"],
31   ["♙", "♙", "♙", "♙", "♙", "♙", "♙", "♙"],
32   ["♖", "♘", "♗", "♕", "♔", "♗", "♘", "♖"]
33 ];
34
```

```
35 const emptyBoard = () => [
36   ["□", "■", "□", "■", "□", "■", "□", "■"],
37   ["■", "□", "■", "□", "■", "□", "■", "□"],
38   ["□", "■", "□", "■", "□", "■", "□", "■"],
39   ["■", "□", "■", "□", "■", "□", "■", "□"],
40   ["□", "■", "□", "■", "□", "■", "□", "■"],
41   ["■", "□", "■", "□", "■", "□", "■", "□"],
42   ["□", "■", "□", "■", "□", "■", "□", "■"],
43   ["■", "□", "■", "□", "■", "□", "■", "□"]
44 ];
45
46 const originField = move => move.slice(0, 2);
47 const targetField = move => move.slice(2);
48
49 const fieldToXPosition = field => letterToChessIndex(field[0]);
50 const fieldToYPosition = field => numberToChessIndex(field[1]);
51 const letterToChessIndex = letter => "abcdefgh".indexOf(letter);
52 const numberToChessIndex = num => 8 - num;
53
54 const history = positionHistoryForMoves(["e2e4", "e7e5",
"f2f4"]);
55
56 console.log(history);
57
58 history.forEach(
59   position => console.log(board2string(position), "\n")
60 );
```

Listing 112 *accompanying_files/22/examples/chess4.js*

22.5   Exercises

Exercise 67: Geoquiz

A school is commissioning the development of a *geoquiz* in which pupils must name the capitals of different countries. Your job is to develop the solution function `capitalOf` which takes a country and returns its capital.

The following code shows you how the data should be structured:

```
"use strict";

const countriesWithCapital = [
  ["UK", "London"],
  ["France", "Paris"],
  ["Germany", "Berlin"],
  ["Switzerland", "Bern"],
```

```
    ["Austria", "Vienna"],
    ["Russia", "Moscow"]
];

const capitalOf = country => /* ??? */;

console.log(capitalOf("Switzerland"));
```

accompanying_files/22/exercises/geo_quiz1.js

Exercise 68: Geoquiz — Part 2

The school now wants to implement an advanced phase of the geoquiz in which pupils name the country associated with a capital. Again, your job is to program a solution function. This time, `countryForCapital` takes a capital and returns the associated country.

The function should use the existing constant `countriesWithCapital`. You may not change the structure of the data in the constant.

Exercise 69: Pokémon — Evolution

Do you know *Pokémon*? All *Pokémon* games have a Pokémon (a fantasy creature) which goes through different stages of evolution. A Pokémon can evolve up to two times — in other words, it may go through a maximum of three stages, its starting stage and up to two subsequent stages. Each of these stages have a new Pokémon name, and none of these names may occur twice. You'll find a good overview of the stages in *Pokémon GO* at *http://www.pokemongoevolution.com*.

1   Write a function `stagesFor` which takes a Pokémon evolution stage and returns all associated evolution stages in the form of an array. You can use the evolution stages of *Pidgey*, *Vulpix* and *Dratini* as your sample data.

2   Develop the functions `stagesAfter` and `stagesBefore` which take a stage and respectively return only the stages after or only the stages before that stage.

You'll find the following template in the exercise material:

```
1  "use strict";
2
3  const evolutionStages = [
4    ["Pidgey", "Pidgeotto", "Pidgeot"],
5    ["Vulpix", "Ninetales"],
6    ["Dratini", "Dragonair", "Dragonite"]
7  ];
8
9  const stagesFor = pokemon => /* ??? */
10
11  const stagesAfter = pokemon => /*??? */
12
13  const stagesBefore = pokemon => /*??? */
14
15  console.log(stagesFor("Vulpix")); // => [ 'Vulpix',
'Ninetales' ]
16  console.log(stagesAfter("Dratini")); // => [ 'Dragonair',
'Dragonite' ]
17  console.log(stagesBefore("Pidgeot")); // => [ 'Pidgey',
'Pidgeotto' ]
18  console.log(stagesBefore("Dragonair")); // => [ 'Dratini' ]
```

accompanying_files/22/exercises/pokemon_evolution.js

You can experiment with calls to log to find out the type of output your functions should generate.

Exercise 70: Happy Mixing with Arrays — Part 3

Fig. 43 Didriks / dinnerseries[49] (CC) Attribution[50]

---

49. *https://www.flickr.com/photos/dinnerseries/*

50. *https://creativecommons.org/licenses/by/2.0/legalcode*

You feel like mixing some more cocktails. But today you just can't decide exactly which cocktail you want. It'd be perfect if you had some way to go through a number of recipes and find out the one you had the right ingredients for. This exercise is a little trickier because you need an array which in turn contains recipes in the form of arrays of ingredients.

The console should print out the ingredients of the first matching cocktail you find.

```
1  "use strict";
2
3  const isMixableWithMyIngredients = cocktailRecipe => /* ???
*/;
4
5  const isMixableWith = (cocktailRecipe,
availableIngredients) =>
6    cocktailRecipe.every(
7      ingredientFromRecipe =>
hasIngredient(availableIngredients, ingredientFromRecipe)
8    );
9
10 const hasIngredient = (listOfIngredients,
searchedIngredient) =>
11   listOfIngredients.includes(searchedIngredient);
12
13 const honoluluFlip = ["Maracuja Juice", "Pineapple Juice",
"Lemon Juice", "Grapefruit Juice", "Crushed Ice"];
14 const casualFriday = ["Vodka", "Lime Juice", "Apple Juice",
"Cucumber"];
15 const pinkDolly = ["Vodka", "Orange Juice", "Pineapple
Juice", "Grenadine", "Cream", "Coco Syrup"];
16 const cocktailRecipes = [honoluluFlip, casualFriday,
pinkDolly];
17
18 const ingredientsFromMyBar = ["Pineapple", "Maracuja
Juice", "Cream", "Grapefruit Juice", "Crushed Ice", "Milk",
"Vodka", "Apple Juice", "Aperol", "Pineapple Juice", "Lime
Juice", "Lemons", "Cucumber"];
19
20 console.log(cocktailRecipes./* ???
*/(isMixableWithMyIngredients));
21 // => [ "Vodka", "Lime Juice", "Apple Juice", "Cucumber" ]
```

accompanying_files/22/exercises/cocktails2.js

Objects of Desire *23*

 Our shop needs to maintain various data on each item. In addition to obvious characteristics like name, category and price, information like how many of an item are still in stock is also important for storekeeping purposes. In addition, customers are often interested in how long we've actually been carrying an item, so they can do things like buy a hot novelty which their neighbors don't have yet.

You'll find many similar situations in the real world. Things like products are represented by different data characteristics (e.g. *title*, *price*, etc.) In addition, you can also apply different operations over these data (e.g. display, store, sale, ship, etc.). As a result, large software systems are generally developed using **object-oriented** concepts. These make it possible to tie together data and operations.

Object-oriented programming (***OOP*** for short) is a standard discipline in our industry. JS has its own approach, which we maintain is modern, useful and often superior to other popular languages. For example, JS provides extremely powerful concepts such as ***duck typing*** and ***dynamic properties*** of which other well-known, popular languages in the industry should be envious.[51]. Unfortunately, JavaScript's suboptimal syntax sometimes detracts from the far-reaching possibilities of the language — a problem that, fortunately, newer ECMAScript versions are rectifying.

A complete examination of the object-oriented philosophy would be far beyond the scope of this class! However, we won't let that stop us from taking a quick look at objects.

23.1   The Program's the Thing — Objects and Properties

A typical function somewhere in the depths of your shop code might look something like this:

---

51. Unfortunately, in an introductory class like this, we won't be able to cover advanced concepts like *duck typing* in greater detail.

```
1 let buyProduct = (customerName, customerFirstname,
customerAddress, productName, productPrice, productCategory,
availableSince, numberInStock) => {
2   // Code that implements the buying process
3 };
```

Even though this code represents no problems technically, functions like that, which contain a large number of parameters, are unwieldy in practice and lead to code which is difficult to read. How do you know which of the following calls is correct?

```
1 buyProduct("Huana", "Marie", "Dragonroad 42, 90411 Puffcity",
"Klingon D`k tahg Letter Opener", 19.99, "Weapons & Office Ware",
2007, 5);
```

or

```
1 buyProduct("Marie", "Huana", "Dragonroad 42, 90411 Puffcity",
"Klingon D`k tahg Letter Opener",   "Weapons & Office Ware", 2007,
5, 19.99);
```

You could always look up the function definition, but that takes valuable time.

It's actually considered poor practice to give functions more than three arguments (see section 17.1.3). So what can you do instead?

Objects offer a solution to this — they make it possible for you to group together related values.

```
1 let customer = {
2   last_name: "Huana",
3   first_name: "Marie",
4   address: "Dragonroad 42, 90411 Smokecity"
5 };
6
7 let product = {
8   name: "Klingon D`k tahg Letter Opener",
9   category: "Weapons & Office Warfare",
10   availableSince: 2007,
11   inStock: 5,
12   price: 19.99
13 };
14
15 buyProduct(customer, product);
```

Now, the likelihood that you'll mix up arguments in a function call is already greatly reduced. You now have only two ways of ordering these arguments — instead of 40320 (8 * 7 * ... * 1) ways. In addition, you can now call `productPrice` just `price`. The fact that it's a product price can be inferred from the fact that it's assigned to the product object — so no one will wonder whether it's actually a special mysterious price added to secretly boost company sales ;)

The object-oriented style lets you group together properties which are related and which together describe a thing — whether that be a customer or a Klingon letter opener. Only instead of things, we call them objects (*thing-oriented programming* would also sound a little silly).

The syntax is quite simple. You group together **properties** within braces `{}` using so-called **key/value pairs**. The **key** (i.e. the name of the property) appears before a colon `:`. This is followed by the **value** of the property. These individual key-value pairs are separated in the object by commas (the comma after the last key-value pair is optional).

```
{
  key1: value1,
  key2: value2,
  ...
}
```

Coding Guideline

Insert a blank space after each colon (between key and value).

You can access a property from outside of an object at any time by using the following dot notation:

```
product.name //=> "Klingon D`k tahg Letter Opener"
```

You can use `console.dir(product)` to get a table listing the individual properties of an object as well as their values:

Property Key	Property Value
availableSince	2007
category	Weapons & Office Warfare
inStock	5

Property Key	Property Value
name	Klingon D`k tahg Letter Opener
price	19.99

You can also change the values of properties:

```
product.price = 24.99;
```

Run `console.log(product)` again to see the modified value. Properties behave like variables. You can assign them a value, you can read their values and you can change their values (i.e. assign them new values).

Alternative Style: Brackets Instead of Dots

Instead of dot notation, you can also use index notation with brackets, with which you're already familiar from working with arrays:

`product.price` is the same as `product["price"]`. Assignment also works with the index operator:

```
product["price"] = 24.99;
```

However, it's generally a better idea to use the shorter dot notation. Only if a key comes from a variable and is not known until run time do you need to use bracket notation e.g.

```
const fieldToZeroOut = "price";
product[fieldToZeroOut] = 0;
```

The code example above sets a field to a value of `0`, but the program doesn't know what field that is until run time. Instead of hardwiring the value of `fieldToZeroOut` to `price`, that value could come from user input, so the key could be specified as anything.

23.2   Adding a Little Life with Dynamic Properties

Adding New Properties

Properties in JavaScript are completely dynamic. In other words, you can add new properties to existing objects at any time, and also remove existing properties. This "at any time" in JS is truly something special. Many other programming languages don't make it possible for properties to be added to or removed from existing objects at run time, or if this is possible, it can only be done with great difficulty.

Example

```
1  let product = {
2    name: "Klingon D`k tahg Letter Opener",
3    category: "Weapons & Office Warfare",
4    availableSince: 2007,
5    inStock: 5,
6    price: 19.99
7  };
8
9  product.description = "for hand-to-hand combat with pesky
   envelopes";
10
11  console.dir(product);
```

Property Key	Property Value
availableSince	2007
category	Weapons & Office Warfare
description	perfect for hand-to-hand combat with pesky envelopes
inStock	5
name	Klingon D`k tahg Letter Opener
price	19.99

In addition, an object doesn't sort the new property and store it at a specific location, as is the case with arrays — individual property names (keys) are not ordered in any relation to one another (however, a function like `console.log` or `console.dir` does sort these alphabetically when printing them out).

Empty Objects

Just like with arrays, you can create objects so that they're completely empty at first. You can then add attributes one at a time. You can specify an empty object as a literal `{}`.

Example

```
1 let product = {};
2
3 product.name = "Klingon D`k tahg Letter Opener";
4 product.description = "for hand-to-hand combat with pesky
envelopes";
5
6 console.dir(product);
```

Property Key	Property Value
description	perfect for hand-to-hand combat with pesky envelopes
name	Klingon D`k tahg Letter Opener

Exercise 71: Geoquiz — Part 3

Revise your *Geoquiz* (exercise 67). This time, use an object for the data instead of an array. Also use a new constant called `countriesWithCapital`:

```
"use strict";

const countriesWithCapital = {
    "UK": "London",
    "France": "Paris",
    "Germany": "Berlin",
    "Switzerland": "Bern",
    "Austria": "Vienna",
    "Russia": "Moscow"
};

const capitalOf = country => /* ??? */;

console.log(capitalOf("Switzerland"));
```

accompanying_files/23/exercises/geo_quiz3.js

First, modify just the function `capitalOf` so that it uses the new data structure.

Note

You may be surprised that the keys are enclosed in quotation marks. Basically, it doesn't matter whether they are quoted or not. Technically, both are possible. In practice, it makes sense to use quotation marks here, because these keys (countries) - just like the values (cities) - have a data-like character. This does not rule out the possibility that at some point in time an extension of the program may include country names containing spaces or special characters (e. g."U. S. A."). The quotation marks would then be mandatory.

Exercise 72: Cracking Codes using Word Analysis ["Brainteaser"]

Your new client is a provider of crypto software designed to crack codes. One of their new algorithms is designed to make it possible for conclusions to be drawn about encrypted text, based on the frequencies of the words in it. Your new client therefore hires you to write a function `wordOccurrence` to calculate word frequencies.

`wordOccurrence` reads in a text string and determines the frequency of all words in it. Its return value should be an object in the form: `{word1: frequency1, word2: frequency2, ...}`.

Example

The following code:

```
const text = 'In cryptology, a code is a method used to
encrypt a message that operates at the level of meaning; that
is, words or phrases are converted into something else. A code
might transform "change" into "CVGDK" or "cocktail lounge". A
codebook is needed to encrypt, and decrypt the phrases or
words.';

console.log(wordOccurrence(text));
```

should print out:

```
{ in: 1,
  cryptology: 1,
  a: 5,
  code: 2,
  is: 3,
  ...
  decrypt: 1 }
```

Tips

➤ Consider uppercase and lowercase letters as identical, e.g: "a" and "A". A
good way to achieve that is to first do something like convert the entire
text to lowercase.

➤ Use `.replace(/[.,"';]/g, "")` to remove all unwanted characters.
These can be removed by replacing them with the empty string `""`.
`/[.,"';]/g` is a so-called ***regular expression***. Regular expressions use
patterns to help you find matching strings. The expression `/[.,"';]/g`
here means: `replace` should replace the characters specified in brackets, and should do this throughout the entire text (i.e. globally, or `g`).

➤ You can get words by using a blank space to split the string.

➤ Store each word in the object as a *key* and increment the frequency in
the corresponding *value* each time the word occurs again.

23.3   JSON, or the Man Behind the Mask

We just realized it would be a lot better if we had the ability to
classify items into more than one category. For example, our *Klingon D`k tahg Letter Opener* should appear both in our *Weapons &
Office Warfare* category and in our *Star Trek* category. Is that possible?

No problem! After all, you have arrays for "many things"! There's no reason why you
can't use arrays within objects and vice versa:

```
1  let product = {
2    name: "Klingon D`k tahg Letter Opener",
3    category: ["Weapons & Office Warfare", "StarTrek"],
4    availableSince: 2007,
5    inStock: 5,
6    price: 19.99
7  };
```

And by "vice versa" we mean something like a list of products:

```
1  let products = [
2    {
3      name: "Klingon D`k tahg Letter Opener",
4      category: ["Weapons & Office Warfare", "StarTrek"],
5      availableSince: 2007,
```

```
 6    },
 7    {
 8      name: "3Doodler 3D Printing Pen",
 9      category: ["Design", "Hits for Kids"],
10      availableSince: 1999,
11    },
12    {
13      name: "8-Bit Legendary Hero Heat-Change Mug",
14      category: ["Coffee Equipment"],
15      availableSince: 2016,
16    }
17  ];
```

In fact, virtually any form of data can be represented in this manner using JS. So you can use JS, in a sense, to build databases in memory, or even better, to send these data sets over the network! Douglas Crockford recognized such possibilities as early as 2001 and even gave this branch of JS its own name: **JSON** (pronounced like the first name *Jason*). Yes, we do realize this sounds exactly like the axe-wielding mass murderer from *Friday the 13th*. But in reality, JSON is an abbreviation for *JavaScript Object Notation* — in other words, a notation which makes use of JavaScript objects.

Fig. 44 *JSON Logo*

Actually, Douglas Crockford isn't considered the *inventor* of JSON but rather its *discoverer*. JSON is virtually a 100% subset of the JavaScript language. Since JSON had already existed as part of JavaScript, Crockford's achievement lay in carving it out and describing it. He created a website with the grammar description (*json.org*[52]), which was later seized on by many other languages so they too could provide JSON support. Practically all modern programming languages these days provide support for JSON. JSON has by now become an international standard (ECMA-404 & RFC7159) as well as probably the most popular language-independent data exchange format in the web.

JSON allows the following data types:

➤ Object
➤ Array
➤ Number
➤ Boolean
➤ String

---

52. *http://json.org*

➤ null

This means you can use the basic data types number, boolean and string, and also structure these as objects and arrays. Objects and arrays can be nested in any fashion. The keyword `null` stands for an empty data set. The following are some examples of valid JSON data sets:

➤ 27.5

➤ [27.5, "Hello"]

➤ {"name": "Ladislaus", "age": 27, "married": false}

➤ [{"name": "Ladislaus", "age": 27}, {"name": "Alice", "hobbies": ["reading", "biking", "stopping mass murderers"]}]

Note here the following essential differences from "normal" JavaScript:

➤ JavaScript allows you to omit quotation marks around an object key if the key doesn't contains any blank spaces, e.g. `{name: "Ladislaus"}` instead of `{"name": "Ladislaus"}`. By contrast, quotation marks in JSON are mandatory.

➤ Strings in JavaScript can be placed in either single or double quotation marks, e.g. `{"name": 'Ladislaus'}`. JSON requires that double quotation marks always be used, e.g. `{"name": "Ladislaus"}`.

If you want to learn even more, the website *json.org*[53] gives a precise description of JSON syntax.

Is there an easy way to import and export our product data?

JS provides a few functions for importing and exporting JSON data:

➤ `JSON.parse`

➤ `JSON.stringify`

`JSON.stringify` converts any JS data set into a JSON string.

Example

```
1  JSON.stringify(
2      {
3         name: "Klingon Letter Opener",
4         inStock: 5,
5         price: 19.99
6      }
7  )
8  // => "{"name": "Klingon Letter Opener","inStock": 5,"price":
   19.99}"
```

`JSON.parse` reads a JSON string, parses it and returns the corresponding JavaScript data.

Example

```
1  JSON.parse(
2    '{"name": "Klingon Letter Opener","inStock": 5,"price": 19.99}'
3  )
4  // => {name: "Klingon Letter Opener", inStock: 5, price: 19.99}
```

Practically all other programming languages can handle JSON strings. As a result, JSON is an excellent format for exchanging data between different languages and platforms.

23.4   Reference

Function	Purpose	Example
Object.keys	Returns the keys of an object as an array	Object.keys(user) //=> ["name", "age"]
Object.values	Returns the values of an object as an array	Object.values(user) //=> ["Ladislaus", 27]
Object.entries	Returns the key-value pairs of an object as an array	Object.entries(user) //=> [["name", "Ladislaus"], ["age", 27]]

Table 23.4 Object functions based on example user = {name: "Ladislaus", age: 27}
Object.values and Object.entries available only in ECMAScript 2017 *and higher versions.*

Objects vs. Higher-Order Functions

Most higher-order functions from lesson 16 (e.g. `map`, `reduce`, ...) cannot be applied directly to an object. So what should you do instead? You have a number of options. The simplest is to use `Object.keys`, `Object.values` or `Object.entries` to create an array out of the object. You can then apply higher-order functions to this new array without any problem.

23.5   Exercises

Exercise 73: Geoquiz — Part 4

Revise your *Geoquiz* (exercise 68). Again, use your new constant `countriesWithCapital`:

```
"use strict";

const countriesWithCapital = {
    "UK": "London",
    "France": "Paris",
    "Germany": "Berlin",
    "Switzerland": "Bern",
    "Austria": "Vienna",
    "Russia": "Moscow"
};

const countryForCapital = capital => /* ??? */;

console.log(countryForCapital("Berlin"));
```

accompanying_files/23/exercises/geo_quiz4.js

Modify the function `countryForCapital` so that it uses the new data structure.

Exercise 74: Happy Mixing with JSON

This time you found a list of cocktails on the Internet — and conveniently enough, it's even in JSON format! Find out what cocktails you can mix using the ingredients in your cocktail cabinet.

This time, print out the names (but not the ingredients) of all cocktails you're able to mix.

```
1  "use strict";
2
3
4  const myMixableCocktails = cocktailList => /* ??? */
5
6  const isMixableWithMyIngredients = cocktailRecipe =>
7    isMixableWith(cocktailRecipe, ingredientsFromMyBar);
8
9  const isMixableWith = (cocktailRecipe,
availableIngredients) =>
10   cocktailRecipe.every(
11     ingredientFromRecipe =>
hasIngredient(availableIngredients, ingredientFromRecipe)
12   );
13
14 const hasIngredient = (listOfIngredients,
searchedIngredient) =>
15   listOfIngredients.includes(searchedIngredient);
16
17 const ingredientsFromMyBar = ["Pineapple", "Maracuja
Juice", "Grapefruit Juice", "Crushed Ice", "Milch", "Vodka",
"Apple Juice", "Aperol", "Pineapple Juice", "Lime Juice",
"Lemons", "Cucumber", "Kaffeelikör"];
18
19 const cocktailRecipesWithNames = {
20   "Honolulu Flip": [
21     "Maracuja Juice",
22     "Pineapple Juice",
23     "Lemon Juice",
24     "Grapefruit Juice",
25     "Crushed Ice"
26   ],
27   "Casual Friday": [
28     "Vodka",
29     "Lime Juice",
30     "Apple Juice",
31     "Cucumber"
32   ],
33   "Pink Dolly": [
34     "Vodka",
35     "Orange Juice",
36     "Pineapple Juice",
37     "Grenadine",
38     "Cream",
39     "coco syrup"
40   ],
```

```
41    "Black Russian": [
42      "Vodka",
43      "Kaffeelikör"
44    ],
45    "White Russian": [
46      "Vodka",
47      "Kaffeelikör",
48      "Cream"
49    ]
50  };
51
52  console.log(myMixableCocktails(cocktailRecipesWithNames));
53  // => [ 'Casual Friday', 'Black Russian' ]
```

accompanying_files/23/exercises/cocktails_json.js

Appetite for Destructuring 24

I was cleaning out our basement the other day and stumbled across a couple of old USB sticks. I found out they contain Excel lists of products we used to offer in our catalog. I'm thinking we'd like to offer some of them for sale again; the only problem is, our shop needs to have the products in JSON format.

Do you think you'd be able to convert that data?

To make it easier for us to work with Marty's data, we first converted it to CSV, or *comma separated values* — a basic text format easily processed by JS. Here's one example of data in CSV format:

```
name, category, price
Klingon Letter Opener, Office Warfare, 19.99
Backpack of Holding, Travel, 29.99
Tardis Alarmclock, Merchandise, 15.99
```

Listing 119 *Products in CSV format*

The first line describes the properties of each product. This is followed the products themselves, line by line. The individual values in each line are separated by commas.

So how do you convert such a list to JSON?

Start by separating the CSV string by line; this is easily done using `split("\n")`. Then throw away the first line which contains just the names of product properties (`slice(1)`). Finally, we'll also want to remove the blank spaces at the beginning and end of each string. We built a small auxiliary function called `trim` for just that purpose. `trim` works using so-called regular expressions. These are a little beyond the scope of this book so we won't go into them further right now — all you need to know is that `trim` removes extraneous blanks, e.g.

```
trim(" Klingon..." ) //=> "Klingon...".
```

```javascript
1  "use strict";
2
3  const trim = s => s.match(/\W*(.+)\W*/)[1];
4
5  const productsFromCSV = csv =>
6    csv
7      .split("\n")
```

```
 8      .slice(1)
 9      .map(trim);
10
11 const productsCSV = `name, category, price
12   Klingon Letter Opener, Office Warfare, 19.99
13   Backpack of Holding, Travel, 29.99
14   Tardis Alarmclock, Merchandise, 15.99`;
15
16 const products = productsFromCSV(productsCSV);
17 console.log(products);
```

Listing 120 accompanying_files/24/examples/products_csv.1.js

Executing the steps described above gives us the following output:

```
[ 'Klingon Letter Opener, Office Warfare, 19.99',
  'Backpack of Holding, Travel, 29.99',
  'Tardis Alarmclock, Merchandise, 15.99' ]
```

This gives us the products as separate array elements, although each product is still in the form of a string. So next, we'll need a function which takes a product in the form of an CSV string and converts it to an object with appropriate properties. This is one approach:

```
 1 "use strict";
 2
 3 const productFromCSV = productString => {
 4   const productArray = productString.split(", ");
 5
 6   const name = productArray[0];
 7   const category = productArray[1];
 8   const price = productArray[2];
 9
10   return {
11     name: name,
12     category: category,
13     price: price
14   };
15 };
16
17 const product = productFromCSV("Backpack of Holding, Travel,
29.99");
18 console.dir(product);
```

Listing 121 accompanying_files/24/examples/products_csv.2.js

We get back the corresponding object:

```
{ name: 'Backpack of Holding',
category: 'Travel',
price: '29.99' }
```

So just exactly how does the function `productFromCSV` work?

`productString.split(", ")` splits a string down into an array which contains the individual product properties, in the same order as in the string: `['Backpack of Holding', 'Travel', '29.99']`. Assignment statements then set the constants `name`, `category` and `price` to the corresponding array elements.

```
const name = productArray[0];
const category = productArray[1];
const price = productArray[2];
```

Finally, the function returns a new object which uses the names of properties as *keys*, and the constants which were just set as *values*.

```
return {
    name: name,
    category: category,
    price:  price
};
```

So our function does exactly what we want it to — however, our code can still be improved a little. To be specific, the constant `productArray` is no longer useful. For one, it doesn't introduce a new name which would improve the readability of the function. In essence, it's a necessary evil, as the function's only purpose is to set the constants `name`, `category` and `price` to the corresponding elements. One way we could dispense with the `productArray` variable is as follows:

```
const name = productString.split(", ")[0];
const category = productString.split(", ")[1];
const price = productString.split(", ")[2];
```

Unfortunately, this isn't an ideal solution either. For starters, the code executes the same `split` three times. Then apart from the code taking three times as long to run as necessary, it's redundant, and also not completely clear nor maintainable. For example, we'd always need to remember to update our array indices whenever we add a new element, e.g.:

```
const name = productString.split(", ")[0];

const description = productString.split(", ")[1];

const category = productString.split(", ")[2]; // Index changed
from 1 to 2
const price = productString.split(", ")[3]; // Index changed from
2 to 3
```

24.1   Taking Arrays Apart Via Destructuring

A feature which entered into the language with ES2015 provides a solution — so-called **destructuring**. This feature breaks arrays down into their individual components and performs an assignment. After the following code is executed, the constants `name`, `category` and `price` will be set to the correct values.

```
const [name, category, price] = ['Backpack of Holding', 'Travel',
'29.99'];
```

This essentially works as follows: On the left side of the assignment statement you specify a **pattern**. JS then tries to identify the matching pattern on the right side (**match** for short) and to assign the individual components correctly. Destructuring is therefore also a form of so-called **pattern matching**. So let's add the following code:

```
1  "use strict";
2
3  const productFromCSV = productString => {
4    const [name, category, price] = productString.split(", ");
5    return {
6      name: name,
7      category: category,
8      price: price
9    };
10 };
11
12 const product = productFromCSV("Backpack of Holding, Travel,
29.99");
13 console.dir(product);
```

Listing 122 accompanying_files/24/examples/products_csv.3.js

As you see, we've omitted our workaround which used the interim variable `productArray`, and our constants can be assigned the proper values directly. In addition, we don't need to specify any indices, so we can easily add other properties whenever we want to without having to update these.

24.2   Shorthand Notation for Objects

We can even take advantage of another small trick to make our code even more compact. You can use a short form for objects whose *keys* and *values* are identical. To do this, just combine *key* and *value* together. So instead of

```
{
  name: name,
  category: category,
  price:  price
}
```

you can use the shorthand version

```
{
  name,
  category,
  price
}
```

So putting everything together, we now get the following code:

```
 1 "use strict";
 2
 3 const trim = s => s.match(/\W*(.+)\W*/)[1];
 4
 5 const productFromCSV = productString => {
 6   const [name, category, price] = productString.split(", ");
 7   return {
 8     name,
 9     category,
10     price
11   };
12 };
13
14 const productsFromCSV = csv =>
15   csv
16     .split("\n")
17     .slice(1)
18     .map(trim)
19     .map(productFromCSV);
20
21 const productsCSV = `name, category, price
22   Klingon Letter Opener, Office Warfare, 19.99
23   Backpack of Holding, Travel, 29.99
```

```
24    Tardis Alarmclock, Merchandise, 15.99`;
25
26 const products = productsFromCSV(productsCSV);
27 console.log(products);
```

Listing 123 accompanying_files/24/examples/products_csv.4.js

And here's our output:

```
[ { name: 'Klingon Letter Opener',
    category: 'Office Warfare',
    price: '19.99' },
  { name: 'Backpack of Holding',
    category: 'Travel',
    price: '29.99' },
  { name: 'Tardis Alarmclock',
    category: 'Merchandise',
    price: '15.99' } ]
```

24.3   Taking Parameters Apart Via Destructuring

There's still another way we can optimize this code — by pulling the functionality
for splitting commas out from the function `productFromCSV`.

```
1 const productFromArray = productArray => {
2    const [name, category, price] = productArray;
3    return {
4       name,
5       category,
6       price
7    };
8 };
9
10 const productsFromCSV = csv =>
11    csv
12       .split("\n")
13       .map(trim)
14       .slice(1)
15       .map(s => s.split(", "))
16       .map(productFromArray);
```

This splitting now needs to take place in the function `productsFromCSV` (note
the products in the plural). To do this, we just add `.map(s => s.split(",
"))` to that function before the result is passed to `productFromArray` (pre-
viously `productFromCSV`). The function `productFromCSV` is now called
`productFromArray` since it takes in an array instead of a CSV string.

However, all of this is just preparation for the next step. Our destructuring can be implemented right in the parameter list of the function:

```
const productFromArray = ([name, category, price]) => {
  return {
    name,
    category,
    price };
};
```

Although `[name, category, price]` is just a single parameter, it consists of multiple parts, and the destructuring sees to it that these parts are passed to the *function body* as separate variables. Also note here the parentheses surrounding the parameter array — unfortunately, we need these for the syntax to be valid.

Thanks to our last refactoring step, the function `productFromArray` now consists of just a return statement. This makes it possible for us to implement one last improvement, to remove the `return`:

```
const productFromArray = ([name, category, price]) => ({
    name,
    category,
    price
});
```

Again, it's essential here that we surround the return object `{name, category, price}` with parentheses — otherwise, JS will try to interpret the braces as a block, or *function body*. Here's the final result:

```
1  "use strict";
2
3  const trim = s => s.match(/\W*(.+)\W*/)[1];
4
5  const productFromArray = ([name, category, price]) => ({
6    name,
7    category,
8    price
9  });
10
11 const productsFromCSV = csv =>
12   csv
13     .split("\n")
14     .slice(1)
15     .map(trim)
16     .map(s => s.split(", "))
17     .map(productFromArray);
18
19 const productsCSV = `name, category, price
```

```
20   Klingon Letter Opener, Office Warfare, 19.99
21   Backpack of Holding, Travel, 29.99
22   Tardis Alarmclock, Merchandise, 15.99`;
23
24 const products = productsFromCSV(productsCSV);
25 console.log(products);
```

Listing 124 accompanying_files/24/examples/products_csv.5.js

And our output is in JSON format, as desired:

```
[ { name: 'Klingon Letter Opener',
    category: 'Office Warfare',
    price: '19.99' },
  { name: 'Backpack of Holding',
    category: 'Travel',
    price: '29.99' },
  { name: 'Tardis Alarmclock',
    category: 'Merchandise',
    price: '15.99' } ]
```

24.4   Taking Objects Apart Via Object Destructuring

Arrays aren't the only thing you can take apart using destructuring — the feature also makes it possible for you to take apart objects with no problem.

Now that our products are in object form, we'll often still need to access their individual elements for further processing. One example of this is in the function `formatProduct`, which creates text formatting which can later be used by say, a product catalog.

```
1 "use strict";
2
3 const formatProduct = product => {
4   const name = product.name;
5   const price = product.price;
6   return `* ${name} — buy now for only $$${price}`;
7 };
8
9 const product = {
10   name: "Klingon Letter Opener",
11   category: "Office Warfare",
12   price: "19.99"
13 };
14
15 console.log(formatProduct(product));
```

Listing 125 accompanying_files/24/examples/products_obj_dest.1.js

Output:

```
* Klingon Letter Opener - buy now for only $19.99
```

Now, instead of assigning our constants the individual attributes of the `product` object like so:

```
const name = product.name;
const price = product.price;
```

we can do this much more elegantly via **object destructuring**.

```
const formatProduct = product => {
  const { name: productName, price: productPrice } = product;
  return `* ${productName} - buy now for only $$${productPrice}`;
};
```

Here, destructuring generates the specified constants `productName` and `productPrice`, at the same time assigning them the corresponding values from the `product` object. Again, this code works according to the **pattern matching** principle. If you would replace `product` with the actual object stored in it, the line of code would look like this:

```
const { name: productName, price: productPrice } = { name:
"Klingon Letter Opener", category: "Office Warfare", price:
'19.99' };
```

For the pattern to match, `productName` must get the value `"Klingon Letter Opener"` and `productPrice` the value `"19.99"`.

It's also convenient that you don't need to specify all attributes — just the ones you need. We can omit the attribute `category` here; the value assignment will just ignore it if we don't specify it.

If we like, we can even give our newly created constants exactly the same names as our object keys:

```
const { name: name, price: price } = product;
```

This gives us the advantage that we can once again make use of shorthand object notation, since *key* and *value* are identical.

```
const { name, price } = product;
```

And here's the entire function once more:

```
const formatProduct = product => {
  const { name, price } = product;
  return `* ${productName} - buy now for only $$${productPrice}`;
};
```

Object destructuring in parameter lists

Since we no longer need to include the original product in the function, we can even go a step further and carry out our destructuring right in the parameter list.

```
const formatProduct = ({ name, price }) => {
  return `* ${name} - buy now for only $$${price}`;
};
```

This makes the function just one line and we can also remove the `return`:

```
const formatProduct = ({ name, price }) =>   `* ${name} - buy now
for only $$${price}`;
```

Here's the entire code once more:

```
 1  "use strict";
 2
 3  const formatProduct = ({ name, price }) =>
 4    `* ${name} - buy now for only $$${price}`;
 5
 6  const product = {
 7    name: "Klingon Letter Opener",
 8    category: "Office Warfare",
 9    price: "19.99"
10  };
11
12  console.log(formatProduct(product));
```

Listing 126 accompanying_files/24/examples/products_obj_dest.2.js

Order in object destructuring

The order of attributes is unimportant in object destructuring. It makes no difference whether we start the function with

```
({ name, price }) =>
```

or

```
({ price, name }) =>
```

The result will still be the same. This is only logical, since we're using an object as a pattern and the order of keys in objects is generally unimportant.

24.5 One "Destructuring" Standard? Destructuring Defaults

Now, let's add product category to our output:

```
const formatProduct = ({ name, price, category }) =>
  `* ${name} [${category}] — buy now for only $$${price}`;
```

Output:

```
* Klingon Letter Opener [Office Warfare] — buy now for only $19.99
```

So what actually happens when we try to print out a product with no category?

```
1  "use strict";
2
3  const formatProduct = ({ name, price, category }) =>
4    `* ${name} [${category}] — buy now for only $$${price}`;
5
6  const product2 = {
7    name: "Backpack of Holding",
8    price: "29.99"
9  };
10 console.log(formatProduct(product2));
```

Listing 127 accompanying_files/24/examples/dest_no_defaults.js

Output:

```
* Backpack of Holding [undefined] — buy now for only $29.99
```

Of course, the `undefined` output here isn't terribly elegant. It'd be very convenient if we were able to declare all products with no category property to be *mis-
cellaneous*. Destructuring provides a very elegant way to do this — default values. You can assign these directly in the object pattern, e.g. `{ name, price,`
`category = "miscellaneous" }`.

```
"use strict";

const formatProduct = ({ name, price, category = "miscellaneous"
}) =>
  `* ${name} [${category}] - buy now for only $$${price}`;

const product2 = {
  name: "Backpack of Holding",
  price: "29.99"
};
console.log(formatProduct(product2));
```

Listing 128 *accompanying_files/24/examples/dest_with_defaults.js*

Our output now looks exactly like we want it to:

```
* Backpack of Holding [miscellaneous] - buy now for only $29.99
```

Note

Unlike default parameters in function definitions, default values
used in object destructuring don't have to put at the end.

Example:

```
const formatProduct = ({ name, price = 10, category})
=>
  `* ${name} [${category}] - buy now for only
$$${price}`;
```

In addition, since parameter order is unimportant, you can conceivably combine default parameters in any way — e.g. just try:

```
const formatProduct = ({ category = "miscellaneous",
name, price = 10 }) =>
  `* ${name} [${category}] - buy now for only
$$${price}`;
```

24.6   Less-Than-Total Destruction or, The Unde-structured Rest

Do you remember the *rest* operator from lesson 21? That's right, this one ... —
the three small dots. The rest operator also works great when you're destructuring
arrays, e.g.

```
1  "use strict";
2
3  const product = ["Klingon Letter Opener", "Office Warfare",
"19.99"];
4
5  const [name, ...everythingElse] = product;
6
7  console.log(everythingElse); // => [ 'Office Warfare', '19.99' ]
```

***Listing 129** accompanying_files/24/examples/dest_rest.1.js*

In principle, it also works with objects:

```
1  "use strict";
2
3  const product = {
4    name: "Klingon Letter Opener",
5    category: "Office Warfare",
6    price: "19.99"
7  };
8
9  const { name, ...everythingElse } = product;
10
11 console.log(everythingElse); // => {category: "Office Warfare",
price: "19.99"}
```

***Listing 130** accompanying_files/24/examples/dest_rest.2.js*

However, you'll have to wait just a little bit longer before you can actually use this
feature. It's officially available since ES2018. While Firefox 56 and Chrome 62 do
provide it, there is currently (at the time of writing) no support for it in Microsoft's
Edge Browser. As always, you can check the *ECMAScript compatibility table*[54] to find
out its actual availability.

---

54.   *http://kangax.github.io/compat-table/esnext/*

Rest Or Spread?

The three-dot-operator . . . is actually called *rest* or *spread*, depending on its position in the assignment. On the left side, in

```
const {a, ...rest} = {a: 1, b: 2, c: 3};
```

it's *rest*. On the ride side like in

```
const spread = {b: 2, c: 3};
const myObject = {a: 1, ...spread};
```

It's called *spread*.

24.7   What's in a Name? More Than You Think! or, Named Parameters

Languages like Ruby and Python have a great feature: **named parameters**. As JS developers, we long envied the improved readability and maintainability that feature brings.

But our envy is now at an end!

With the help of destructuring, named parameters are now entering into JS, in indirect form. So exactly what does the feature provide?

It's not clear, in functions with a large number of parameters, what parameter is what. For example, consider a function like this:

```
const transferMoney = (targetAccount, sourceAccount, amount) => {
...
}
```

This function transfers money from one account to another. However, it's not clear in what order the parameters belong unless you look through the function definition. But interchanging the parameters could have unpleasant consequences...

Even when you do call the function, you can't really see what's happening:

```
transferMoney(companyAccount, customerAccount, 10000)
```

Who's paying $10,000, and to whom?

Named parameters provide a solution to this problem. The trick here lies in passing the function an object whose attribute serve as arguments, instead of passing the function multiple arguments. Sound confusing? It's actually pretty straightforward, as this example shows:

```
transferMoney({targetAccount: customerAccount, sourceAccount:
companyAccount, amount: 10000})
```

In this function call, it's immediately obvious who's transferring what, and to whom. Even better, you can change the order of parameters, and the function will still work flawlessly.

```
transferMoney({sourceAccount: companyAccount, amount: 10000,
targetAccount: customerAccount})
```

The advantages are obvious:

➤ **Fewer errors** occur.

➤ The function call is much more **understandable**, and you don't have to look up the function definition every time you call it (it could appear in an entirely different location of your code, or even in an entirely different file).

➤ Your code is much more **maintainable**. You can add new arguments any time you want without having to worry about whether you're changing attribute order.

The function definition itself doesn't bring too many surprises:

```
const transferMoney = ({targetAccount, sourceAccount, amount}) => {
...
}
```

It's a completely normal object destructuring of parameters. You only need to add a couple of extra parentheses — a small price to pay for such a great feature.

My recommendation for parameter lists

I'm a big fan of clarity. All too often I'm gotten burned by using parameter lists which were too long, and have later had to spend a lot of my time searching for errors. In general, I try to write functions which require only one or two parameters. If they do need three or more, I use *named parameters* — sometimes I even use the feature when I have only two parameters, if their order isn't completely clear.

But wait, there's more! Named parameter variants

You can also destructure multiple parameters in the same function with no problem. For example, consider the following function called `sendMessage`:

```
person1 = {firstName: "Ladislaus", lastName: "Coolio"}
person2 = {firstName: "Heribert", lastName: "West"}

const sendMessage = (from, to) => {
… //a lot of crazy stuff here
}

sendMessage(person1, person2)
```

Instead of the direct parameters `from` and `to`, you can use destructuring here as well:

```
const sendMessage = (
  {firstName: fromFirstName, lastName: fromLastName},
  {firstName: toFirstName, lastName: toLastName}
) => {
  ...
}
```

You can even combine with normal parameters:

```
const sendMessage = (
  message,
  {firstName: senderFirstName, lastName: senderLastName},
  {firstName: receiverFirstName, lastName: receiverLastName}) => {
  ...
}

sendMessage("Hallo", person1, person2)
```

Actually, in this case we'd be more likely to use `from` and `to` as *keys* in order to avoid confusion between the sender and recipient:

```
const sendMessage = (message,  {from: sender, to: receiver}) => {
  ...
}

sendMessage("Hallo", {from: person1, to: person2})
```

Hardcore destructurers could also use this variant:

```
const sendMessage = (
  message,
  {
    from: {firstName: senderFirstName, lastName: senderLastName},
    to: {firstName: receiverFirstName, lastName: receiverLastName}
  }
) => {
  ...
}

sendMessage("Hallo", {from: person1, to: person2})
```

Nesting at any level is possible since destructuring is a recursive process. Or to put this another way, you can use any JSON structure as a destructuring pattern. But beware — if you take nesting too far, this will lead to confusing code faster than you can say "*destructure*".

24.8 Named Parameter With Default Values

Of course, we can also use destructuring defaults with named parameters:

```
1  "use strict";
2
3  const foo = ({ a = 1, b = 2 }) => `a: ${a}, b: ${b}`;
4
5  console.log(foo({ a: 7 })); // => a: 7, b: 2
6  console.log(foo({ b: 7 })); // => a: 1, b: 7
7  console.log(foo({ a: 7, b: 8 })); // => a: 7, b: 8
```

Listing 131 accompanying_files/24/examples/named_params.1.js

As long as we pass our function an object, everything'll work great. We could even pass in an empty object and get back all our parameters:

```
console.log(foo({})); // => a: 1, b: 2
```

However, a typical problem arises when we call the function without any parameters at all:

```
console.log(foo()); // => TypeError: Cannot match against
'undefined' or 'null'.
```

Instead of the printout, JS terminates with an error message. JS cannot "match" an `undefined` parameter. If we do need to make it possible for a function to be called even without arguments, we'll need to use something different — something you already know — *defaults for missing function arguments*!

We can even combine both default variants (destructuring defaults and defaults for missing function arguments) with no problem:

```
1 "use strict";
2
3 const foo = ({ a = 1, b = 2 } = { a: 3, b: 4 }) => `a: ${a}, b:
${b}`;
4
5 console.log(foo({ a: 7 })); // => a: 7, b: 2
6 console.log(foo({})); // => a: 1, b: 2
7 console.log(foo()); // => a: 3, b: 4
```

Listing 132 accompanying_files/24/examples/named_params.2.js

Admittedly this does look a little strange, but it does solve the problem described above. The function can now be called even without passing it any arguments, and it'll just use the default value. In real life, it's generally a good idea to make the defaults the same.

```
const foo = ({ a = 1, b = 2 } = { a: 1, b: 2 }) => `a: ${a}, b:
${b}`;
```

This often prevents unpleasant surprises.

24.9   Exercises

Exercise 75: First Name first and Last Name last or Last Name first and First Name last?

If reading the name of this exercise confused you as much as it did us when we were writing it, it's because the order of first names and last names isn't always obvious. Sometimes it needs to be *John Doe*, and sometimes it needs to be *Doe, John*. So that users of the function `logTransformedName` (from exercise 34) won't be as confused, you might do better to convert it to use `named parameters`.

```
1 "use strict";
2
3 let logTransformedName = (firstName, lastName) =>
4     console.log(lastName + ", " + firstName.charAt(0) + ".");
5
6 logTransformedName("Ladislaus", "Jones");
```

accompanying_files/13/solutions/ladislaus.js

Exercise 76: And Triangular It Shall Be (Named Parameter Remix)

```
 1  "use strict";
 2
 3  const triangle = height => buildTriangle(height, 1, "*");
 4
 5  const buildTriangle = (height, topLineWidth, character) =>
 6    topLineWidth > height
 7      ? ""
 8      : line(topLineWidth, character) + "\n"
 9      + buildTriangle(height, topLineWidth + 1, character);
10
11  const line = (length, character) =>
12    length === 0
13      ? ""
14      : character + line(length - 1, character);
15
16  console.log(triangle(10));
```

accompanying_files/19/solutions/triangle.js

Modify the solution from so that you eliminate a function and the call to the function `triangle` looks as follows:

```
console.log(triangle({ height: 10 }));
```

Your modification should make it possible to specify the character to be used, e.g.:

```
console.log(triangle({ height: 10, character: "#" }));
```

If a user calls `triangle` without parameters, the function should create a triangle of height `5` using asterisks (`*`).

Exercise 77: How Much Further? Are We There Yet?

The formula to calculate distance is:

```
Math.sqrt((yDestination - yOrigin) ** 2 + (xDestination - xOrigin) ** 2)
```

Write a function called `distance` which you can call as follows:

```
distance({ x: 1, y: 1 }, { x: 5, y: 1 }) // => 2
```

The End

PS: If you liked the course, we would be very happy about a book review at *Amazon*[55]. Five stars would be great - if you didn't like it, you don't have to write anything ;)

No seriously, write your honest opinion. The reviews help us to continue this work and to develop new, ever better courses.

---

55. *https://www.amazon.com/Learning-JavdeaScript-non-boring-beginners-programming-ebook/dp/B07DNCPJ84*

Appendix A: Language Versions and Transpilers

25.1 JavaScript, JScript, LiveScript, ECMAScript, WhatTheHeckIsThisScript?

Unfortunately, the multitude of terms used in the field of JS is enormous, and it can be tough for a beginner to keep track of all of them. We'll give you an overview of the most important terms and try not to fall into a long-winded lesson of the language's history.

Brendan Eich developed JavaScript in December 1995 for the **Netscape Navigator** browser. The language has since been standardized by *Ecma International* as **ECMA-262** or **ECMAScript** (: **ES** for short). You could say that ECMAScript is a stable, standard subset of the language shared by various JavaScript-type implementations (e.g. Microsoft's *JScript*). Many developers actually mean *ECMAScript* when they say *JavaScript* — we generally do this as well. One reason for this might be the fact that ECMAScript sounds a little like a skin disease (at least, according to the language's inventor Brendan Eich) (2006, 2008).

Since the various implementations of JavaScript have their own features and extensions but are still compatible with ECMAScript (*ES* for short), it probably makes more sense to look at versions of ES rather than JavaScript. Let's say we want to use a language feature in ECMAScript 5.1 (take `Array.prototype.map`). How can you find out whether your language version supports that feature?

Actually, it doesn't matter whether you're using JavaScript version 1.85 in Mozilla Firefox or Node.js version 0.12. You can use the feature in any implementation as long as the implementation conforms to ES5.

Fig. 46 *Cover of* ECMAScript 2015 *standard*

The version supported by most browsers is *ECMAScript 5.1*. The successor to ECMAScript 5.1 was originally called **ECMAScript 6** (**ES6** for short), but finally appeared in mid-2015 under the name **ECMAScript 2015**[56]. Mozilla Firefox, Google Chrome and Microsoft Edge support this standard almost fully (as of September 2016). However, by using a transpiler (we'll explain what this is shortly in section 25.2.2) ES6 can also be used in older browsers.

---

56. Based on the cover of the specification (Ecma International 2015), or officially as *ECMA-262-6* (this is read as "ECMA-262, 6th edition"). (Wirfs-Brock 2015)

A Short History Lesson: The Whole Truth about JavaScript

JavaScript has quite an eventful history — it'd be very easy for us to come up with another book or class on just that. It's not without reason that JavaScript is considered one of the most misunderstood programming languages in the world (Crockford 2001). Even the details presented in this highlight box only represent a brief outline of that history.

The main contestants during the "browser wars" were Netscape and Microsoft, who vied to integrate the latest technologies and top features into their products. In 1995, Netscape hired Brendan Eich to develop a lightweight language alternative for its browser. Brendan Eich had just ten days in which to develop an initial prototype (Severance 2012). In light of the short time, you can imagine that the language design was somewhat less than perfect (JavaScript Flaws, 2010). Even today, we still need to puzzle over one or another of those design issues.

Originally the language was called *Mocha* and then a little later, *LiveScript*. Finally, Netscape changed the name once more, to *JavaScript* — after contractual partner Sun Microsystems granted Netscape the rights to it (Eich, Krill 2008).

Then in 1996, Microsoft responded with *JScript* in *Internet Explorer 3.0*. Because of brand protection, the language couldn't be called JavaScript. When I (Marco) worked for Markant Software in the mid-90s, we were programming almost everything twice — once for Netscape Navigator and once for Microsoft Internet Explorer. In addition to the enormous additional effort, users of other browsers were often left out. Then fortunately, in order to prevent further rampant growth, *ECMA International* assumed the task of creating a common language standard. *ECMA International* is a standardization body similar to the ISO or W3C which has dedicated itself to the standardization of information technology and electronics systems.

The standard *ECMA-262* now represents the common base shared by JavaScript and JScript (a co-standardization also exists, in the form of ISO/IEC 16262:2011). The standard itself has quite an eventful history. For example, committee members were unable to come to agreement on version 4. There were significant discrepancies with regard to the future development of ECMAScript. In the end, the committee completely rejected ES4. Agreement was finally reached with ES5 (originally ES3.1) a full ten years after version 3. In the process, Macromedia (later bought out by Adobe) had already implemented large portions of ES4 in *ActionScript* — a language which, along with its Flash/Flex environment, was now decreasing in importance.

> ES6 (better yet, ES2015) contained many features originally planned for ES4, and fortunately these were thought out much better and were better implemented. The change of the name to ES2015 was due to the fact that in 2015 the language switched over to an annual release cycle (Wirfs-Brock 2015).
>
> While ES6/ES2015, following the many years of stagnation, brought with it a huge package of changes and enhancements, newer releases (ES2016, ES2017, etc.) are intentionally kept small. Instead of occasional large releases, there are now smaller updates released more frequently.
>
> If this history still hasn't been enough for you, you'll find more detailed examinations of the language in Young (2010) and Mills (2012).

25.2   Of JavaScript Machines, Environments and Transpilers

25.2.1   The Engine Just Keeps Going and Going and Going…

You can't do a whole lot with just JS alone. It requires a program which can read and execute JS code — a so-called *JavaScript engine*. These engines used to be just pure *interpreters*, i.e. programs which actually read and interpreted the code. Modern engines often use hybrid technologies which also pre-compile portions of the code: They translate JS code either directly into machine code which the CPU can execute (*just-in-time compilers*), or into an intermediate code which is then interpreted. Modern engines are highly optimized and compete to provide the best performance.

JS in the Browser

All popular browsers provide JS engines. Here's a brief overview:

Engine	Browser
Chakra	Microsoft Edge
Nitro	Apple Safari
SpiderMonkey	Mozilla Firefox
V8	Chromium Google Chrome Opera

JS in Desktop Software

For some time, JavaScript engines have been available in more than just browsers. For example, there are JS engines like *Rhino*[57] and *Nashorn*[58] which make it possible to integrate JS code into Java programs, and *QtScript*[59] which integrates JS code into Qt/C++. Even Adobe's *Acrobat Reader* and *Photoshop* contain JS engines to carry out scripting functions.

25.2.2   Transpiling and JS as a Transpile Target

In addition to JS, browsers can also execute other languages, e.g. *Dart* (Chrome) or *VBScript* (Internet Explorer).

However, JavaScript is the only language which actually works in **all** browsers (or at least in all current browsers). A favorite trick is to write an application in one language and translate it into JS — so-called **transpiling**. In contrast to a compiler, a transpiler doesn't translate a program into machine code, but into another language which has approximately the same level of abstraction as the source language. This makes it possible to use languages such as Ruby (e.g. *Opal*[60], *RubyJS*[61]), Python (e.g. *PyJs*[62]), Java (e.g. *GWT*[63]) or Clojure (e.g. *ClojureScript*[64]) in the browser.

Some languages were developed for the sole purpose of being transpiled into JavaScript. These include *CoffeeScript*[65] and*LiveScript*[66].

Jeremy Ashkenas (who developed CoffeeScript and Backbone) maintains a *list*[67] of all languages which have JS as a transpiler target.

---

57. *https://developer.mozilla.org/en-US/docs/Mozilla/Projects/Rhino*

58. *http://openjdk.java.net/projects/nashorn*

59. *http://doc.qt.io/qt-4.8/scripting.html*

60. *http://opalrb.org/*

61. *http://en.wikipedia.org/wiki/RubyJS*

62. *http://pyjs.org*

63. *http://www.gwtproject.org/*

64. *https://github.com/clojure/clojurescript*

65. *http://coffeescript.org/*

66. *http://livescript.net/*

67. *https://github.com/jashkenas/coffeescript/wiki/List-of-languages-that-compile-to-JS*

I have an especially high regard for CoffeeScript and LiveScript, and have already collaborated in a large CoffeeScript project. Nevertheless, the importance of such languages in practice is actually quite low. Their use is always associated with additional effort and can also lead to losses in performance. I would generally recommend not using GWT since it makes error searching significantly more difficult. Even if you do choose to use a lightweight extension language like CoffeeScript in a project, you still need to understand the JS code it generates. So in short, it's always a good idea to take the time to learn JS properly right from the start — that way you'll never make an error no matter what route you decide to take! You'll find more on the topic of transpilers in *Fowler (2013)*[68] and *Fenton (2012)*[69].

25.3   From JS To JS

It's intriguing that you can also transpile JS into JS. What sense does that make? Simple — it gives you the ability to code right now in the ultra-modern ECMAScript standard of next year, but you can still execute your code in an old browser which can maybe only master ECMAScript 5.1. There're even a few backward transpilers of this nature! These are listed in *Juriy Zaytsev's ECMAScript Compatibility Table*[70], next to browsers. You can use the table to find out what features of ECMAScript 2015/16/17 are available in what browser, or what transpiler can translate these back. The transpiler **Babel** currently has the best coverage in terms of new language features. You can use it for all your real world programming needs without a problem.

JavaScript is the assembly language of the Internet.

---

68. *http://martinfowler.com/bliki/TransparentCompilation.html*

69. *https://www.stevefenton.co.uk/Content/Blog/Date/201211/Blog/Compiling-Vs-Transpiling/*

70. *http://kangax.github.io/compat-table/es6/*

Appendix B: Coding Guidelines

This appendix compiles together all the coding guidelines we specified in the lessons. These coding guidelines are neither mandatory nor compulsory. Use these guidelines for the purpose of this course. Of course, you can also use them as a starting point for your own projects. As you progress, you should then gradually tailor them to meet your own requirements and/or those of your team.

26.1   ESLint

Many of the following guidelines can be automatically checked using the **linter** *ESLint*. Linters are tools which assist you in complying with guidelines — they point out and sometimes even fix rules violations. ESLint is the best-known linter for modern JS code.

A detailed presentation of ESLint would be beyond the scope of this class, but you can find all important information on the *ESLint website*[71].

Each of the following guidelines is followed by a reference to the corresponding ESLint rule in parentheses.

26.2   General

➤ Use `"use strict"` at the beginning of JS files (strict: global).
➤ Always use exactly one line for exactly one statement (max-statements-per-line).
➤ End each command with a semicolon (semi).
➤ You should normally use double quotes to delimit strings, example: `"Hello world"`.
➤ Use parentheses when you're unsure of the order of evaluation in an expression or if you think they'll make your code easier to read.
➤ Avoid *magic numbers* (no-magic-numbers).

➤ Put a blank space before and after each operator with two operands (e.g. addition operator, assignment operator, etc.) (space-infix-ops).

➤ Never use more than two empty lines in a row to show logical separations in your code (no-multiple-empty-lines).

26.3   Variables & Constants

➤ Don't use global variables (no-undef).

➤ Avoid variables (`let`) — try to work with constants (`const`) instead (no-var, prefer-const).

➤ When declaring variables or constants, select their scope to be as small as possible.

26.4   Variable & Constant Identifiers

➤ Always select identifiers which are meaningful and self-explanatory. Singular nouns are generally the best choice for variable identifiers.

➤ Never use special characters or made-up abbreviations in identifiers.

➤ Write variable and constant identifiers in lowerCamelCase (camelcase). **Exception:** Continue to write constants which serve to configure your program, i.e. whose value is already defined before your program runs, in SCREAMING_SNAKE_CASE.

26.5   Code Blocks

Use 1 true brace style (brace-style: 1tbs):

➤ The opening brace `{` of a body is on the same line as the corresponding keyword (e.g. `if`).

➤ A line break follows the opening brace of a body.

➤ Each statement within a body is indented using 2 blank spaces. (indent: 2)

➤ The closing brace `}` of a body appears on a new line and is left-aligned with the corresponding keyword.

26.6   Keywords

➤ A keyword (e.g. `if`, `else`, `let` etc.) should be followed by exactly one space (keyword-spacing).

26.7 Functions

➤ Function identifiers are either verbs or start with a verb. Use the imperative if at all possible!

➤ Function identifiers begin with a lowercase letter (a through z).

➤ Omit braces and the keyword `return` in one-line functions. The arrow is followed by a blank space, with the expression immediately after that.

➤ Limit functions to 10 statements at the most (max-statements: 10).

➤ Use functions without side effects whenever possible.

27 *Appendix C: Sources & References*

27.1   APA Style

We use so-called *APA Style* to list references, sources and related literature. APA Style is one system, among others, used to indicate references. The system was developed by the *American Psychological Association* (APA).

You'll find more information on *Wikipedia*[72] or in the *Online Writing Lab*[73]. An APA Style reference usually consists of last name and year. Here're two examples:

> *Another indication of the meaningfulness of an identifier is its length. Variables which consist of only a single character are usually problematic (Kellerwessel 2002).*

> *Douglas Crockford (2008) even calls* == *the evil twin.*

You can then look up the references listed in the following list of sources.

27.2   Sources

Beck K., Beedle M., van Bennekum A., Cockburn A., Cunningham W., Fowler M., Grenning J., Highsmith J., Hunt A., Jeffries R., Kern J., Marick B., Robert C. M., Mellor S., Schwaber K., Sutherland J., Thomas D. (2001). Manifesto for Agile Software Development. Website, see *agilemanifesto.org*[74]

Beck K., Andres C. (November 2004). Extreme Programming Explained: Embrace Change, Second Edition. Addison Wesley Professional

Crockford D. (2001). JavaScript: The World's Most Misunderstood Programming Language. Douglas Crockford's Wrrrld Wide Web (private website). Seen on March 19, 2015 at*http://javascript.crockford.com/javascript.html*

Crockford D. (May 2008). JavaScript: The Good Parts: Working with the Shallow Grain of JavaScript. O'Reilly

---

72. *http://en.wikipedia.org/wiki/Apa_style*
73. *https://owl.english.purdue.edu/owl/resource/560/01/*
74. *http://agilemanifesto.org*

Ecma International (June 2015). ECMAScript 2015 Language Specification. Standard ECMA-262, 6th Edition / June 2015

Ecma International (June 2011). ECMAScript Language Specification. Standard ECMA-262, 5.1 Edition / June 2011

Eich B. (October 2006). Will there be a suggested file suffix for es4?. E-Mail in der ES4-discuss Mailing-Liste. Seen on January 16, 2015 at*https://mail.mozilla.org/pipermail/es-discuss/2006-October/000133.html*

Eich B., Krill P. (June 2008). JavaScript creator ponders past, future. An interview with Brandon Eich posted on Infoworld.com. Seen on March 19, 2015 at*http://www.infoworld.com/article/2653798/application-development/javascript-creator-ponders-past--future.html*

Evans E.J. (August 2003). Domain-Driven Design: Tackling Complexity in the Heart of Software. Addison Wesley

Fenton S. (November 2012). Compiling vs. Transpiling. Blog post on Fenton's home page. Seen on March 20, 2015 at*https://www.stevefenton.co.uk/Content/Blog/Date/201211/Blog/Compiling-Vs-Transpiling/*

Flanagen D. (April 2011). JavaScript: The Definitive Guide: Activate Your Web Pages. Edition: 6. O'Reilly Media

Fowler M., Beck K., Brant J., Opdykeet. W. (1999). Refactoring, Improving the Design of Existing Code, Amsterdam: Addison-Wesley Longman

Fowler M. (2002). Patterns of Enterprise Application Architecture. Amsterdam: Addison-Wesley Longman

Fowler M. (February 2013). TransparentCompilation. Blog post in Fowler's Bliki. Seen on March 20, 2015 at*http://martinfowler.com/bliki/TransparentCompilation.html*

Goldberg A. (August 1981). Introducing the Smalltalk-80 System. Byte Magazine, Vol. 06 No. 08 – Smalltalk, 14-26. see*https://archive.org/details/byte-magazine-1981-08*

Goodman D., Morrison M. (2004). The JavaScript Bible, 5th Edition. Wiley

JavaScript Flaws. (2010). Article in Ward Cunningham's C2-Wiki. Seen on March 23, 2015 at *http://c2.com/cgi/wiki?JavaScriptFlaws*

Kellerwessel H. (2002). Programmierrichtlinien in der Praxis. MITP

Münz S. (2003). JavaScript Referenz. Franzis

Oestereich B. (1998). Objektorientierte Softwareentwicklung: Analyse und Design mit der Unified Modeling Language. 4th updated edition. Munich; Vienna: Oldenbourg. See *www.oose.de/uml*[75]

Mills C. (June 2012) A Short History of JavaScript. Entry in W3C-Wiki. Seen on March 19, 2015 at
https://www.w3.org/community/webed/wiki/A_Short_History_of_JavaScript

Rauschmayer A. (March 2014). Speaking JavaScript: An In-Depth Guide for Programmers. O'Reilly & Associates

Robson D. (August 1981). Object-Oriented Software Systems. Byte Magazine, Vol. 06 No. 08 – Smalltalk, 74-86. See*https://archive.org/details/byte-magazine-1981-08*

Sawall A. (April 2009). Oracle kauft Sun. News article on Golem. Seen on March 22, 2015 on *http://www.golem.de/0904/66578.html*

Severance C. (February 2012). JavaScript: Designing a Language in 10 Days. Computer, Vol. 45, No. 2. Seen on March 22, 2015 at*http://www.computer.org/csdl/mags/co/2012/02/mco2012020007-abs.html*

Ullenboom C. (May 2014). Java ist auch eine Insel: Das umfassende Handbuch. Galileo Computing; edition: 11

Vermeulen A. et al. (2000). The Elements of Java Style. Sigs Reference Library

Wirfs-Brock A. (January 2015). Commentary on the public mailing list *es-discuss@mozilla.org*. Seen on March 23, 2015 at*https://esdiscuss.org/topic/javascript-2015#content-54*

Wirfs-Brock R., McKean A. (November 2002). Object Design: Roles, Responsibilities, and Collaborations. Pearson Education

Young A. (May/July 2010). History of JavaScript: Parts 1 – 8. Blog post on DailyJs.com. Seen on March 19, 2015 at*http://dailyjs.com/tags.html#hoj*

Zakas N. C. (unpublished). Understanding ECMAScript 6. Leanpub.com

---

75. *http://www.oose.de/uml*

Solutions (Exercises)

Exercise 1: Logged into the Console

```
1 console.log("Christin");
```

accompanying_files/02/solutions/logged.js

Exercise 2: Sound the Alarm!

```
1 alert("Alert! Your console is on fire! Hurry! Write an email to
the firefighters or tweet with the hashtag
#helpMyComputerIsOnFire");
```

accompanying_files/02/solutions/alert.js

Exercise 3: 2000 Seconds

```
1 "use strict";
2
3 console.log(2000 / 60);
4 console.log(2000 % 60);
```

accompanying_files/03/solutions/2000_secs.js

Exercise 4: Lucky Numbers & Name Codes

```
1 "use strict";
2
3 console.log("Christin".length * "Marit".length);
4 console.log("Marco".length * "Emrich".length);
```

accompanying_files/03/solutions/lucky_number.js

Exercise 5: Hmmm...So What are You Really?

```
String
```

Exercise 6: Just a Few More Calculations...

Expression	Return value
3 + 4	7
3 * 12	36
25 + 12	37
(12 - 3) / 3	3
12 % 3	0
12 * (44 / 11) / 3 + 67	83

Exercise 7: But You Don't Ask Someone Something Like That!

```
1  "use strict";
2
3  let userAge = prompt("Please let me know your age!");
4
5  console.log(userAge);
```
accompanying_files/04/solutions/age.js

Exercise 8: Imposing More Taxes

```
1  "use strict";
2
3  const TAX_PERCENTAGE = 22;
4
5  let price = 150;
6  let totalPrice = price * TAX_PERCENTAGE / 100 + price;
7
8  console.log(totalPrice);
```
accompanying_files/04/solutions/tax.js

Exercise 9: Think Up Some Good Variable Identifiers!

Variable Description	Variable Identifier
Price of a book in an online shop	price
Number of users currently logged in	numberOfCurrentUsers

Variable Description	Variable Identifier
Title of a web page	title
Cost of a house on a real estate site	price
Model of a monitor on a manufacturer's website	model
Vehicle identification number of a car being serviced on the website of a car repair shop	vehicleId

These answers are just suggestions. It depends on the context. Usually you won't have a variable `bookPrice` in an online store, since there are various products. It could also be `productPrice`, if `price` alone is not enough to understand what `price` means in the context.

Exercise 11: Mmmmmmmmm...

1.

```
1 "use strict";
2
3 let favoriteFood = prompt("Please let me know your favorite
food");
4 let favoriteDrink = prompt("Please let me know your favorite
drink");
```

accompanying_files/06/solutions/mmm1.js

2.

```
1 "use strict";
2
3 let favoriteFood = prompt("Please let me know your favorite
food");
4 let favoriteDrink = prompt("Please let me know your favorite
drink");
5
6 console.log("My favorite food is " + favoriteFood + " and my
favorite drink is " + favoriteDrink + ".");
```

accompanying_files/06/solutions/mmm2.js

3.

```
1 "use strict";
2
3 let favoriteFood = prompt("Please let me know your favorite
food");
4 let favoriteDrink = prompt("Please let me know your favorite
drink");
5
6 console.log(`My favorite food is ${favoriteFood} and my favorite
drink is ${favoriteDrink}.`);
```

accompanying_files/06/solutions/mmm3.js

4.

```
1 "use strict";
2
3 let favoriteFood = prompt("Please let me know your favorite
food");
4 let favoriteDrink = prompt("Please let me know your favorite
drink");
5
6 console.log(`My favorite food is ${favoriteFood} and my favorite
drink is ` + favoriteDrink + `.`);
```

accompanying_files/06/solutions/mmm4.js

Exercise 12: String "Calculations"

Expression	Return value
"Hello" + "world"	"HelloWorld"
"Hello" + " world"	"Hello world"
"1" + "1"	"11"
1 + 1	2
"1 + 1"	"1 + 1"

Exercise 13: Errors in Detail

```
1 "use strict";
2
3 let tale = "Three hicks were working on a telephone tower –
Steve, Bruce and Jed. Steve falls off and is killed instantly.\n\
```

```
nAs the ambulance takes the body away, Bruce says, 'Someone should
go and tell his wife.'\n\nJed says, 'OK, I'm pretty good at that
sensitive stuff, I'll do it.'\n\nTwo hours later, he comes back
carrying a case of beer.\n\nBruce says, 'Where did you get that,
Jed?'\n\n'Steve's wife gave it to me,' Jed replies.\n\n'That's
unbelievable, you told the lady her husband was dead and she gave
you beer?'\n\n'Well, not exactly', Jed says. 'When she answered the
door, I said to her, \"You must be Steve's widow\".'\n\nShe said,
'No, I'm not a widow!'\n\nAnd I said, 'I'll bet you a case of
Budweiser you are.'";
4
5 console.log(tale);
```

accompanying_files/06/solutions/bugs_everywhere.js

Exercise 14: Just Exactly What Kinds of Expressions are These?

Expression	Return Value	Data Type
"1.5" * 2	3	Number
"1.5" * 2	NaN	number
"1.5" + 2	"1.52"	String
Number("1.5") * 2	3	Number
Number("1,5") * 2	NaN	Number
Number("3 days") * 7	NaN	Number
Number("Page 20") + 5	NaN	Number
"9,2" + Number("11.7");	"9,211.7"	String
(NaN - 2) * (4 / 2)	NaN	Number
alert(Number(17 / 2 + 1.3))	Undefined	Undefined
typeof 12.25	"number"	String
typeof typeof 12.25	"string"	String

Exercise 15: Maximum Distance & Consumption

1.

```
1  "use strict";
2
3  let totalGasConsumed = prompt("How much fuel did you consume?");
4  let distance = prompt("How many km did you travel?");
5  let consumption = totalGasConsumed / distance * 100;
6
7  console.log(`Your car has a consumption of ${consumption} liter
per 100 kilometers`);
```

accompanying_files/07/solutions/gasoline1.js

2.

```
1  "use strict";
2
3  let totalGasConsumed = prompt("How much fuel did you consume?");
4  let distance = prompt("How many km did you travel?");
5  let tankSize = prompt("How many liters of gasoline fits in your
tank?");
6
7  let consumption = totalGasConsumed / distance * 100;
8  let maxDistance = tankSize * distance / totalGasConsumed;
9
10 console.log(`Your car has a consumption of ${consumption} liter
per 100 kilometers .\nYou can travel ${maxDistance} km with a full
tank.`);
```

accompanying_files/07/solutions/gasoline2.js

Exercise 16: 2000 Seconds, Part 2

```
1  "use strict";
2
3  let minutes = Math.floor(2000 / 60);
4  let seconds = 2000 % 60;
5
6  console.log(`2000 seconds equals ${minutes}:${seconds}`);
```

accompanying_files/08/solutions/2000_secs2.js

Exercise 17: Lotto (or the "49-Sided Die")

```
1  "use strict";
2
3  console.log(Math.floor(Math.random() * 49) + 1);
```

accompanying_files/08/solutions/lotto.js

Exercise 18: Maximum Distance & Consumption, Part 2

```
 1  "use strict";
 2
 3  let totalGasConsumed = prompt("How much fuel did you consume?");
 4  let distance = prompt("How many km did you travel?");
 5  let tankSize = prompt("How many liters of gasoline fits in your
tank?");
 6
 7  let consumption = Math.round(totalGasConsumed / distance * 100);
 8  let maxDistance = Math.round(tankSize * distance /
totalGasConsumed);
 9
10  console.log(`Your car has a consumption of ${consumption} liter
per 100 kilometers .\nYou can travel ${maxDistance} km with a full
tank.`);
```

accompanying_files/08/solutions/gasoline.js

Exercise 19: Just Exactly What Kinds of Expressions are These? — Part 2

Expression	Return Value	Data Type
"computer" === "problems"	false	boolean
19 >= 19	true	boolean
19 >= 19.2	false	boolean
5 * 7 === 36 - 1	true	boolean
3 + 3 !== 2 * 3	false	boolean
"42" === 42	false	boolean
"42" + 1 === 43	false	boolean
"2" * "4" === Number(17 / 2)	false	boolean
"42" === "forty-two"	false	boolean
isNaN("3" + "4")	false	boolean
"two" < "three"	false	boolean
"seven" < "nine"	false	boolean
"nine" < "seven"	true	boolean

Exercise 20: The Dark Side of JavaScript

```javascript
1  "use strict";
2
3  let username = prompt("Welcome. Please tell me your name");
4  alert(`Hey ${username}. Nice to meet you.`);
5
6  let playerFitness = prompt(`So ${username}. Let me know: Are you
   ready to fight?\nPlease answer with yes or no"`);
7
8  if (playerFitness === "yes") {
9    let fightOne = prompt("Great! Let start to play! I´m sure
   you´ll make it.\nWhich Operators has the higher priority: * or +
   ?");
10   if (fightOne === "*") {
11     alert(`Yeah, you got it. ${fightOne} is right! The dark side
   has no chance at this point.`);
12   }
13   if (fightOne !== "*") {
14     alert("Damn! Please don´t give up and try again.");
15   }
16 }
17
18 if (playerFitness !== "yes") {
19   alert(`${username}, I´m very disappointed about you. The force
   of dark side of JavaScript grows up.`);
20 }
```

accompanying_files/10/solutions/dark_side_of_js.js

Exercise 21: The Dark Side of JavaScript

```javascript
1  "use strict";
2
3  let username = prompt("Welcome. Please tell me your name");
4  alert(`Hey ${username}. Nice to meet you.`);
5
6  let playerFitness = prompt(`So ${username}. Let me know: Are you
   ready to fight?\nPlease answer with yes or no"`);
7
8  if (playerFitness === "yes") {
9    let fightOne = prompt("Great! Let start to play! I´m sure
   you´ll make it.\nWhich Operators has the higher priority: * or +
   ?");
10   if (fightOne === "*") {
11     alert(`Yeah, you got it. ${fightOne} is right! The dark side
   has no chance at this point.`);
12   } else {
13     alert("Damn! Please don´t give up and try again.");
14   }
```

```
15 } else {
16     alert(`${username}, I´m very disappointed about you. The force
of dark side of JavaScript grows up.`);
17 }
```

accompanying_files/10/solutions/dark_side_of_js_else.js

Exercise 22: Occurrence of Leap Years

```
1  "use strict";
2
3  let year = Number(prompt("Enter a year"));
4
5  if (year % 400 === 0) {
6    console.log(`${year} is a leap year`);
7  } else {
8    if (year % 100 === 0) {
9      console.log(`${year} is NOT a leap year`);
10   } else {
11     if (year % 4 === 0) {
12       console.log(`${year} is a leap year`);
13     } else {
14       console.log(`${year} is NOT a leap year`);
15     }
16   }
17 }
```

accompanying_files/10/solutions/leap_year.js

Exercise 23: The Dark Side Strikes Back...

```
1  "use strict";
2
3  let username = prompt("Welcome. Please tell me your name");
4  alert(`Hey ${username}. Nice to meet you.`);
5
6  let playerFitness = prompt(`So ${username}. Let me know: Are you
ready to fight?\nPlease answer with yes or no"`);
7  if (playerFitness === "yes") {
8    let fightOne = prompt("Great! Let start to play! I´m sure
you´ll make it.\nWhich Operators has the higher priority: * or +
?");
9    if (fightOne === "*") {
10     alert(`Yeah, you got it. ${fightOne} is right! The dark side
has no chance at this point.`);
11     let fightTwo = prompt(`Yeah, you got it. ${fightOne} is
right! The dark side has no chance at this point.\nWhat's the
German word for if?`);
12     if (fightTwo === "wenn" || fightTwo === "falls" ) {
13       alert("That's a small step for a programmer, but a giant
```

```
leap in this fight!");
14      let fightThree = prompt("That's a small step for a
programmer, but a giant leap in this fight!\nNow, please enter
string with a length between 8 and 15 characters…");
15      if (fightThree.length >= 8 && fightThree.length <= 15) {
16        alert("You've rocked. For this time the bad JavaScript
is defeated!");
17      } else {
18        alert("That's tragic. Just a step before winning...");
19      }
20    } else {
21      alert("There is no time for a break. Try again!");
22    }
23  } else {
24    alert("Damn! Please don't give up and try again.");
25  }
26 } else {
27   alert(`${username}, I'm very disappointed about you. The force
of dark side of JavaScript grows up.`);
28 }
```

accompanying_files/11/solutions/dark_side_of_js.js

Exercise 24: Of Good and Evil Input

```
1  "use strict";
2
3  let name = prompt("What's your name?");
4  let firstName = prompt("What's your first name?");
5  let gender = prompt("Are you a lord (m) or lady (f)?");
6  let age = prompt("How old are you?");
7
8  let errorMessage = "";
9
10 if (name.length < 2 || name.length > 100) {
11   errorMessage += "name ";
12 }
13
14 if (firstName.length < 2 || firstName.length > 100) {
15   errorMessage += "first name ";
16 }
17
18 if (gender !== "f" && gender !== "m") {
19   errorMessage += "gender ";
20 }
21
22 if (isNaN(age) || age >= 150) {
23   errorMessage += "age ";
24 }
25
26 if (errorMessage === "") {
```

```
27   console.log("OK!");
28 } else {
29   console.log("KO! The following entries are invalid: " +
errorMessage);
30 }
```

accompanying_files/11/solutions/inputs.js

Exercise 25: Occurrence of Leap Years — Part 2

```
1 "use strict";
2
3 let year = Number(prompt("Enter a year"));
4
5 if (year % 400 === 0 || (year % 4 === 0 && year % 100 !== 0)) {
6   console.log(`${year} is a leap year`);
7 } else {
8   console.log(`${year} is NOT a leap year`);
9 }
```

accompanying_files/11/solutions/leap_year2.js

Exercise 26: When a First Name Just isn't Enough...

```
1 "use strict";
2
3 let name = "Ladislaus Coolio Jones";
4 let spacePosition = name.lastIndexOf(" ");
5 let firstName = name.substr(0, spacePosition);
6 let lastName = name.substr(spacePosition + 1);
7
8 console.log(firstName);
9 console.log(lastName);
```

accompanying_files/12/solutions/first_name.js

Exercise 27: A Heribert Split

```
1 "use strict";
2
3 let name = "Heribert  Gold ";
4 let spacePosition = name.trim().lastIndexOf(" ");
5 let firstName = name.substr(0, spacePosition).trim();
6 let lastName = name.substr(spacePosition + 1).trim();
7
8 console.log(firstName);
9 console.log(lastName);
```

accompanying_files/12/solutions/heribert.js

Exercise 28: Ladislaus Transformed

```
1  "use strict";
2
3  let name = "Ladislaus Jones";
4  let spacePosition = name.indexOf(" ");
5  let firstName = name.substr(0, spacePosition);
6  let lastName = name.substr(spacePosition + 1);
7
8  console.log(lastName + ", " + firstName.charAt(0) + ".");
```

accompanying_files/12/solutions/ladislaus.js

Exercise 30: If Someone Could Just Find That Needle in the Haystack...

```
1  "use strict";
2
3  let haystack = "haystack haystack haystack haystack haystack
   haystack haystack needle haystack haystack haystack haystack
   haystack haystack haystack haystack haystack";
4
5  console.log(haystack.indexOf("needle"));
```

accompanying_files/12/solutions/needle.js

Exercise 31: Valuable Zeros, Part 1

```
1  "use strict";
2
3  let itemNumber = "123";
4  let correctedItemNumber = (itemNumber.charAt(0) === "0" ? "" :
   "0") + itemNumber;
5
6  console.log(correctedItemNumber);
```

accompanying_files/12/solutions/zeroes.js

Exercise 32: Logged into the Console, Part 2

```
1  "use strict";
2
3  let showName = () => {
4    console.log("Christin");
5  };
6
7  showName();
```

accompanying_files/13/solutions/logged.js

Exercise 33: Hello, Mr. ${recipient}... or maybe Ms.?

```
1  "use strict";
2
3  let newsletterFor = recipient => `
4    Hello Mr ${recipient},
5
6    We're happy to inform you that you've won $100.000!
7
8    Congratulations!
9    Please write us an email with your banking information and we will
10   transfer the money.
11   Sincerely, the Win-Team`;
12
13 let showNewsletterFor = recipient =>
14   console.log(newsletterFor(recipient));
15
16 showNewsletterFor("Heribert");
17 showNewsletterFor("Goldy");
18 showNewsletterFor("Ladislaus");
```
accompanying_files/13/solutions/hello_mr_recipient1.js

```
1  "use strict";
2
3  let newsletterFor = (recipient, salutation) => `
4    Hello ${salutation} ${recipient},
5
6    We're happy to inform you that you've won $100.000!
7
8    Congratulations!
9    Please write us an email with your banking information and we will
10   transfer the money.
11   Sincerely, the Win-Team`;
12
13 let showNewsletterFor = (recipient, salutation) =>
14   console.log(newsletterFor(recipient, salutation));
15
16 showNewsletterFor("Heribert", "Mr.");
17 showNewsletterFor("Goldy", "Ms.");
18 showNewsletterFor("Ladislaus", "Mr.");
```
accompanying_files/13/solutions/hello_mr_recipient2.js

```
1  "use strict";
2
3  let newsletterFor = (recipient, salutation) => `
4    Hello ${salutation} ${recipient},
5
6    We're happy to inform you that you've won
```

```
${prizeFor(salutation)}
7
8    Congratulations!
9    Please write us an email with your banking information and we
will
10   transfer the money.
11   Sincerely, the Win-Team`;
12
13 let showNewsletterFor = (recipient, salutation) =>
14   console.log(newsletterFor(recipient, salutation));
15
16 let prizeFor = salutation =>
17   salutation === "Mr"
18     ? "an incredible Ferrari and $20.000!"
19     : `a voucher from Tiffany & Co. (worth $50.000),
20   a luxury trip to New York and an extra $50.000 for shopping
and more!`;
21
22 showNewsletterFor("Heribert", "Mr.");
23 showNewsletterFor("Goldy", "Ms.");
24 showNewsletterFor("Ladislaus", "Mr.");
```

accompanying_files/13/solutions/hello_mr_recipient3.js

Exercise 34: Ladislaus Transformed, Part 2

```
1 "use strict";
2
3 let logTransformedName = (firstName, lastName) =>
4     console.log(lastName + ", " + firstName.charAt(0) + ".");
5
6 logTransformedName("Ladislaus", "Jones");
```

accompanying_files/13/solutions/ladislaus.js

Exercise 35: Ladislaus Transformed, Part 3

```
1 "use strict";
2
3 let transformName = (firstName, lastName) =>
4     lastName + ", " + firstName.charAt(0) + ".";
5
6 console.log(transformName("Ladislaus", "Jones"));
```

accompanying_files/14/solutions/ladislaus.js

Exercise 36: Maximum Distance & Consumption, Part 3

```
1  "use strict";
2
3  let askForFuelLoad = () => prompt("How much fuel did you
consume?");
4  let askForDistance = () => prompt("How many km did you travel?");
5  let askForTankSize = () => prompt("How many liters of gasoline
fits in your tank?");
6
7  let fuelLoad = askForFuelLoad();
8  let distance = askForDistance();
9  let tankSize = askForTankSize();
10
11 let consumption = () => Math.floor(fuelLoad / distance * 100);
12 let fuelRange = () => Math.floor(tankSize * distance / fuelLoad);
13
14 console.log(`Your car has a consumption of ${consumption()}
liter per 100 kilometers .\nYou can travel ${fuelRange()} km with a
full tank.`);
```

accompanying_files/14/solutions/gasoline.js

Exercise 37: Hot, Hot, Hot

```
1  "use strict";
2
3  let fahrenheit = celsius => celsius * 9 / 5 + 32;
4
5  let celsius = Number(prompt("How hot is it, Baby? (In degree
celsius!)"));
6
7  console.log(fahrenheit(celsius));
```

accompanying_files/14/solutions/hot.js

Exercise 38: Baking Cookies Using Arrays

```
1  "use strict";
2
3  let ingredients = ["1/4 cup rapeseed oil", "1 separated egg",
4    "1/2 cup sugar", "1 tsp baking powder"];
5  ingredients.push("1 tbsp flour");
6  ingredients.unshift("1 cup rolled oats");
7  ingredients.splice(1, 1, "1/3 cup butter");
8
9  let ingredientsText = ingredients.join("\n");
10 let ingredientsTitel = "Rolled oat cookies";
11 let directions = "Melt the butter in a pan, add the rolled oats
and mix everything well. Remove the mixture from heat and let it
```

cool. Add the sugar to the egg white and beat until stiff. Mix in the yolk, baking powder and flour. Now mix in the cooled oat mixture. Shape small mounds of batter onto a baking sheet. These mounds should not be too large, since the batter will spread out a little as it is baked. Bake for 15 minutes at 350 °F in a pre-heated oven.";

```
12
13 console.log(ingredientsTitel + "\n\n" + ingredientsText + "\n\n"
+ directions);
```

accompanying_files/15/solutions/cookies.js

Exercise 39: The Short Trip, or When You Don't Have the Right Change

```
1 "use strict";
2
3 const LINE_46 = [
4   "Nordostbahnhof",
5   "Theresienkrankenhaus",
6   "Teutoburger Str.",
7   "Leipziger Str.",
8   "Dresdener Str.",
9   "Spitalhof",
10  "Hubertusstr.",
11  "Tattersall",
12  "Martha-Maria-Krkhs."
13 ];
14
15 let busStopsFromTo = (departureStation, destinationStation) => {
16   let positionDeparture = LINE_46.indexOf(departureStation);
17   let positionDestination = LINE_46.indexOf(destinationStation);
18   return LINE_46.slice(positionDeparture, positionDestination +
1);
19 };
20
21 let myBusStops = busStopsFromTo("Nordostbahnhof",
"Hubertusstr.");
22
23 console.log(myBusStops);
```

accompanying_files/15/solutions/short_trip_solution.js

Exercise 40: Old Lists

```
1 "use strict";
2
3 let handleCsv = string => string.split(", ").sort();
4
5 let productList = "3Doodler 3D Printing Pen, Game of Thrones Wax
```

Seal Coasters, 10th Doctor Sonic Screwdriver Exclusive Programmable
TV Remote, Electronic Butterfly in a Jar, Aquafarm: Aquaponics Fish
Garden, Cassette Adapter Bluetooth, Marvel Comics Lightweight
Infinity Scarf, Ollie - The App Controlled Robot, Sound Splash
Bluetooth Waterproof Shower Speaker, PowerCube, Backpack of
Holding, Retro Duo Portable NES/SNES Game System, Universal Gadget
Wrist Charger, USB Squirming Tentacle, USB Fishquarium, Space Bar
Keyboard Organizer & USB Hub Pop,USB Pet Rock, Powerstation 5- E.
Maximus Chargus, Dual Heated Travel Mug, Crosley Collegiate
Portable USB Turntable, Meh Hoodie, Magnetic Accelerator Cannon,
8-Bit Legendary Hero Heat-Change Mug";

```
6
7 console.log(handleCsv(productList).join("\n"));
```

accompanying_files/15/solutions/csv_lists.js

Exercise 41: City, Country, River

```
1  "use strict";
2
3  let sortByLength = category => category.sort((a, b) => b.length
   - a.length);
4
5  let city = ["Barcelona", "Basel", "Belgrade", "Berlin",
   "Budapest"];
6  let country = ["Belgium", "Bulgaria", "Brazil", "Bolivia",
   "Bosnia and Herzegovina"];
7  let river = ["Bode", "Brahmaputra", "Beuvron", "Black River",
   "Belaja"];
8
9  console.log(sortByLength(city));
10 console.log(sortByLength(country));
11 console.log(sortByLength(river));
12
```

accompanying_files/16/solutions/city_country_river.js

Exercise 42: Fill in the Blanks Using map

```
1  "use strict";
2
3  let result;
4  let inputs = [1, 2, 3, 4, 5, 6, 7, 8, 9, 10];
5
6  //double
7  result = inputs.map(x => x * 2);
8  console.log(result); // => [2, 4, 6, 8, 10, 12, 14, 16, 18, 20]
```

```
9
10 //squares
11 result = inputs.map(x => x * x);
12 console.log(result); // => [1, 4, 9, 16, 25, 36, 49, 64, 81, 100]
```

accompanying_files/16/solutions/koans_map.js

Exercise 43: Ladislaus Transformed, Part 4

```
1 "use strict";
2
3 let transformName = (firstNames, lastName) =>
4         firstNames.map(name => name.charAt(0) + ".").join(" ")
5         + " " + lastName;
6
7 console.log(transformName(["Ladislaus", "Coolio", "Barry"],
"Jones"));
```

accompanying_files/16/solutions/ladislaus.js

Exercise 44: Friedemann Friese

```
1 "use strict";
2
3 let startsWithLetterF = game => game.startsWith("F");
4
5 let boardgames = [
6   "Caverna",
7   "Puerto Rico",
8   "Agricola",
9   "Black Friday",
10  "Funny Friends",
11  "Fauna",
12  "Eclipse",
13  "Codenames",
14  "Dominion",
15  "Fast Flowing Forest Fellers",
16  "Fearsome Floors"
17 ];
18 let boardgamesStartingWithF =
boardgames.filter(startsWithLetterF);
19
20 console.log(boardgamesStartingWithF); // => [ 'Funny Friends',
'Fauna', 'Fast Flowing Forest Fellers', 'Fearsome Floors']
```

accompanying_files/16/solutions/friedemann_friese.js

Exercise 45: Fill in the Blanks Using filter

```
1  "use strict";
2
3  let result;
4
5  //even numbers
6  let inputs = [1, 2, 3, 4, 5, 6, 7, 8, 9, 10];
7  result = inputs.filter(x => x % 2 === 0);
8  console.log(result); // => [2, 4, 6, 8, 10]
9
10 //names ending with letter 'e' or 'a'
11 let names = ["Heribert", "Friedlinde", "Tusnelda", "Oswine",
"Ladislaus"];
12 result = names.filter(n => n.endsWith("a") || n.endsWith("e"));
13 console.log(result); // => [ 'Friedlinde', 'Tusnelda', 'Oswine' ]
14
15 //word with at least three letters
16 let text = "Hi this is a short text";
17 result = text.split(" ").filter(word => word.length >= 3).join("
");
18 console.log(result); // => "this short text"
```

accompanying_files/16/solutions/koans_filter.js

Exercise 46: Fill-in-the-Blank Exercise for Higher-Order Functions

```
1  "use strict";
2
3  let result;
4  let inputs = [1, 2, 3, 4, 5, 6, 7, 8, 9, 10];
5  let text = "Hi this is a short text";
6  let names = ["Heribert", "Friedlinde", "Tusnelda", "Oswine",
"Ladislaus"];
7
8  //odd numbers
9  result = inputs.filter(x => x % 2 !== 0);
10 console.log(result); // => [ 1, 3, 5, 7, 9 ]
11
12 //sum
13 result = inputs.reduce((sum, x) => sum + x, 0);
14 console.log(result); // => 55
15
16 //product
17 result = inputs.reduce((product, x) => product * x, 1);
18 console.log(result); // => 3628800
19
20 //longest word length
21 result = text.split(" ")
```

```
22    .map(x => x.length)
23    .reduce((longest, x) => Math.max(longest, x));
24 console.log(result); // => 5
25
26 //longest word
27 result = text.split(" ")
28    .reduce((res, word) => res.length > word.length ? res : word);
29 console.log(result); // => short
30
31 //avg word length
32 result = text.split(" ")
33    .map(x => x.length)
34    .reduce((sum, x) => sum + x)
35    / text.split(" ").length;
36 console.log(result); // => 3
37
38 //sort by 3rd letter
39 result = names.sort(
40    (a, b) => a.charAt(2) > b.charAt(2)
41 );
42 console.log(result); // => [ "Ladislaus", "Friedlinde",
"Heribert", "Tusnelda", "Oswine" ]
43
44 // Are there names with more than 8 letters?
45 result = names.some(name => name.length > 8);
46 console.log(result); // => true
47
48
49 // Has every name at least 8 letters?
50 result = names.every(name => name.length > 8);
51 console.log(result); // => true
52
53
54 // What is the lowest value from the inputs?
55 result = inputs.reduce((a, b) => Math.min(a, b));
56 console.log(result); // => 1
```

accompanying_files/16/solutions/koans.js

Exercise 47: Happy Mixing with Arrays — Part 1

Step 1

```
1 "use strict";
2
3 let hasIngredient = (listOfIngredients, searchedIngredient) =>
4    listOfIngredients.includes(searchedIngredient);
5
6 let honoluluFlip = ["Maracuja Juice", "Pineapple Juice", "Lemon
```

```
Juice", "Grapefruit Juice", "Crushed Ice"];
7
8 console.log(hasIngredient(honoluluFlip, "Maracuja Juice")); // =>
true
```

accompanying_files/16/solutions/cocktails1.1.js

Step 2

```
1  "use strict";
2
3  let hasIngredient = (listOfIngredients, searchedIngredient) =>
4    listOfIngredients.includes(searchedIngredient);
5
6  let isMixableWith = (cocktailRecipe, availableIngredients) =>
7    cocktailRecipe.every(ingredientFromRecipe =>
8      hasIngredient(availableIngredients, ingredientFromRecipe)
9    );
10
11 let honoluluFlip = [
12   "Maracuja Juice",
13   "Pineapple Juice",
14   "Lemon Juice",
15   "Grapefruit Juice",
16   "Crushed Ice"
17 ];
18 let ingredientsFromMyBar = [
19   "Pineapple",
20   "Maracuja Juice",
21   "Cream",
22   "Lemon Juice",
23   "Grapefruit Juice",
24   "Crushed Ice",
25   "Milk",
26   "Apple Juice",
27   "Aperol",
28   "Pineapple Juice",
29   "Limes",
30   "Lemons"
31 ];
32
33 // honoluluFlip isMixableWith ingredientsFromMyBar?
34 console.log(isMixableWith(honoluluFlip, ingredientsFromMyBar));
// => true
```

accompanying_files/16/solutions/cocktails1.2.js

Exercise 48: Sum of its Parts

```
1 "use strict";
2
3 let digitSum = number =>
String(number).split("").map(Number).reduce(add, 0);
4 let add = (x, y) => x + y;
5
6 console.log(digitSum(4242)); // => 12
```

accompanying_files/16/solutions/digitSum.js

Exercise 49: Assorted Sums

```
1 "use strict";
2
3 let byDigitSum = (a, b) => digitSum(a) - digitSum(b);
4 let digitSum = number =>
String(number).split("").map(Number).reduce(add, 0);
5 let add = (x, y) => x + y;
6
7 let numbers = [99, 5, 8, 12, 111, 123];
8
9 console.log(numbers.sort(byDigitSum)); // => [ 12, 111, 5, 123,
8, 99 ]
```

accompanying_files/16/solutions/sort_by_digitSum.js

Exercise 50: Friedemann Friese, Part 2

```
1 "use strict";
2
3 let isFerdinandsBoardgame = game => hasAtLeastTwoWords(game) &&
allWordsStartWithF(game);
4 let hasAtLeastTwoWords = game => words(game).length >= 2;
5 let allWordsStartWithF = game =>
words(game).every(startsWithLetterF);
6 let startsWithLetterF = word => word.startsWith("F");
7 let words = game => game.split(" ");
8
9 let boardgames = [
10   "Caverna",
11   "Puerto Rico",
12   "Agricola",
13   "Black Friday",
14   "Funny Friends",
15   "Fauna",
16   "Eclipse",
17   "Codenames",
18   "Dominion",
```

```
19   "Fast Flowing Forest Fellers",
20   "Fearsome Floors"
21  ];
22  let ferdinandsBoardgames =
boardgames.filter(isFerdinandsBoardgame);
23
24  console.log(ferdinandsBoardgames); // => [ 'Funny Friends',
'Fast Flowing Forest Fellers', 'Fearsome Floors' ]
```

accompanying_files/16/solutions/friedemann_friese2.js

Exercise 51: Maximum Distance & Consumption, Part 4

```
1  "use strict";
2
3  const promptForPositiveNumber = question => {
4    const value = prompt(question);
5    if (!isNaN(value) && value > 0) return value;
6    return promptForPositiveNumber("Please enter a positive
number.");
7  };
8
9  const askForFuelLoad = () => promptForPositiveNumber("How much
fuel did you consume?");
10  const askForDistance = () => promptForPositiveNumber("How many
km did you travel?");
11  const askForTankSize = () => promptForPositiveNumber("How many
liters of gasoline fits in your tank?");
12
13  const fuelLoad = askForFuelLoad();
14  const distance = askForDistance();
15  const tankSize = askForTankSize();
16
17  const consumption = () => Math.floor(fuelLoad / distance * 100);
18  const fuelRange = () => Math.floor(tankSize * distance /
fuelLoad);
19
20  console.log(`Your car has a consumption of ${consumption()}
liter per 100 kilometers .\nYou can travel ${fuelRange()} km with a
full tank.`);
```

accompanying_files/18/solutions/gasoline.js

Exercise 52: I'm Thinking of a Number

```
1  "use strict";
2
3  const MAX_NUMBER = 10;
4  const MIN_NUMBER = 1;
5
```

```
 6  const play = randomNumber => {
 7    const playersNumber = Number(prompt("Guess a number!"));
 8
 9    if (randomNumber === playersNumber) {
10      displayVictoryMessageFor(randomNumber);
11    } else {
12      displayFeedbackFor(randomNumber, playersNumber);
13      play(randomNumber);
14    }
15  };
16
17  const displayVictoryMessageFor = randomNumber =>
18    alert(`Yeah! ${randomNumber} is right`);
19
20  const displayFeedbackFor = (randomNumber, playersNumber) =>
21    alert(`Your number ist too ${lowOrHigh(randomNumber,
playersNumber)}`);
22
23  const lowOrHigh = (randomNumber, playersNumber) =>
24    (playersNumber < randomNumber) ? "low" : "high";
25
26  const generateRandomNumber = () => Math.floor(Math.random() *
MAX_NUMBER) + MIN_NUMBER;
27
28  play(generateRandomNumber());
```

accompanying_files/18/solutions/guess_a_number.js

Exercise 53: It Should Have Three Sides...

```
 1  "use strict";
 2
 3  const triangle = height => buildTriangle(height, 1, "*");
 4
 5  const buildTriangle = (height, topLineWidth, character) =>
 6    topLineWidth > height
 7      ? ""
 8      : line(topLineWidth, character) + "\n"
 9      + buildTriangle(height, topLineWidth + 1, character);
10
11  const line = (length, character) =>
12    length === 0
13      ? ""
14      : character + line(length - 1, character);
15
16  console.log(triangle(10));
```

accompanying_files/19/solutions/triangle.js

Exercise 54: I'm Thinking of a Number, Part 2

```
1  "use strict";
2
3  const MAX_NUMBER = 10;
4  const MIN_NUMBER = 1;
5
6  const play = (randomNumber, round) => {
7    const playersNumber = Number(prompt(`Round: ${round} \nGuess a
number!`));
8
9    if (randomNumber === playersNumber) {
10     displayVictoryMessageFor(randomNumber);
11   } else {
12     displayFeedbackFor(randomNumber, playersNumber);
13     play(randomNumber, round + 1);
14   }
15 };
16
17 const displayVictoryMessageFor = randomNumber =>
18   alert(`Yeah! ${randomNumber} is right`);
19
20 const displayFeedbackFor = (randomNumber, playersNumber) =>
21   alert(`Your number ist too ${lowOrHigh(randomNumber,
playersNumber)}`);
22
23 const lowOrHigh = (randomNumber, playersNumber) =>
24   (playersNumber < randomNumber) ? "low" : "high";
25
26 const generateRandomNumber = () => Math.floor(Math.random() *
MAX_NUMBER) + MIN_NUMBER;
27
28 play(generateRandomNumber(), 1);
```

accompanying_files/19/solutions/guess_a_number.js

Exercise 55: Everything in Its Place? ["Brainteaser"]

```
1  "use strict";
2
3  const isSorted = list =>
4    list.length === 1
5      || (list[0] < list[1] && isSorted(list.slice(1)));
6
7  const customersOnline = ["Heribert", "Friedlinde", "Tusnelda",
"Oswine", "Ladislaus", "Goldy"];
8  //const customersOnline = ["Friedlinde", "Goldy", "Heribert",
"Ladislaus", "Oswine", "Tusnelda"]; // sorted list for testing
9
10  console.log(isSorted(customersOnline));
```

accompanying_files/19/solutions/everything_in_place.js

Exercise 56: The Most Wonderful Time of the Year

```
"use strict";

const times = (n, fn) => {
  const result = new Array(n);
  for (let i = 0; i < n; i += 1) result[i] = fn(i);
  return result;
};

times(3, () => console.log("Ho!"));
```

accompanying_files/20/solutions/ho_ho_ho.js

Exercise 57: Wallpaper Time

```
"use strict";

const rectangle = (width, height, character) =>
  times(height, () => line(width, character)).join("\n");

const line = (length, character) =>
  times(length, () => character).join("");

const times = (n, fn) => {
  const result = new Array(n);
  for (let i = 0; i < n; i += 1) result[i] = fn(i);
  return result;
};

console.log(rectangle(25, 12, "°"));
```

accompanying_files/20/solutions/rectangle_times.js

Exercise 58: Valuable Zeros, Part 2

With recursion

```
1  "use strict";
2
3  const ARTICLE_NUMBER_LENGTH = 7;
4
5  const fillUp = itemNumber =>
6    ARTICLE_NUMBER_LENGTH === String(itemNumber).length
7      ? String(itemNumber)
8      : fillUp("0" + itemNumber);
9
10 console.log(fillUp(477));
```

accompanying_files/20/solutions/zeroes_recursive.js

With times function

```
1  "use strict";
2
3  const ARTICLE_NUMBER_LENGTH = 7;
4
5  const fillUp = itemNumber =>
6    times(numberOfMissingZeros(itemNumber), () => "0").join("")
7    + itemNumber;
8
9  const numberOfMissingZeros = number =>
10   ARTICLE_NUMBER_LENGTH - String(number).length;
11
```

```
12  const times = (n, fn) => {
13    const result = new Array(n);
14    for (let i = 0; i < n; i += 1) result[i] = fn(i);
15    return result;
16  };
17
18  console.log(fillUp(477));
```

accompanying_files/20/solutions/zeroes_times.js

Without recursion or times function

```
1   "use strict";
2
3   const ARTICLE_NUMBER_LENGTH = 7;
4   const SEVEN_ZEROS = "0000000";
5
6   const fillUp = itemNumber =>
7     SEVEN_ZEROS.substr(0, numberOfMissingZeros(itemNumber))
8     + itemNumber;
9
10  const numberOfMissingZeros = number =>
11    ARTICLE_NUMBER_LENGTH - String(number).length;
12
13  console.log(fillUp(477));
```

accompanying_files/20/solutions/zeroes_simple.js

Exercise 59: Learning How to Count

```
1   "use strict";
2
3   const range = (startOrEnd, end, step) =>
4     end
5       ? rangeFromStartToEnd(startOrEnd, end, step)
6       : rangeFromStartToEnd(0, startOrEnd);
7
8   const rangeFromStartToEnd = (start, end, step = 1) => {
9     const length = Math.max(Math.ceil((end - start) / step), 0);
10    const result = Array(length);
11    const sign = step / Math.abs(step);
12    let index = 0;
13    for (let value = start; value * sign < end * sign; value +=
step)
14      result[index++] = value;
15    return result;
16  };
17
18  console.log("70 to 130\n");
19  console.log(range(70, 131).join("\n"));
20
```

```
21  console.log("\n\n200 to 20\n");
22  console.log(range(200, 19, -1).join("\n"));
23
24  console.log("\n\n10 to 50 - only even\n");
25  console.log(range(10, 51, 2).join("\n"));
```

accompanying_files/20/solutions/counting.js

Exercise 60: 6 Correct?

Step 1

```
1   "use strict";
2
3   const lotteryNumbers = count => times(count, () =>
lotteryNumber());
4   const lotteryNumber = () => Math.floor(Math.random() * 49) + 1;
5
6   const times = (n, fn) => {
7     const result = new Array(n);
8     for (let i = 0; i < n; i += 1) result[i] = fn(i);
9     return result;
10  };
11
12  console.log(lotteryNumbers(6));
```

accompanying_files/20/solutions/lotteryNumbers1.js

Step 2

```
1   "use strict";
2
3   const MAX_NUMBER = 49;
4
5   const lottoNumbers = (count, remainingLottoNumbers) =>
6     times(count, () =>
pickRandomLottoNumber(remainingLottoNumbers));
7
8   const pickRandomLottoNumber = remainingLottoNumbers =>
9
remainingLottoNumbers.splice(randomNumberTo(remainingLottoNumbers.length),
1)[0];
10
11  const randomNumberTo = n => Math.floor(Math.random() * n);
12
13  const range = (startOrEnd, end, step) =>
14    end
15      ? rangeFromStartToEnd(startOrEnd, end, step)
16      : rangeFromStartToEnd(0, startOrEnd);
```

```
17
18  const rangeFromStartToEnd = (start, end, step = 1) => {
19    const length = Math.max(Math.ceil((end - start) / step), 0);
20    const result = Array(length);
21    const sign = step / Math.abs(step);
22    let index = 0;
23    for (let value = start; value * sign < end * sign; value +=
step)
24      result[index++] = value;
25    return result;
26  };
27
28  const times = (n, fn) => {
29    const result = new Array(n);
30    for (let i = 0; i < n; i += 1) result[i] = fn(i);
31    return result;
32  };
33
34  const allLottoNumbers = range(1, MAX_NUMBER + 1);
35
36  console.log(lottoNumbers(6, allLottoNumbers));
```

accompanying_files/20/solutions/lotteryNumbers2.js

Exercise 61: Prime Numbers

```
 1  "use strict";
 2
 3  const primesUpTo = n => range(2, n + 1).filter(isPrime);
 4  const isPrime = n => range(2, n).every(divider => !divisible(n,
    divider));
 5  const divisible = (n, divider) => n % divider === 0;
 6
 7  const range = (startOrEnd, end, step) =>
 8    end
 9      ? rangeFromStartToEnd(startOrEnd, end, step)
10      : rangeFromStartToEnd(0, startOrEnd);
11
12  const rangeFromStartToEnd = (start, end, step = 1) => {
13    const length = Math.max(Math.ceil((end - start) / step), 0);
14    const result = Array(length);
15    const sign = step / Math.abs(step);
16    let index = 0;
17    for (let value = start; value * sign < end * sign; value +=
    step)
18      result[index++] = value;
19    return result;
20  };
21
22  console.log(primesUpTo(97));
```

accompanying_files/20/solutions/primes_range.js

Exercise 62: Lotto Statistics ["Brainteaser"]

```
 1  "use strict";
 2
 3  const MAX_NUMBER = 49;
 4  const NUMBER_OF_PLAYS = 10000;
 5  const MY_GUESS = [2, 12, 19, 21, 42, 43];
 6
 7  const lottoStats = () => range(NUMBER_OF_PLAYS)
 8    .map(() => numberOfHits(play(), MY_GUESS))
 9    .reduce((stats, numHits) =>  {
10      stats[numHits] += 1;
11      return stats;
12    }, [0, 0, 0, 0, 0, 0]);
13
14  const numberOfHits = (draw, guess) =>
15    intersection(draw, guess).length;
16
17  const intersection = (a, b) => a.filter(v => b.includes(v));
18
19  const play = () => lottoNumbers(6, allLottoNumbers());
```

```
20  const allLottoNumbers = () => range(1, MAX_NUMBER + 1);
21
22  const lottoNumbers = (count, remainingLottoNumbers) =>
23    times(count, () =>
pickRandomLottoNumber(remainingLottoNumbers));
24
25  const pickRandomLottoNumber = remainingLottoNumbers =>
26
remainingLottoNumbers.splice(randomNumberTo(remainingLottoNumbers.length),
1)[0];
27
28  const randomNumberTo = n => Math.floor(Math.random() * n);
29
30  const range = (startOrEnd, end, step) =>
31    end
32      ? rangeFromStartToEnd(startOrEnd, end, step)
33      : rangeFromStartToEnd(0, startOrEnd);
34
35  const rangeFromStartToEnd = (start, end, step = 1) => {
36    const length = Math.max(Math.ceil((end - start) / step), 0);
37    const result = Array(length);
38    const sign = step / Math.abs(step);
39    let index = 0;
40    for (let value = start; value * sign < end * sign; value +=
step)
41      result[index++] = value;
42    return result;
43  };
44
45  const times = (n, fn) => {
46    const result = new Array(n);
47    for (let i = 0; i < n; i += 1) result[i] = fn(i);
48    return result;
49  };
50
51  console.log(lottoStats());
```

accompanying_files/20/solutions/lottery_statistic.js

Exercise 64: Letter Thief

```
1  "use strict";
2
3  const letterThief = word =>
4    word.split("").map((letter, i) => word.slice(0, i)).reverse();
5
6  console.log(letterThief("dance"));
7  // => [ 'danc', 'dan', 'da', 'd', '' ]
```

accompanying_files/21/solutions/letter_thief.js

Exercise 65: ISBNx — The Secret of Checksums ["Brainteaser"]

```
 1  "use strict";
 2
 3  const checksumDigit = isbn => (10 - completeChecksum(isbn) % 10)
% 10;
 4
 5  const completeChecksum = isbn =>
 6    isbn
 7      .split("")
 8      .map(Number)
 9      .filter(d => !isNaN(d))
10      .reduce((sum, d, i) => sum + multiplyerByPosition(i) * d, 0);
11
12  const multiplyerByPosition = position => even(position) ? 1 : 3;
13  const even = number => number % 2 === 0;
14
15  console.log(checksumDigit("4567"));
16
17  console.log(checksumDigit("978151705411"));
18
19  console.log(checksumDigit("978-3-86680-192"));
```

accompanying_files/21/solutions/isbn_x.js

Exercise 66: Chess: Different Positions

```
"use strict";

const board2string = board =>
  board.map(row => row.join("")).join("\n");

const execMoves = moves => moves.reduce(execMove,
boardInStartPosition());

const execMove = (board, move) => {
  const originX = fieldToXPosition(originField(move));
  const originY = fieldToYPosition(originField(move));
  const targetX = fieldToXPosition(targetField(move));
  const targetY = fieldToYPosition(targetField(move));

  board[targetY][targetX] = board[originY][originX];
  board[originY][originX] = emptyBoard()[originY][originX];
  return board;
};

const boardInStartPosition = () => [
  ["♖", "♘", "♗", "♕", "♔", "♙", "♘", "♖"],
```

```
  ["♟", "♟", "♟", "♟", "♟", "♟", "♟", "♟"],
  ["□", "■", "□", "■", "□", "■", "□", "■"],
  ["■", "□", "■", "□", "■", "□", "■", "□"],
  ["□", "■", "□", "■", "□", "■", "□", "■"],
  ["■", "□", "■", "□", "■", "□", "■", "□"],
  ["♙", "♙", "♙", "♙", "♙", "♙", "♙", "♙"],
  ["♖", "♘", "♗", "♕", "♔", "♗", "♘", "♖"]
];

const emptyBoard = () => [
  ["□", "■", "□", "■", "□", "■", "□", "■"],
  ["■", "□", "■", "□", "■", "□", "■", "□"],
  ["□", "■", "□", "■", "□", "■", "□", "■"],
  ["■", "□", "■", "□", "■", "□", "■", "□"],
  ["□", "■", "□", "■", "□", "■", "□", "■"],
  ["■", "□", "■", "□", "■", "□", "■", "□"],
  ["□", "■", "□", "■", "□", "■", "□", "■"],
  ["■", "□", "■", "□", "■", "□", "■", "□"]
];

const originField = move => move.slice(0, 2);
const targetField = move => move.slice(2);

const fieldToXPosition = field => letterToChessIndex(field[0]);
const fieldToYPosition = field => numberToChessIndex(field[1]);
const letterToChessIndex = letter => "abcdefgh".indexOf(letter);
const numberToChessIndex = num => 8 - num;

console.log(board2string(boardInStartPosition()));

console.log("\n");

console.log(board2string(
  execMove(boardInStartPosition(), "e2e4")
));

console.log("\n");

console.log(board2string(
  execMoves(["e2e4", "e7e5", "f2f4"])
));
```

accompanying_files/22/solutions/chess_execMoves.js

Exercise 67: Geoquiz

```
"use strict";

const countriesWithCapital = [
  ["UK", "London"],
  ["France", "Paris"],
  ["Germany", "Berlin"],
  ["Switzerland", "Bern"],
  ["Austria", "Vienna"],
  ["Russia", "Moscow"]
];

const capitalOf = country => {
  const capitalIndex = 1;
  const countryIndex = 0;
  return countriesWithCapital.find(
    countryWithCapital => countryWithCapital[countryIndex] ===
country
  )[capitalIndex];
};

console.log(capitalOf("Switzerland"));
```

accompanying_files/22/solutions/geo_quiz1.js

Exercise 68: Geoquiz — Part 2

```
"use strict";

const countriesWithCapital = [
  ["UK", "London"],
  ["France", "Paris"],
  ["Germany", "Berlin"],
  ["Switzerland", "Bern"],
  ["Austria", "Vienna"],
  ["Russia", "Moscow"]
];

const countryForCapital = capital => {
  const capitalIndex = 1;
  const countryIndex = 0;
  return countriesWithCapital.find(
    countryWithCapital => countryWithCapital[capitalIndex] ===
capital
```

```
  )[countryIndex];
};


console.log(countryForCapital("Berlin"));
```

accompanying_files/22/solutions/geo_quiz2.js

Exercise 70: Happy Mixing with Arrays — Part 3

```
1  "use strict";
2
3  const isMixableWithMyIngredients = cocktailRecipe =>
4    isMixableWith(cocktailRecipe, ingredientsFromMyBar);
5
6  const isMixableWith = (cocktailRecipe, availableIngredients) =>
7    cocktailRecipe.every(
8      ingredientFromRecipe => hasIngredient(availableIngredients,
ingredientFromRecipe)
9    );
10
11 const hasIngredient = (listOfIngredients, searchedIngredient) =>
12   listOfIngredients.includes(searchedIngredient);
13
14 const honoluluFlip = ["Maracuja Juice", "Pineapple Juice",
"Lemon Juice", "Grapefruit Juice", "Crushed Ice"];
15 const casualFriday = ["Vodka", "Lime Juice", "Apple Juice",
"Cucumber"];
16 const pinkDolly = ["Vodka", "Orange Juice", "Pineapple Juice",
"Grenadine", "Cream", "Coco Syrup"];
17 const cocktailRecipes = [honoluluFlip, casualFriday, pinkDolly];
18
19 const ingredientsFromMyBar = ["Pineapple", "Maracuja Juice",
"Cream", "Grapefruit Juice", "Crushed Ice", "Milk", "Vodka", "Apple
Juice", "Aperol", "Pineapple Juice", "Lime Juice", "Lemons",
"Cucumber"];
20
21 console.log(cocktailRecipes.find(isMixableWithMyIngredients));
22 // => [ "Vodka", "Lime Juice", "Apple Juice", "Cucumber" ]
```

accompanying_files/22/solutions/cocktails2.js

Exercise 71: Geoquiz — Part 3

```
"use strict";

const countriesWithCapital = {
  "UK": "London",
  "France": "Paris",
```

```
    "Germany": "Berlin",
    "Switzerland": "Bern",
    "Austria": "Vienna",
    "Russia": "Moscow"
};

const capitalOf = country => countriesWithCapital[country];

console.log(capitalOf("Switzerland"));
```

accompanying_files/23/solutions/geo_quiz3.js

Exercise 72: Cracking Codes using Word Analysis ["Brainteaser"]

```
"use strict";

const wordOccurrance = text => text
    .toLowerCase()
    .replace(/[.,"';]/g, "")
    .split(" ")
    .reduce(addWord, {});

const addWord = (wordOccurances, word) => {
  if (!wordOccurances[word]) wordOccurances[word] = 0;
  wordOccurances[word] += 1;
  return wordOccurances;
};

const text = 'In cryptology, a code is a method used to encrypt a
message that operates at the level of meaning; that is, words or
phrases are converted into something else. A code might transform
"change" into "CVGDK" or "cocktail lounge". A codebook is needed
to encrypt, and decrypt the phrases or words.';

// console.log(addWord({hello: 1}, "hello"));

console.log(wordOccurrance(text));
```

accompanying_files/23/solutions/word_occurrance.js

Exercise 73: Geoquiz — Part 4

```
"use strict";

const countriesWithCapital = {
  "UK": "London",
```

```
  "France": "Paris",
  "Germany": "Berlin",
  "Switzerland": "Bern",
  "Austria": "Vienna",
  "Russia": "Moscow"
};

const countryForCapital = capital =>
  Object.keys(countriesWithCapital).find(
    country => capital === countriesWithCapital[country]
  );


console.log(countryForCapital("Berlin"));
```

accompanying_files/23/solutions/geo_quiz4.js

Exercise 74: Happy Mixing with JSON

```
 1  "use strict";
 2
 3
 4  const myMixableCocktails = cocktailList =>
 5    Object.keys(cocktailList).filter(
 6      cocktailName =>
isMixableWithMyIngredients(cocktailList[cocktailName])
 7    );
 8
 9  const isMixableWithMyIngredients = cocktailRecipe =>
10    isMixableWith(cocktailRecipe, ingredientsFromMyBar);
11
12  const isMixableWith = (cocktailRecipe, availableIngredients) =>
13    cocktailRecipe.every(
14      ingredientFromRecipe => hasIngredient(availableIngredients,
ingredientFromRecipe)
15    );
16
17  const hasIngredient = (listOfIngredients, searchedIngredient) =>
18    listOfIngredients.includes(searchedIngredient);
19
20  const ingredientsFromMyBar = ["Pineapple", "Maracuja Juice",
"Grapefruit Juice", "Crushed Ice", "Milch", "Vodka", "Apple Juice",
"Aperol", "Pineapple Juice", "Lime Juice", "Lemons", "Cucumber",
"Kaffeelikör"];
21
22  const cocktailRecipesWithNames = {
23    "Honolulu Flip": [
24      "Maracuja Juice",
25      "Pineapple Juice",
26      "Lemon Juice",
27      "Grapefruit Juice",
```

```
28       "Crushed Ice"
29     ],
30     "Casual Friday": [
31       "Vodka",
32       "Lime Juice",
33       "Apple Juice",
34       "Cucumber"
35     ],
36     "Pink Dolly": [
37       "Vodka",
38       "Orange Juice",
39       "Pineapple Juice",
40       "Grenadine",
41       "Cream",
42       "coco syrup"
43     ],
44     "Black Russian": [
45       "Vodka",
46       "Kaffeelikör"
47     ],
48     "White Russian": [
49       "Vodka",
50       "Kaffeelikör",
51       "Cream"
52     ]
53 };
54
55 console.log(myMixableCocktails(cocktailRecipesWithNames));
56 // => [ 'Casual Friday', 'Black Russian' ]
```

accompanying_files/23/solutions/cocktails_json.js

Exercise 75: First Name first and Last Name last or Last Name first and First Name last?

```
1 "use strict";
2
3 const logTransformedName = ({ firstName, lastName }) =>
4   console.log(`${lastName}, ${firstName.charAt(0)}.`);
5
6 logTransformedName({ firstName: "Ladislaus", lastName: "Jones" });
```

accompanying_files/24/solution/ladislaus.js

Exercise 76: And Triangular It Shall Be (Named Parameter Remix)

```
1  "use strict";
2
3  const triangle = ({ height, topLineWidth = 1, character = "*" })
=>
4    topLineWidth > height
5      ? ""
6      : `${line(topLineWidth, character)}\n${triangle({
7          height,
8          topLineWidth: topLineWidth + 1
9        })}`;
10
11 const line = (length, character) =>
12   length === 0 ? "" : character + line(length - 1, character);
13
14 console.log(triangle({ height: 10 }));
```
accompanying_files/24/solution/triangle.js

```
1  "use strict";
2
3  const triangle = (
4    { height, topLineWidth = 1, character = "*" } = {
5      height: 5,
6      topLineWidth: 1,
7      character: "*"
8    }
9  ) =>
10   topLineWidth > height
11     ? ""
12     : `${line(topLineWidth, character)}\n${triangle({
13         height,
14         topLineWidth: topLineWidth + 1
15       })}`;
16
17 const line = (length, character) =>
18   length === 0 ? "" : character + line(length - 1, character);
19
20 console.log(triangle());
```
accompanying_files/24/solution/triangle2.js

Exercise 77: How Much Further? Are We There Yet?

```
1  "use strict";
2
3  const distance = (
4    { x: xOrigin, y: yOrigin },
5    { x: xDestination, y: yDestination }
```

```
6  ) => Math.sqrt((yDestination - yOrigin) ** 2 + (xDestination -
xOrigin) ** 2);
7
8  console.log(distance({ x: 1, y: 1 }, { x: 5, y: 1 }));
```

accompanying_files/24/solution/distance.js

Index

We Want Your Feedback!

We would love to know what you think about this book. What did you like best, what wasn't so good? Have you missed any content or should we have shortened certain topics? How did you cope with knowledge questions and exercises?

Give us your opinion!

Send an email to the OWL Team at *feedback@owl.institute*

98501887R00181

Made in the USA
Middletown, DE
09 November 2018